Also by Serge Kahili King, Ph.D.:

Imagineering for Health
Kahuna Healing
Mastering Your Hidden Self
Pyramid Energy Handbook

URBAN SHAMAN

SERGE KAHILI KING, PH. D.

A FIRESIDE BOOK
Published by Simon & Schuster
New York London Toronto Sydney
Tokyo Singapore

Fireside

Rockefeller Center
1230 Avenue of the Americas
New York, New York 10020

Designed by Diane Stevenson, SNAP·HAUS GRAPHICS
Manufactured in the United States of America

10

Library of Congress Cataloging in Publication Data
King, Serge.
    Urban shaman / Serge Kahili King, Ph.D.
        p. cm.
    "A Fireside book."
    1. Shamanism—Hawaii.   2. Self-realization—Religious aspects.
3. Spiritual healing.   I. Title.
BL2370.S5K58 1990
299'.92—dc20   90-39839
                                                                    CIP

ISBN 0-671-68307-1

Pili kau, pili ho'oilo
(together in the dry season,
together in the wet season)

With grateful and abundant thanks to the many friends
I have had the privilege of training in the Hawaiian
shaman tradition,
and who taught me that when the teacher is ready, the
student will appear.

CONTENTS

URBAN SHAMAN

THE PREPARATION

Ho'omoe wai kahi ke kao'o
(Let's all travel together like water
flowing in one direction)

This is a book about shamanism, especially the Hawaiian tradition of shamanism, and about being an
"urban shaman." In order for you to get the most out of this
book, I'd like to define what it is that we're talking about
right at the beginning.

According to the French historian Mircea Eliade, shamanism is a practice found all over the world, including Asia,
the Americas, and the Pacific. The word *shaman* is derived
from the Tungusic language of Siberia and is now used as a
convenient term by scientists and laymen alike to describe
the practitioner and his or her practice. Most cultures have
their own term in their own language for such a person,
such as *kupua* in Hawaiian. A lot of people have different
ideas about what a shaman is and does, but like Eliade, I
tend toward a strict definition. Not every medicine man is a
shaman, but a shaman might be a medicine man. Not every

tribal priest is a shaman, but a shaman might be a tribal priest. Not every psychic healer is a shaman, but a shaman might be a psychic healer. For the purposes of this book and my teachings, I define a shaman as a healer of relationships: between mind and body, between people, between people and circumstances, between humans and Nature, and between matter and spirit.

In practicing his or her healing, the shaman has a view of reality very different from the one most of the world uses, and it is this unique viewpoint (which will be covered extensively in the rest of the book) which really sets the shaman apart from other healers. It also leads to some rather unusual healing techniques commonly associated with shamanism, such as shapechanging, communicating with plants and animals, and journeying to the "underworld." If some of these things sound strange, don't let it bother you. You will find as you continue that many, if not most, of these practices will have a curious familiarity. This is because shamans base their art on natural human experience. You will discover that you already know more about shamanism than you thought you did.

Hawaiian Shamanism

Shamanism is a distinct form of healing, and Hawaiian shamanism is a distinct form of shamanism. The outstanding quality of the shaman, regardless of culture, is the inclination toward engagement, or creative activity. Knowledge and understanding are not enough, nor does passive acceptance hold any appeal. The shaman plunges into life with mind and senses, playing the role of cocreator. There is a type of soul content to admire the shape and place of a fallen tree. The shaman is more like a sculptor who views the tree and is seized by the desire to transform it into some semblance of an internal image . . . or a useful tool. There is respect and admiration for the tree as it is, *as well as* the impulse to join with the tree and produce something new. This activism is expressed in the primary function of a shaman: that of a healer. Regardless of culture, location, or social environment a shaman is, by purpose, a healer of mind, body, and circumstance. It is this bent toward social and environmental benefit, in fact, which distinguishes the shaman from the sorcerer of Castaneda's model who follows a path of strictly personal power and enlightenment. And yet, while all shamans are healers, the majority follow the "way of the warrior"; some, a minority which includes the Hawaiian shaman tradition, follow what we might call "the way of the adventurer."

A "warrior" shaman tends to personify fear, illness, or disharmony and to focus on the development of power, control, and combat skills in order to deal with them. An "adventurer" shaman, by contrast, tends to depersonify these conditions (i.e., treat them as effects, not things) and deal with them by developing skills of love, cooperation, and harmony. As a simple example of the different approaches, if you had to deal with a person who was emotionally upset, a warrior shaman might help you build a strong psychic shield to protect yourself from the other person's negative energy. The adventurer shaman, on the other hand, would be more likely to teach you how to harmonize your energy so that you remain calm and even become a source of healing for the other person. In addition, the warrior shaman's path is often quite lonely, while the adventurer's path is, by its very nature, quite social. Nevertheless, it is difficult, if not impossible, to tell the difference between masters of either path because the more powerful you are, the more loving you are (since there is less and less to fear); and the more loving you are, the more powerful you are (since there is greater and greater confidence). I have walked both paths, and I choose and teach the Hawaiian adventurer way because I believe it is the most practical and beneficial, but I have great respect for the warrior shamans and their healing.

The Urban Shaman

The title of this book is *Urban Shaman* because that is the focus and purpose of my teaching. Although shamanism is usually associated with primitive or wilderness settings, its application in urban environments is both natural and needed. First of all, a shaman is a healer, regardless of culture or environment. Secondly, there are more people living in urban areas today than in nonurban areas (suburbs and towns are considered urban), and it is these people who need the most healing. And thirdly, shamanism, especially the Hawaiian variety, is well adapted to modern times and needs for several reasons:

1. It is completely nonsectarian and pragmatic. Shamanism is a craft, not a religion, and you can practice it alone or with a group.
2. It is very easy to learn and apply, although, as with any craft, the full development of certain skills may take a while.
3. The Hawaiian version in particular may be practiced anywhere at any time, including at home, at work, at school, at play, or while traveling. This is mainly because the Hawaiian shamans primarily worked with the mind and body alone. They did not use drums to induce altered states and they did not use masks to assume other forms or qualities.
4. The nature of shamanism is such that while you are healing others you are healing yourself, and while you are transforming the planet you are transforming yourself.

Apprenticeship

In days long past, when people lived in fairly isolated villages and one's world view was limited to one's valley or mountain or island, then it was appropriate for someone who had mastered the shaman path to have one, two, or maybe three apprentices over a lifetime because that small number could fill all the village's needs. Today, however, we live in a Global

Village with billions of people, and at the very least, we need thousands of urban shamans to help maintain a harmonious, healthy existence. People just like you.

I was raised as an urban shaman. My father was exceptionally well traveled and well versed in the cultures and traditions of most of the world, and he underwent deep training in the Hawaiian shaman tradition. He was highly skilled in the ways and crafts of bush and jungle, forest and farm, desert and tundra, and I learned a great deal about Nature from him. But he was first and foremost an urban man, a holder of medical and engineering degrees, and quite at home in business and government circles. I came into his life at the beginning of a war and he left mine at the end of one. A large portion of the years between were spent in travel between urban centers. In the seventeen years that we knew each other, the shamanism I learned through example and training was mostly applied in the environments of cities, towns, and schools.

I speak of training, but it wasn't in classes or sit-down sessions with my father acting as instructor and I as student. The kind of training I had would be considered very traditional because it took place in the course of ordinary activities. In the middle of a conversation about vegetables, say, my father might give me a technique for plant communication to practice on my own and then discuss with him later. Or he might set up a situation during the day which would give me an opportunity to apply recently learned skills, and then comment on my application (or nonapplication). And he would frequently drop intriguing hints, ideas, and suggestions for me to follow up on by myself. It was training because it was consciously intended and I certainly learned from it, but it was not organized like a school at all.

After my father's death my shaman training continued in the same way with members of our Hawaiian family, but the application was still primarily in cities, towns, and schools, plus an interlude in the Marine Corps. I used the knowledge I gained in very practical ways, as it was meant to be used. It helped to increase my health and my strength, and helped me to recover quickly when I forgot my knowledge and became unhealthy or injured. It helped me at the University of Colorado to carry an overfull academic load and hold three jobs at the same time, and to graduate with a degree in Asian Studies and a Phi Beta Kappa pin. I used the knowledge again as I worked my way through the American Graduate School of International Management in Arizona for a bachelor's and a master's degree with honors, and much later when I got my Ph.D. in psychology at California Western University.

When my marriage was three years old and my first son was two, we moved to West Africa to live for seven years. About half of that time I spent in the bush—jungle, forest, and desert—and I learned much more about different aspects of shamanism there, but the primary application was still urban. I have used it to keep my relationship with my wife happy and full; to keep my sons (eventually three) in good physical and academic health, and to have them be close friends with me and among themselves; to heal and teach pets; to help family, friends, and neighbors to be healthier and more successful; and to further my career and to reach out to share my knowledge with people around the world. I use it to keep vehicles and computers in good working order, to ensure the cooperation of airlines and weather during my travels, and to increase the speed of learning of the shamans and others I train. I use it in innumerable ways to benefit myself and my social and physical environment, wherever I am. I have learned many things in my life and have studied many systems of religion (e.g., Christianity, Judaism, Buddhism, Hinduism, Confucianism, Islam, voodoo), philosophy (mainly Taoism, Yoga, Zen, Western pragmatism), and healing (massage, herbs, energy work, faith healing, hypnosis, to name a few), and shamancraft has enhanced my knowledge of every one. Today, as I live in Hawaii and direct Aloha International, a worldwide network of shaman healers which promotes the Hawaiian healing tradition through courses and seminars, museums, and local chapters, urban shamancraft is evident in all our activities.

In this book I intend to show that the ideas and practices of Hawaiian shamanism are well suited to use in modern urban society, as well as in settings considered closer to Nature. As previously noted, some of the concepts, examples, and exercises will seem familiar, and some of them might seem quite strange. The material is taken from two shaman training courses that I give, and is presented in approximately the same order that I give it. In this book format, however, we can explore many of the ideas in much more depth than is possible in a workshop.

An Open-Door Policy

I am presenting freely and openly many things that are considered deep secrets in some traditions. Some fear a misuse of the knowledge, some fear the knowledge will be less potent if everyone knows it, and some fear retribution from a hierarchy which gave an order not to let things be known.

However, a true shaman keeps no secrets about knowledge that can help and heal. The difficulty is not in keeping knowledge secret, but in getting people to understand and use it. As for misuse, that only comes from ignorance. The more knowledge everyone has about how to change things, the less inclination and opportunity there will be for misuse. Widely spread knowledge actually has more potency than secrets locked up and unused. Knowledge held secret is about as useful as money under a miser's mattress. And the sacredness of knowledge lies not in its reservation for a few, but in its availability to many. More likely such a fear of free expression has to do with a baser fear that the guardian of knowledge really hasn't much to guard or doesn't understand what he has. And finally, shamans recognize no hierarchy or authority in matters of the mind; if ever a group of people could be said to follow a system of spiritual democracy, it would be the shamans of the world.

The Hawaiian Heritage

The Hawaiians have a very rich spiritual, psychological, cultural, and practical heritage, and I can only present the small
part of it that I was privileged to receive. Their heritage is
so rich, in fact, that a number of traditions have grown up
within it and not all Hawaiians or students of Hawaiiana
agree on what the heritage consists of. So what you receive
from me comes through my adoptive Hawaiian father and
his ancestors, through my natural father and his Hawaiian
brother and sister by adoption, and then through me and
my particular personality and outlook. So even though this
is traditional wisdom presented in modern terms for today's
conditions, I take full responsibility for everything I say.

A great part of the heritage maintained by the Hawaiians
is in their language. It is deceptively simple, having only
twelve letters and no form of the verb *to be*. Yet it contains
the most profound concepts you can imagine about spiritual
awareness, psychological constructs, the nature of reality,
love, power, achievement, and on and on. Because it will
be so unfamiliar to most of you, I have limited its use to
those areas where an English translation just isn't quite good
enough. If you want to try your hand at pronunciation, I
will risk the wrath of Hawaiian language purists and tell you
that it's easiest to pronounce the consonants as in English
(*k, p, h,* etc.) and the vowels as in Spanish (*a* as in *father,
e* as in *prey, i* as in *pita, o* as in *mote, u* as in *duty*).

And so this is the beginning of my story and here is the
knowledge I have to share. May it help you to find as well
as enjoy greater peace, love, and power.

THE FIRST ADVENTURE:

THE EVOLUTION OF HAWAIIAN SHAMANISM

Waiho wale kahiko
(Old secrets are now revealed)

Thunder crashed, the wind roared, torrents of rain filled the air, and mountainous waves rose and fell, yet still the mighty Maui pulled and heaved on his magic fishhook. Finally, with the sound of a thousand waterfalls the islands of Hawaii rose slowly from the sea. Maui had triumphed once again and mankind had new land to explore and cultivate.

The evolution of Hawaiian shamanism begins with the myths of Maui. Magician, trickster, demigod, miracle worker, luck bringer—Maui was known as all these things from one end of Polynesia to the other, the only male figure of Polynesian myth to be so renowned. The only female mythological being in Polynesia with as widespread a reputation was Hina, goddess of the moon and mother of Maui.

The stories told of Maui as abundantly recorded in Beckwith's *Hawaiian Mythology*, Andersen's *Myths and Legends of the Polynesians*, and Fornander's *An Account of the Polynesian*

Race make it clear that he was an archetypal shaman in the same ancient tradition found elsewhere in the world, with a Polynesian touch. Besides pulling up the islands of Hawaii (a discovery myth), he slowed down the sun so his mother could dry her clothes (another discovery myth of finding lands in high northern latitudes), visited the Upper World and tricked the gods into giving up the secret of fire (a myth of creative intuition through shamanic trance), visited the Underworld to overcome various monsters (another myth of shamanic trance for healing), was able to use magic and magical items, and spoke freely with birds, animals, and the natural elements. Maui was the most popular figure in Polynesian myth because of his helpfulness, his adventurousness, his irreverence for authority, and his accessibility. As a demigod (more properly, a human with magical abilities), he was never worshiped, but he could be called on for luck. In New Zealand, where the Maori carved his likeness in wood or jade in the form of a human embryo and often wore it as a charm, he was called "Maui Tikitiki"; in Hawaii, where no likeness of him was ever made, he was called "Maui Kupua." Both names can be translated as "Maui the Shaman."

The Kahuna Orders

Very early in Polynesia (some traditions, such as those of the Kahili family—which adopted me—and those recorded by Leinani Melville in *Children of the Rainbow,* are said to go back as far as the lost continent of Mu, although in fairness there are many who disagree with that) there came into being a philosophy of life called *Huna*—the "secret" or the "hidden knowledge." The name did not refer to any desire to keep the knowledge away from others, but rather it referred to a knowledge of the hidden or unseen side of things. The expert or master practitioners of this philosophy were called *kahuna* in Hawaiian, *tahuna* in Tahitian, and *tohunga* in Maori. At some point these experts formed themselves into three loosely formed separate groups. The existence of these three groups is noted by many sources (e.g., Malo's *Hawaiian Antiquities* and The Kamehameha Schools' *Ancient Hawaiian Civilization*), but most of the specifics that follow were given to me by Ohialaka Kahili and Wana Kahili, my aunt and uncle by Hawaiian-style adoption. When I was seventeen I was *hanai'd* (adopted) by the Kahili family, after my natural father had died. This is not a legal form of adoption, but for the Hawaiians it means being taken into their family as one of their own.

One of the groups mentioned above focused on the arts of physical therapy, ceremonial religion, politics, and war. In Hawaii it was known as the Order of *Ku*. A second group focused on the spiritual and material aspects of crafts and sciences such as fishing and farming, shipbuilding and navigation, wood carving and herbalism. This was the Order of *Lono* in Hawaii. The third group, the Hawaiian Order of *Kane*, focused on magic, mysticism, and psychology, and these were the shamans. Each order had many subcategories, and while there were healers in each one, the art of healing through spirit became the primary activity of the shamans. *Ku*, *Lono*, and *Kane* (pronounced "kah-nay") were archetypes or personifications of Body, Mind, and Spirit. The full name of *Kane* was originally *Kanewahine*, which may be translated as "manwoman," and refers to an understanding of polarities similar to the yin/yang concept of Taoist shamans. *Kane* was an archetypal god of forests, high places, water sources, and peace. This is significant because the Hawaiians as a rule only inhabited the shorelines of their islands. Apart from special forays for sandalwood, tall trees for oceangoing canoes, and feathers for capes, the only Hawaiians who spent much time in the forests and uplands were the shamans.

As a guild, the Order of *Kane* was roughly divided into apprentices, journeymen, and masters, though different teachers might change the number of categories. When I was being trained I started out as an apprentice and then mastered different areas as I progressed. Hawaiian shamans, like shamans everywhere, have no hierarchy among themselves.

The apprentices are students and colleagues, not followers, and the master is a master of knowledge, not of people. The Hawaiian word for master in the sense of someone with spiritual and material expertise in a given area is *kahuna*, as mentioned above. That word is used very loosely nowadays, but in proper usage, and to have any real meaning, it should always have a qualifier added. For instance, a master healer who uses herbs, massage, and energy work is a *kahuna lapa'au;* a master of prayer and ceremony is a *kahuna pule;* and a master shaman is a *kahuna kupua*. As an aside, the "big kahuna" of the surfing beaches would be a *kahuna he'e nalu*. And the black magician or sorcerer was called a *kahuna 'ana'ana*.

A great deal of nonsense has been written and presented about the *kahuna*s of Hawaii, ranging from the red flash in the eye one is supposed to see on meeting a real *kahuna*, to their healing broken bones instantly without fail, to raising the dead, and to the infamous "death prayer." Since much of the credit or blame for these things is laid on the shamans, I would like to clarify these issues here and now.

To begin with, the belief in the red flash (which has even appeared on television) came about because of a play on words, so greatly enjoyed by Polynesians. The word used for flash is *makole*, which means "red eyed" and refers even to conjunctivitis. But the same word also means "rainbow" and that is a symbol for the presence of chiefs, gods, or spirits. As applied to a *kahuna*, it is a word of respect.

The instant healing of a broken bone is possible for any healer *under the right conditions*. Specifically, it can occur when there is abundant energy and faith, and no doubt. The *kahuna*s' reputation for this skill is mostly due to a single story in a book by Max Freedom Long entitled *The Secret Science Behind Miracles*. In the book he tells of a female *kahuna* who instantly healed the leg of a man who broke it while he was drunk. Obviously, the *kahuna* had the energy and the faith, and the man was probably too drunk to have any doubt. Not even *kahuna*s can do it every time without fail, however.

Raising the dead has taken place in every culture, sometimes spontaneously without a shaman or healer present. In such cases the "dead" person is actually in a deep coma or trance, or on the way to the other side. It might be wise to believe Jesus was right when he said the girl he was bringing back to life was only asleep. A typical *kahuna* shaman technique for reviving someone apparently dead was to push the person's wandering spirit back into the body through the big toe. Amazingly astute when you consider that squeezing the big toe is a well-known method for reviving someone who has fainted.

Now for the big one, the so-called "death prayer." This was only engaged in by the *'ana'ana*, the black magicians or sorcerers who were despised by the *kahuna*s of all the orders. These renegades were usually apprentices of one of the orders who had received some knowledge and who had been dropped or kicked out of their guild because of their negative personality or behavior. It was the Europeans who first gave them the title *kahuna* and the missionaries who put out the idea that all *kahuna*s were evil sorcerers. The "death prayer" itself was no more than a cursing chant designed to work openly and telepathically on the victim's fear. No fear, no effect. There were certain *kahuna*s who specialized in undoing the attempts of the *'ana'ana*, either by working directly on the sorcerer or by empowering the victim, and sometimes these "countersorcerers" were called *kahuna 'ana'ana* as well.

Shaman Training

Shaman training in Polynesia may be formal or informal, depending on the area. In old New Zealand, Maori candidates attended the Whare Wananga, or "Psychic School," and underwent rigorously controlled training and examinations. The Hawaiian tradition was much more family oriented, with candidates picked out of or adopted into the family of a master shaman and trained informally by the shaman or his or her advanced students. In the Maori system you were given specific things to accomplish and were tested on those things. In the Hawaiian system you were given experiences, demonstrations, hints, and suggestions and were then left to develop your own initiative and self-discipline to master those things or not. When you felt you were ready, you came to the master and asked to demonstrate your skill. Then he or she would either give you some suggestions to improve your skill or acknowledge your expertise and give you a new challenge—if you asked for it.

The Hawaiian system, in my opinion, is much the tougher of the two because the guidelines are so unclear. For instance, my Hawaiian *kahuna* uncle, Wana Kahili, once said to me without any preamble, "It is a good thing to understand the energies of stone and stonelike things." So I asked him, "Does that mean you think I should study them?" "No," he replied. "Do you want me to?" I persisted. "No," he said again. At first I couldn't figure out why he had mentioned it, but thanks to previous experiences with my father and M'Bala, my African shaman mentor, I finally got a flash of inspiration and asked him, "How does one get to understand the energies of stone?" "Well, you might begin by . . ." And then he offered several suggestions for starting. If I hadn't asked the right question, he would not have helped me to extend my knowledge into that area. In Hawaiian shamanism initiative is highly prized and rewarded.

A novel aspect of Polynesian shamanism, compared to the more well known Amerindian shamanism, is its lack of masks and its use of drumming and dance. Masks as representations of gods, spirits, or animals were not used anywhere in Polynesia, though some people think the Melanesian masks of New Guinea are Polynesian. If the dancers, shamans, or priests of Polynesia wanted to convey the presence or activities of gods, spirits, or animals they would do so by sound and gesture only. Even the elaborate facial tattooing of the Polynesians was intended as an enhancement of beauty, not as a mask. And drumming was not used as a means of going into trance. It was used for communication, for maintaining rhythm, and for energizing. As for the sacred hula, a performer would go into a kind of trance by meditating on the god, spirit, or intention to be represented before the dance. The dance itself was a carefully choreographed affair whose power came from the dancer's skill in connecting with the spirit or intent being expressed. A deeper trance or focus might occur as a side effect, but the primary purpose of the sacred hula was to teach or move the audience. Ecstatic or trance-inducing dance was not part of the Polynesian culture.

Polynesian shamans were trained as healers in seven areas, and though to become a *kahuna* shaman you had to develop a certain degree of mastery in all seven, not everyone was equally adept in each area because of differences in natural talent and interest. Basically, the shaman was trained as a psychic, as a releaser of mental and physical blocks, as a manifester of events, as a shapechanger, as a peacemaker, as a teacher, and as an adventurer. The form of the training would differ with each teacher, but invariably the process would emphasize self-esteem, inner authority, and the power of words to direct energy, evoke imagery, and create beliefs. Generally, apprentices were given chant formulas that we would recognize today as affirmations, images to meditate on and explore, and elemental, animal, or plant forms to emulate or model. Any formal training would usually take place from dawn to noon, but the apprentice was expected to apply his or her learning at every opportunity throughout the day or night. Breathing exercises were also important for increasing spiritual energy and directing thought.

As a psychic the shaman was trained in telepathy and clairvoyance, but also in journeying to other worlds, inner and outer; in communication with spirits; in channeling; in dreamwork; and in communication with plants, animals, and the natural elements of the earth. All of these were actually conceived of as forms of telepathy, probably the most important of all shaman skills. Tools such as casting stones, scrying stones, and divining wands were often used to train and enhance the mental skills.

As a releaser of blocks the shaman was trained in the use

of energy to relieve physical, emotional, and mental stress, and in methods of changing limiting beliefs. Energy release was most often based on *lomi-lomi,* a Hawaiian form of massage combining elements resembling Swedish and Esalen massage, rolfing, polarity therapy, acupressure, laying on of hands, and other variations. However, personal and environmental geomancy was also used for such release. The dissolving of limiting beliefs could be done in a number of ways, but a common method used was a kind of talk therapy often including affirmations that could be done by oneself, one-on-one, or in a group.

As a manifester the shaman was trained to do things like change the weather, increase prosperity (perhaps by inducing a more abundant crop or attracting a bigger catch of fish), and bring about various events (like finding an island or causing a meeting of chiefs). Among several methods used was a form of contemplation or passive focused attention similar to certain yogic practices in which an idea is calmly held in awareness until it attracts enough energy to manifest in form. Also included in this training was astral travel and psychokinesis.

As a shapechanger he or she was trained to take on various roles through singing, acting, or dancing, to take on the characteristics of animals or objects, to merge with the elements of Nature and influence them by resonance, and at the highest levels of the skill, to disappear or appear to others in a different form.

As a peacemaker the shaman was trained to create harmony within him- or herself, within others, between people, between people and Nature, and within Nature. A shamanic society in Tahiti, the Arioi, specialized in this peacemaking process. With song, dance, and poetry as their medium, they would travel from island to island and give their performances. Respect for them was so great that any current wars had to cease as long as they were present. Through the recounting of myth and legend they would remind combatants of their common origin and purpose, and through ribald and irreverent humor they would attempt to make the antagonists see the error of their ways. This emphasis on peace is one of the distinguishing characteristics of Polynesian shamans. Whereas most shamans of the world follow the way of the warrior, with its focus on power and the conquering of self, Polynesian shamans follow what I call the way of the adventurer, with its focus on love (*aloha*) and the expansion of self.

As teachers, shamans were trained to demonstrate and share their knowledge, helping people to discover their own power to change their lives. A shaman would very seldom become a *kahuna a'o*, a master teacher who speaks in front of groups. More often the teaching would be done by example, suggestion, and counseling.

As an adventurer the shaman was trained to be flexible, to be comfortable with change and to direct it in a positive way, to be free to explore new ways and means of doing things, and to constantly update and expand his or her knowledge by travel and study with other teachers.

The Fall and Rise of Hawaiian Shamanism

Given such powers and abilities, people often ask, how did Polynesia ever get taken over by outsiders? Why didn't the shamans prevent it? Since this has a direct bearing on the evolution of shamanism in Polynesia, I will answer that important question here. Each area of Polynesia had its local variations on this theme, but the experience of Hawaii was typical enough to serve as an example for all.

As recorded by Fornander in *An Account of the Polynesian Race*, about the year 1200 A.D., during the Age of Chivalry in Europe and the rule of Genghis Khan in Asia, a man named Paao, a powerfully motivated and determined *kahuna* of the Order of *Ku*, led an expedition with a Samoan chief and Samoan and Tahitian warriors to Hawaii. At this time Hawaii was a fairly peaceful place, with various parts of the different islands ruled by local chiefs who were more like village headmen. The boatyards of Hawaii were busy and oceangoing canoes traveled regularly for trade and migration between the Hawaiian Islands, Samoa, and Tahiti. The Order of *Ku*, mentioned by Malo in *Hawaiian Antiquities*, already existed in Hawaii as a ceremonial priesthood in charge of most of the temples and celebrations dedicated to agriculture, fishing, and healing. Until the arrival of Paao, the priests of *Ku* lived in relative harmony with shamans of *Kane* and the professionals (herbalists, astrologers, navigators, boat-wrights, etc.) of the Order of *Lono*. Life was more than peaceful, it was complacent. If any did suspect what was coming they would not have been listened to. This was paradise— what could go wrong?

Paao had a special talent which, when combined with his ambition, was to change Hawaiian society profoundly. He was a genius at organization. As soon as he landed (some say he started on the Big Island), he established a base of operations with his imported chief and warriors. Then he set about using his powerful personality and organizing ability to turn the local Order of *Ku* into a strongly hierarchical and exclusive structure of acolytes and priests. At some point he introduced human sacrifice into the ceremonies for the first time in Hawaii with the usual justification that, since human life is so sacred, it makes the most powerful sacrifice. As the Order of *Ku* became stronger organizationally, Paao began expanding politically with the help of his warriors. As each new area was taken over, with the help of the local priesthood, Paao replaced the headman system of the local chiefs with the new aristocratic system. Whereas before all the land was held in common, now it belonged solely to the new form of chief who could allocate it and take it away at will. The aristocracy had its own hierarchy, of course, much like the feudal system in Europe, and Paao made sure that its power over the people was linked inextricably with the power of the priesthood so that each should be dependent on and serve as a check for the other, again much as in Europe. However, even though he was able to change the rough class system of Hawaii into a more strict caste system, he was never able to establish serfdom. The common people were tenants, but not serfs. The chiefs did not own them, and if a commoner was not satisfied with one chief he could move to another area under a different chief.

Only two sources gave Paao any real or potential opposition: the shamans and the professionals. So Paao and his followers set out to eliminate them both. One of the first things to go was the commerce with the other islands of the South Pacific. No more oceangoing canoes were allowed to depart (it was against the will of the gods), and any that arrived were confiscated, so very soon all interchange ceased. Without the commerce there was no need for boat building, so the boatyards were closed down. And of course, there was no need for boatwrights and navigators, so those two professions dwindled and their mastery was lost. Since most of the astrologers were also navigators, much of that knowledge was lost as well. Seven hundred years before the Iron Curtain descended in Europe, Paao had brought down his even more effective "Ocean Curtain" in Hawaii.

The Order of *Lono* suffered greatly under Paao and virtually the only ones to survive over the next five hundred years until the coming of Cook were the master farmers, fishermen, and herbalists who were undeniably useful and posed no threat to the new order. The shamans of *Kane* were actually the greatest threat to Paao because of their teaching of freedom and individual power, but in a way they were also the least able to resist him. The shamans could, and did, protect themselves by withdrawing into the forests and highlands where few others desired or dared to go; however, they could only influence the people in ways in which the people wanted to be influenced. Paao offered absolute security in return for giving up personal freedom and responsibility, using fear as the motivation for going along with his way of doing things. Security was maintained not only by the soldiers of the new rulers, but by a class of executioners hired by the rulers and the priesthood to go out by night and punish enemies and gather victims for the sacrifices. The general populace went along with the new order and the shamans were neither numerous enough nor organized enough to oppose the policies of Paao directly. So they re-treated into the wilderness, letting their whereabouts be known to only a few, healing those who could find them and maintaining a very low profile within their own society.

By the time of Cook's discovery of Hawaii at the end of the eighteenth century, the priesthood of *Ku* had a rigid hold on the area even though all the islands were at war with each other. The Order of *Lono* had lost most of its knowledge and had become practically a minor branch of the priest-hood, and the shamans of *Kane* were shadowy figures in the hinterlands to be consulted in times of emergency but oth-erwise avoided. Only on Kauai did the shamans maintain any significant influence. When the brilliant King Kame-hameha conquered Hawaii, Maui, Oahu, and Molokai with the help of Western advice and technology, it was the sha-mans of Kauai who twice helped prevent him from con-quering Kauai by force with their magic. Kamakau reports in *Ka Po'e Kahiko (The People of Old)* that in 1796 Kameha-meha set sail with ten thousand warriors across the channel separating Oahu and Kauai, but a strong wind arose and threatened to wipe out his entire fleet so he retreated. Again in 1804 Kamehameha gathered over seven thousand troops for an invasion of Kauai, armed with muskets, cannon, swivel guns, mortars, and armed schooners as well as canoes. This time it was a disease similar to typhoid that destroyed his army completely and prevented the invasion. In *Kauai: The Separate Kingdom*, his account of this period, Edward Joesting says, "Throughout the islands Kauai was noted for the religious nature of its people (and was) often referred to as 'Kauai *pule o'o'*—Kauai of strong prayers."

Neither the entry of Kauai into Kamehameha's union through negotiation, the disruption and virtual destruction of the priesthood shortly after the great king's death, the arrival of the missionaries, nor the acquisition of Hawaii by the United States had very much effect on the shamans of Hawaii and their way of life. Once a number of them did come out of the wilderness to participate in King Kalakaua's attempt to revive the ancient healing arts, but when the influence of political activists known as "The Missionary Group" became strong enough to force the king to disband his *kahuna*-led Board of Health, they silently disengaged and disappeared again.

Throughout the years of suppression of Hawaiian culture by the missionaries and the new American economic and political elite, the island shamans continued much as they had during the centuries of suppression initiated by Paao. Masters at blending in with their environment, they either remained in the uplands out of sight, or mixed right in with their peers as apparently perfectly ordinary folk. In both cases their skills were inaccessible except to family, friends, and the very needy. The law in Hawaii which made it a crime to be or to call oneself a *kahuna* had very little effect on their activities.

The seeds of change among Hawaiian *kahuna*s were sown by the social revolution of the sixties and the sprouts of change continued to grow into the seventies and eighties. Like other peoples elsewhere, the Hawaiians slowly began to feel again their pride in being Hawaiian, and the bravest among them began to revive and improve upon the best aspects of their ancient culture. Arts and crafts and dance and song in traditional old and uniquely new styles became more popular, and somewhere along the way the law against *kahuna*s was taken off the books. As Hawaiian pride grew, so did the activities of Hawaiian *kahuna*s. However, the suppression by church and state had taken a serious toll in that there were very few genuine *kahuna*s of any kind left, and there were even fewer apprentices in training. As proud of their heritage as the Hawaiians might be, the churches had still made a deep impression by associating all *kahuna* lore with black magic. Even those Hawaiians who dare seek out the healing aspects of this great tradition do so with more than a little fear. Nevertheless, their numbers continue to grow.

Today, however, the great healing, metaphysical, and shamanic traditions of Hawaii are being kept alive primarily by the same race that almost destroyed them completely. With-

out the audiences of white mainlanders, even the few Hawaiian teaching *kahuna*s would have virtually no one to
teach. A Hawaiian *kahuna* friend of mine told me that the
Hawaiians won't return to the ancient *Huna* lore until
enough whites say that it is good. And another Hawaiian
kahuna attending one of my lectures to hear what this *haole*
kahuna was saying ended up confirming what I had learned
and giving me his blessing for sharing it, while at the same
time expressing the strange feelings it gave him to hear this
knowledge so openly taught after so many years of suppression. On the other hand, there are some Hawaiians, though
not *kahuna*s to my knowledge, who feel that Hawaiian sacred
traditions should only be shared with Hawaiians.

In a way it is both fortunate and unfortunate that *kahuna*
wisdom—*Huna*—is being taught mostly to mainland Caucasians today. Fortunate because their numbers and interest
and relative fearlessness ensure that the knowledge will be
maintained and enhanced; unfortunate only because the
knowledge could be so useful to the Hawaiians themselves
in their modern quest for self-esteem and self-determination.
At the present time there are less than a half dozen teaching
*kahuna*s, all teaching primarily on the mainland. Only one
of those is of the Order of *Kane,* and he also happens to be
a *haole*—white. That teacher is me. None of the remaining
kahuna shamans I know have any desire to teach, but at
least some *kahuna*s of the other orders are starting to come
forward and share their healing skills and knowledge. I do
have great hopes for the few Polynesian apprentices I have,
yet we seem to be moving into a period of history where
differences are becoming less and less important. Hawaiian
shamanism and the spirit of *aloha* on which it is based represent a way of life with great value for all of humanity. It
is a coming together time for all, and the best use of all
shamanism, urban and otherwise, would be for the cause of
peace, inner and outer. As an old Hawaiian proverb says:
He ali'i ka la'i, he haku na ke aloha (Peace is a chief, the lord
of love). May peace and love be our guide and our purpose
as we work on healing the world today.

THE SECOND ADVENTURE:

HEART, MIND, AND SPIRIT

'A'ohe pau ka 'ike i ka halau ho'okahi
(All knowledge is not taught in the
same school)

The Hawaiian shaman system is similar to other systems of thought which deal with the mind and its effect on the Universe, but some of the differences are considerable. Many centuries ago Hawaiian spiritual masters came to the same conclusions reached by others in various times and places: that there is an aspect of consciousness which operates covertly and indirectly (the subconscious); that there is an aspect of consciousness which operates openly and directly (the conscious mind); and that there is an aspect of consciousness which transcends yet includes them both (the superconscious). The differences in Hawaiian thought have to do with their nature, their functions, and their relationships. In the title of this chapter I have called them heart, mind, and spirit, and understanding what they are and how they work from the Hawaiian point of view can be one of the most practical things you will ever learn.

The Three Aspects of Consciousness

The concept of three aspects is a way of dividing the complex nature of a human being into three convenient parts, each with its own function and motivation. There is nothing in Polynesian thought to imply that these three aspects are actually separate. It is more like dividing a papaya into three parts called skin, pulp, and seeds. Those three parts are actually a whole papaya which came from one source, but sometimes it is more convenient to speak of the skin, pulp, and seeds separately. Nor is there anything inherent in the nature of a human being which would prevent us from making a division into, say, fourteen aspects. Three is simply useful, convenient, and therefore accepted as a working truth. In Hawaiian they are called *ku* (the heart, body, or subconscious), *lono* (the mind, or conscious mind), and *kane* (the spirit, or superconscious).

The Heart Aspect—*Ku*

The primary function of this aspect of consciousness is memory. It is thanks to the *ku* that we can learn and remember, develop skills and habits, maintain the integrity of the body, and keep a sense of identity from day to day. It is a close equivalent to the Western concept of the subconscious, but it is not identical.

The most important thing to know about memory is that it is stored in the body as a vibration or movement pattern. Genetic memory is, of course, stored at the cellular level, while experiential or learned memory is stored at one or more of the many muscular levels. Under the right stimulation—internal or external, mental or physical—the movement occurs and the memory is released. This then gives rise to mental, emotional, or physical behavior. If the movement is inhibited, say by tension or stress, then the related memory is inhibited, too. This holds true for both genetic and learned memory.

In the case of genetic memory, the body only knows what its ancestors knew. That is such a rich store, however, that physical and emotional behavior and reactions are usually influenced to a greater or lesser degree by learned memory. In a stressful situation the *ku* first goes to ancestral memory for a way to cope and then, if there are several potential choices, it goes to learned memory for specifics. Let's suppose you are in a stressful situation involving your self-worth, which usually manifests in the chest. And let's suppose that genetic memory offers you the choices of a chest cold, an anxiety attack, or asthma. If, within the past week or so, your *ku* learned from another person or from television all about chest cold symptoms, the likelihood is high that your *ku* will make that choice.

Genetic memory is stored in every cell, but learned memory seems to be stored in specific areas of the body muscle tissue. The area of storage seems to be related to which part of the body was active or energized during the learning. When the part of the body in which memory was stored is under sufficient tension, then that memory is inhibited or even inaccessible. During a hiking trip with a friend into a wilderness area of Kauai, we found ourselves unable to locate our return trail. We agreed that it was on the other side of a stream, but we couldn't agree on what the site looked like, so we spent a whole day tramping up and down a stream looking for a place that both of us would recognize. The next day, after sleeping in a wet and muddy swamp, I decided to use our knowledge of the *ku*. With careful mutual questioning we discovered that in her memory of the trail site there was a peculiar mud bank nearby which I didn't remember at all, and in my memory there was a tributary with a large boulder nearby which she didn't remember at all. So we walked the stream until we found both attributes close to each other, and there was the trail, right in between.

When muscle tension is released, any memory stored in that area and inhibited by the tension is also released. This is common knowledge to anyone who gives or receives a lot of massages, but there are many ways to create tension and release it either consciously or unconsciously. A frequent experience people have is that of forgetting someone's name. You might be able to have a clear image of their face in your mind, but the name just won't come. It's because that part of your body in which the name is stored is under too much stress at the moment. Usually if you let it be and go about your business the name will sort of slip into your mind when you least expect it. And that is because in the meantime the muscles that held the name had relaxed enough to let the memory out. One time in Africa I was under high stress when I brought my wife to a party to meet the new U.S. ambassador, and when it came time to introduce her I couldn't remember her name! I assured the ambassador I had lived with her for several years and knew her well, but he was understandably skeptical. When Gloria finally said her own name that triggered the right muscle release and I could say, "Right, that's it, Gloria."

Severe shock which produces generalized stress may also result in amnesia, a condition in which large areas of memory are blocked. As various muscle groups are relaxed memory begins to return. Very interestingly, language is almost never forgotten by amnesiacs even though one's personal name might be blocked. This is probably because the components of language (letter sounds) are used so frequently that they are stored in many areas of the body. Nevertheless, there are still cases in which a person may be shocked speechless in actual fact.

I still blush when I recount the story about forgetting my wife's name. What is noteworthy is that I blush while I am recounting it, while the memory is vividly present in my mind. This tells us something else important about memory and the *ku*. The *ku*, your subconscious body-mind, does not distinguish between past, present, and future. As far as it is concerned the present is all there is. When you call a memory to mind you get physiological reactions in the present moment whose intensity depends on the vividness of that which you are recalling. For instance, you are more likely to get stronger physiological reactions from recalling a memory of being severely criticized at age seven than you are from recalling a memory of lunch a week ago Tuesday, unless that luncheon was even more traumatic. This means that whatever memories you dwell on will be affecting your body in the present moment, producing more or less the same chemical and muscular reactions that occurred when the event first happened. A good memory can produce endorphins and a bad memory can produce toxins, all in the present moment. Obviously, the longer you dwell on the memory, the greater the present effect.

Exploring Memory

Give yourself about fifteen seconds to recall an unpleasant memory and pay close attention to your body while you do so. Then immediately recall a very pleasant memory for about the same time, also paying close attention to your body. You will find that the unpleasant memory tends to make you feel tired, tense, contracted, depressed and/or unhappy, while the pleasant memory tends to make you feel lighter, expanded, relaxed and/or happy. Besides the fact that the two types of memories made you feel differently right here and now, note how fast the change took place. One moment you were feeling bad, and the next moment you were feeling good. And all it took was a shift of focus. One way to control your emotions and your health, then, is to choose what memories you allow yourself to dwell on.

As I said, I blush when I recall the incident about my wife's name. Blushing is an emotional reaction, and emotions are triggered by memories. That is the one and only source of emotions, or what are usually called feelings. They do not occur all by themselves. They are energy reactions set off by memory patterns. No one walks around full of anger, for instance. But people do walk around dwelling on memories that keep restimulating anger, or with muscle tension that suppresses memories which would release anger if they were brought to conscious awareness. As an example, brand-new knowledge or experience totally unrelated to past knowledge or experience, in and of itself, does not produce emotion. The only way in which brand-new knowledge or experience could produce an emotion would be if you already had a memory pattern (in the form of habit or expectation) of how to react when presented with brand-new knowledge or experience. If you had a pattern to remind you that brand-new knowledge or experience was a) exciting or b) scary, then your reaction would be appropriate to that pattern. Otherwise your reaction would be more on the order of "Huh?" or "That's nice." The point of all this is that if emotions are generated by memories of how to react in given situations, then one way to indirectly control emotions is by changing the memories. Ways and means to do this will be discussed farther on in the book.

Emotions can also be controlled indirectly by teaching your *ku* a new trick. This is based on the fact that emotions, particularly negative emotions like fear and anger, are always accompanied by muscle tension.

Exploring Emotions

Sit or stand comfortably with all your muscles relaxed (keep tense enough only to remain sitting or standing). Now, using your memory or imagination, go ahead and get as angry as you can, *but don't tense a single muscle.* What you will find, if you can keep your muscles relaxed, is that it is physiologically impossible to get angry. Anger *cannot* exist without muscle tension, and neither can fear. Therefore, training yourself to relax your muscles at will can help you recall knowledge and skills more easily, as well as enable you to prevent or free yourself in the middle of fear or anger. Not only that, it can help you break many unpleasant and unhealthy habit pat-

terns by giving your *ku* a new memory of how to act
or react in different situations.

I was with a friend, the same one who hikes with me, in
a town called Kapaa waiting for my wife to pick us up. The
friend offered me a taste of her ice cream cone, which I took,
and it was very good. In a little while she offered me another
taste, which I refused because I was cutting down on the fat
in my diet. Later she asked me how I was able to refuse a
second taste of such good ice cream. It was easy, I told her.
All I had to do was keep my shoulder muscles so relaxed
that I couldn't lift my arms to take the cone.

Another very important thing to know about the *ku* and
memory is that every experience, regardless of its source, is
stored as a body memory. The *ku* does not make fine distinctions about whether the experience came from an internal or external source, whether it came from an actual
physical situation or from a book, movie, TV program,
dream, psychic intuition, or your imagination. It's all stored
as body memory. All the *ku* cares about is the intensity of
the experience; that is, how much physiological (emotional,
chemical, muscular) reaction occurred during the experience. That is the *ku*'s only basis for how "real" the experience
was. The practical side of this is that an intensely imagined
experience is just as good as the real thing, at least as far as
memory-based behavior is concerned. Hawaiian and other
shamans have used this bit of wisdom for untold ages as a
tool for healing and self-development. Recently this ancient
shamanic understanding has been put to modern use by
Olympic athletes, among others, with extremely effective
results. By using full sensory imagination in which they perform perfectly every time, the athletes create body memories
which make the physical performance easier and better. The
same process can be used to train yourself in any skill, state,
or condition whatsoever.

Exploring Imagination

Recall a scene from a book you've read or from a favorite daydream. Then recall a vacation or trip you have taken. For about thirty seconds recall first one and then the other. Now, excluding differences in content (degree of vividness or type of activity, or conscious decision about which is real), attempt to determine any difference between the two as memories. You will find that, *as memories*, there is no difference. You can recall one as easily as the other and, in fact, the scene from the book or the daydream might have a stronger present effect on you than the "real" memory. The point: *ku* does not make distinctions between memories, regardless of the source. For the *ku* the ones that are most real are the ones with the greatest sensory impact.

The primary function of the *ku* is memory, and its primary motivation is pleasure. To put it more accurately, the *ku*'s motivation is toward pleasure and away from pain. All of your habitual—i.e., memory-based mental, emotional, or physical—behavior has this motivation. This is why you like to do certain things and why you don't like others, why some things are easier to do than others, and why you procrastinate even when there is something important to do. The *ku* quite automatically moves toward what is pleasurable and does its best to avoid what is painful.

If you create a "future" memory—in other words, if you imagine what will happen if you do a certain thing—your *ku*'s behavior will be strongly influenced by whether the memory carries the expectation of pain or pleasure. If you have created the expectation/memory that human encounters may result in painful rejection, you will find it hard to meet or be with people, to make phone calls (especially sales calls), and possibly even to write letters. On the other hand, if the thought of such encounters evokes an expectation/

memory of pleasurable contact, then such things will be easy and enjoyable for you. And if, as is very common, your *ku* holds both expectation/memories, then the ease or difficulty of these activities will vary according to your present level of self-confidence and self-esteem (also called your "mood").

There are occasions when the only choice available to the *ku* is the choice between two pains. The *ku* cannot make creative choices; it cannot invent new solutions. It can only do what it has learned from past experience or what it can copy from others in the present. When faced with a painful situation, the normal inclination of the *ku* is to move toward a pleasurable resolution, but it can only do this by remembering, copying, or taking directions from the conscious mind. If the conscious mind is not participating in the solution, and if no pleasurable solution is available in the present or past, then the *ku* must use the present or past to come up with the solution that produces the least pain. If you are working in a place which causes you to react with increasing stress that threatens the integrity of the body and you are not consciously doing anything about it (because you need the money, say), the *ku* may look around or remember and give you the flu to get you out of there. From the *ku*'s point of view the flu is not pleasant, but it is better than the pain of staying on the job. You get well when you quit, when you get fired, or when the pain of the flu becomes greater than the remembered pain of the job (the role of viruses will be considered in the chapter on healing the body).

Sometimes you will go through great mental, emotional, or physical pain to accomplish something. Athletes, mountain climbers, salespeople, scientists, students, and many others may experience this. What happens here is the addition of a factor called "importance." People will knowingly go through pain, even severe pain, only when some other part of them has decided that the end result or goal of what they are doing is more important—and therefore contains more potential pleasure—than the pain they have to go through, *and* when the potentially pleasurable goal is kept in mind.

The gain has to be greater than the pain. The athlete wants the pleasure of winning, the mountain climber wants the pleasure of reaching the top, the salesperson wants the pleasure of more money, the scientist wants the pleasure of solving a problem, the student may just want the pleasure of finishing. The point is that all behavior, habits, and action are influenced by the motivation toward pleasure.

In order to operate its memory function and engage its motivation, the *ku* uses its primary tool of sensation. According to this concept, all memory is kinesthetic, or body related; all pleasure and pain is as well; and all experience, even of emotions and ideas, produces physical sensations. As an urban shaman, you will want to develop and fine-tune this important tool of sensation, or sensory awareness. The part of you that can do this is the subject of the next section.

The Mind Aspect—*Lono*

The *lono* is that part of yourself which is consciously aware of internal and external input; of memories, thoughts, ideas, imaginings, intuitions, hunches, and inspirations, as well as sensory impressions of sight, sound, touch, taste, smell, depth, movement, pressure, time, and others. It hangs out on the border, so to speak, between the inner and outer worlds. The primary function of the *lono* is decision making. Since the process of decision making includes such things as attention, intent, choosing, and interpretation, I'll discuss each in turn with a lot of overlapping.

One of the decisions that the *lono* has to make frequently is where to focus attention. There are so many things to be aware of in any given moment that an attempt to be aware of all of them at once would soon reduce one to total ineffectiveness. Total awareness requires inaction, because action requires exclusion. To do any one thing means not to do a lot of other things. To increase awareness of one thing means to decrease awareness of a lot of other things. So part of the *lono*'s role is to make decisions that result in selective awareness in order to increase the individual's skill or effectiveness. In other words, *lono* decides what is important and what is not and attention follows the decision. Most such decisions are based on *ku*'s memory pattern of pleasure and pain, but *lono* may have a multitude of other reasons for attributing importance based on other kinds of decisions. When attention is focused on something important by *lono*'s standards, the focus might be narrow or broad depending on how much of the potential awareness is considered important.

Exploring Awareness

Find a small object to look at about ten or more feet away from you. While keeping your attention centered on the object allow your awareness to expand around it to include other objects above, below, and to the sides of it. Now look at the first object more closely and discover some detail about its appearance. In this case the importance was implied by the directions of the experiment itself. When you first directed your attention to the object of focus, most everything else in your awareness was dimmed. Then you expanded your focus to increase your awareness. Finally you will note that when your attention was drawn to a detail about the first object, your awareness of most everything else dimmed again. This experiment simply illustrates how importance operates and how flexible attention is.

Intent is a kind of decision making that directs awareness as well as activity. It is a powerful way to manage your *ku*, with tremendous effects on health, happiness, and success when used properly. Management theory recognizes three main styles of operation: authoritarian, democratic, and laissez-faire. These also happen to describe the three main ways that people deal with their own *ku*. To make our discussion more clear we'll call them controlling, cooperative, and uncontrolled styles.

When you intend to walk across the room, the intention is followed by awareness, which is followed by action. A controlling style of *ku* management will involve the *lono* constantly monitoring and correcting the *ku* to make sure it doesn't do anything wrong. The usual effect of such control is stiff and awkward movement or, at worst, clumsy and spastic movement (if there is any movement at all). The cooperative style involves the *lono* holding the intent and trusting the *ku* to do what it already knows how to do. The usual effect of this is smooth movement or, at best, movement that is fluid and graceful. The uncontrolled style usually results in never getting to the other side of the room at all because too many pleasurable or additional important things distract the attention. When you are speaking to someone with the intention of expressing something definite, the *ku* searches its memory and in a miraculous fashion that no one can yet explain, it vibrates the vocal cords and moves the jaw, tongue, and lips in such a way that more or less meaningful sounds are produced. A controlling *lono* interferes with the process by trying to make sure that the right words are said in the right way and usually creates havoc in the form of halting speech with a lot of "uh"s or "ya know"s or even stuttering. The cooperative *lono* holds the intent and lets the *ku* do its thing, which often produces spontaneous humor and unexpectedly good insights or phrases. The uncontrolling *lono* lets the *ku* wander off the subject a lot or even speak gibberish. What the *ku* knows it knows well, and that includes everything from how to heal itself to how to perform skills it has learned. I heard not long ago that hang gliders are designed to fly perfectly every time. The only accidents in hang gliding are caused by overcontrol on the part of fearful human beings. As we shall see shortly, it is the *lono* that generates fear. The *ku* is very much like a perfectly designed hang glider. Overcontrolled, it will not function properly; under cooperative guidance it will go and do whatever you want; without direction it will go wherever the currents of life take it.

Choosing is what most people think of as decision making. Choosing is making a decision to turn your attention in one direction rather than another, or to do one thing rather than another (the actual doing is done by the *ku*). Many people experience great difficulty in making such decisions, and they usually say that they are afraid of making the wrong decision and having things turn out wrong because of it. What they are really afraid of is either being disappointed or receiving disapproval. Well, first of all, no one can make a wrong decision about the future because a present decision does not create a future event. Present decisions can only create present events. Future events are created by future decisions, or rather, decisions made when the future is a present moment experience. If two people living in St. Louis, Missouri, one a positive thinker and one a negative thinker, are both making a decision about whether to move to Honolulu or New York and they both choose Honolulu, the high likelihood is that the positive thinker will have a positive experience and the negative thinker will have a negative experience. There is also a high likelihood (unless they have read this book) that each will praise or blame the decision about the move depending on their experience. In fact, if each had chosen New York instead the situation would have been the same.

A decision does not make the future turn out a certain way. It is how you continue to think after making a decision that makes the future turn out the way it does. As for disappointment, this is nothing more than a decision to feel bad about an outcome. And not making a decision because you are afraid of being disappointed is like saying that you are afraid you might make a decision to feel bad in the future regardless of the outcome, or that you are afraid the outcome might not be what you want it to be. I don't know about you, but that sounds pretty silly to me. It's like not getting out of bed because you might decide to feel unhappy about something, or because everything might not go according to plan. As we'll see, the decision about unhappiness has nothing to do with events, and (I almost hate to tell you this) things rarely go according to plan. If your thinking is right they often go better. In terms of choosing what to focus on or what to do, then, it really doesn't matter what you choose. Some things you choose might be easier than others, but that has to do with existing *ku* memory and habits rather than what is chosen. Much more important than such choices are the decisions you make about interpreting experience.

Interpretation is a decision about the meaning or validity of experience. This kind of decision sets up patterns of expectation and filtering that have great bearing on future experience. Interpretation is done either by evaluation or analysis. Evaluation is basically a decision that something is good or bad, right or wrong, while analysis is a decision that something is or isn't. When you evaluate an employee's performance you look for things to fault or to praise; you make decisions about which aspects of his or her performance are bad and which are good. When you analyze an employee's performance you make decisions about effectiveness and efficiency. A set goal is either achieved within a given time period or it isn't. Once you make a value judgment with your *lono* about effectiveness or efficiency, you are out of analysis and into evaluation. The difference is quite important for clear thinking because evaluation usually generates emotional responses of happiness, fear, or anger, while pure analysis does not. This is because "goodness" stimulates expectation patterns of pleasure (approval, acceptance) and "badness" stimulates expectation patterns of pain (disapproval, rejection). Mere existence only stimulates interest or indifference (based on decision patterns of importance).

I spoke of the primary motivation of the *ku* being pleasure, which explains a lot of human behavior. Even more behavior can be explained by the primary motivation of the *lono*, which is order. Order doesn't necessarily mean neatness, although some *lono*s may interpret it that way. It has more to do with rules, categories, and understanding. Human *lono*s just love logic, even when the logic is based on silly assumptions; and they love explanations, as long as the explanations are based on *ku* memory and motivation, or if they bring order out of disorder. Some people spend their entire lives classifying plants, for example, and that's fine if they enjoy it. But Nature isn't *really* divided into genus, family, and species. Those are just categories invented by human *lono*s to bring a sense of order into the overwhelming variety of Nature. And some people insist on knowing *why* things are the way they are before they will give themselves permission to change. Understanding isn't necessary in order to bring about positive change, but a lot of people feel better if they have explanations first. When fear is present, the motivation for order becomes a motivation for security.

The primary tool of the *lono* is imagination. Since the *lono* is the only part of you under your direct control, the development of this tool is of supreme importance for the urban shaman. It is through your imagination that you influence and direct your aspects and the world around you.

The Spirit Aspect—*Kane*
The *kane* is conceived of as a "source" aspect, a purely spiritual essence which manifests or projects into reality our physically oriented being. It might also be called the soul or oversoul as long as you don't get the idea that it is something that can be lost or separated from you. For that reason it is often called the god-self or High Self [but it comes from an even greater source, which might be called the godhead or any other term you prefer]. In Hawaiian tradition it is often called the *aumakua,* and may be symbolically related to one's ancestors or grandparents.

The primary function of the *kane* is creativity in the form of mental and physical experience. Simplified, the *lono* generates a pattern by deciding that something is true, *ku* memorizes the pattern, and *kane* uses the pattern to manifest experience. At the same time, *kane* is constantly giving inspiration to improve the pattern because its primary moti-

vation is harmony. That inspiration might come mentally,
as in meditation, or it might come physically by means of
an omen contained in the movement of birds, animals, or
clouds or perhaps, in modern times, in the content of a
conversation, a book, or even a TV program. However it
comes, the motivation is to help the whole self integrate its
patterns more harmoniously with others in the community
and environment.

Kane never interferes with experience unless there is some
possibility of moving off your life path. This is not the same
as predestination. The idea is that you-as-*kane* decided to
accomplish certain things during this lifetime and accomplish
them you will: kicking and screaming or laughing and dancing, you will accomplish your mission. It's something like
having decided to set sail from one shore of an ocean to the
other. The destiny you've assigned yourself is to get to the
other side, but the specific direction you take, the currents
you follow, the kinds of sails you use, the sort of crew you
take on, the islands you stop at, and the attitudes you develop
along the way are all up to you. The only time *kane* inter-
venes directly is when an event is about to occur that would
lead, directly or indirectly, to not reaching the other side.
These occasions usually take the form of little "accidents"
that break a train of thought which you then can't regain.
It might be something as simple as being bumped by a
passerby or stubbing your toe. Once I was having dinner
with some fellow shamans in a Chinese restaurant on Kauai
and a woman to my right was just starting to tell us a story
about something or other when I reached for a dish in the
middle of the table. Halfway there my hand suddenly jerked
to the right and knocked a glass of wine all over the woman
telling the story. Immediately we helped her clean it up, but
afterward she couldn't remember what she'd been talking
about and neither could anyone else. Weeks later the woman
still couldn't remember what she'd been saying or been
about to say. I apologized at the time, of course, but I was
completely unembarrassed about it because I had a strong
intuition about what had happened. It was clear to me that

kane had intervened because the story would have had detrimental consequences (in terms of the life path) on one or more people present.

The primary tool of the *kane* is energy. The universe is made of energy and it is energy that sustains and maintains and changes the dreams of life. The imagination of the *lono* directs the energy and the sensation of the *ku* lets us experience its effects.

Many traditions and teachings express the idea that getting in touch with your spirit aspect is an arduous, long-term process involving great self-discipline and special techniques. I'm telling you here and now that it's simple and easy. It must be. For nothing is so intimately a part of you as your own spirit.

Exploring Spiritual Connection

it comfortably and close your eyes; take a few deep breaths and be aware of your body. Now imagine something beautiful, as beautiful as you can. It may be something from your memory, something you've seen or read about, or something you make up right now. Just think about it strongly. In a moment or so you may feel sensations of relaxation, pleasure, or energy. That is the *ku* telling you that you are now in direct, conscious contact with your *kane*. This is also a good time for conscious communication. One of the best ways for communicating directly with your *kane* is to say "thank you." Thank you for the good things that are and for the good that is coming. Take a few moments, being as specific as you like, and finish with some phrase that signifies to you a completion and positive expectation. "So be it," "amen," or the Hawaiian "*amama*" are examples.

To the degree you believe and trust, you will get results. That's what we'll deal with next.

THE THIRD ADVENTURE:

THE FUNDAMENTAL PRINCIPLES

Hili hewa ka mana'o ke 'ole ke kukakuka
(Ideas run wild without discussion)

I was told by my teachers that a very long time ago some wise healers got together to share their observations on life and healing and to put them in a form that could easily be taught and remembered as a craft. Although they could have picked a hundred ideas, they chose to express their wisdom as seven basic principles because of the esoteric symbolism of the number seven. These are essentially principles of manifestation, of the hidden or inner cause of outer events, and in many ancient traditions the number seven represents this inner knowledge because it is made up of the numbers three and four, which in turn represent the primal masculine and feminine forces or polarities of the universe. Not all traditions agree on which is which, however. In Hawaiian the number seven is *hiku*, composed of two syllables—*hi*, the feminine principle (meaning "to flow") and *ku*, the masculine principle (meaning "to stand firm").

The Seven Shaman Principles

I learned the seven principles in their Hawaiian form as seven individual words with many extended meanings, but in order to teach this knowledge in Western culture I had to translate each word into a basic phrase. It soon became clear that the basic phrases couldn't capture enough of the essence of each principle, so I added several "corollaries" for each phrase.

The principles and corollaries that follow represent a workable philosophy of life and guide to the practice of urban shamancraft.

The First Principle: *IKE*—The World Is What You Think It Is

Depending on your point of view a water gourd can be half-empty or half-full. Depending on your plans the rain can be good for the crops or bad for the picnic. Depending on your attitude a problem can be an obstacle or a challenge. These are clear, obvious, and understandable ways in which our thinking affects our experience. In a more subtle way— but a way very well documented in the fields of psychosomatics, psychoimmunology, and motivational psychology— we know that thoughts of fear, worry, anger, and resentment can make us sick and diminish our effectiveness, while thoughts of confidence, determination, love, and forgiveness can make us well and increase our performance. Extending into the metaphysical realm, we come across the idea that thoughts will telepathically attract their equivalent. In other words, to put it very simply, positive thoughts will attract positive people and events, and negative thoughts will attract negative people and events. This is less obvious than the previous examples, but millions of people acknowledge the concept and a careful and honest appraisal of your thoughts and your life will clearly demonstrate the effect. Then there is the deeper esoteric idea shared by many spiritual teachers around the world that your experience is determined by your faith, by what you believe in. And both ancient and contemporary history are full of examples of the power of thought in the form of prayer, faith, and conviction to change physical conditions, events, and circumstances. All of these ideas are included in the first principle of this philosophy. Plus a bit more.

Corollary: Everything is a dream

In addition to recognizing the effects on experience of attitude, expectation, telepathy, and belief, shamans also hold the exceptionally subtle idea that life is a dream; that, in fact, we dream our lives into being. This does not mean that life is an illusion. It means that dreams are real and reality is a dream. It means that the reality that you are experiencing right now is only one of many dreams. Now at first this sounds so weird that it's confusing and seems illogical because you can knock your hand against a wall and feel its solidity, you can hear the sound around you, and you can see lots of objects in great detail. What's so dreamlike about that? But think a moment. The wall you knocked your hand against isn't really solid, and neither is your hand. Both are composed of molecules which are composed of atoms which are mostly energy fields vibrating at different frequencies. The only reason your hand didn't go through the wall was because both it and the wall are vibrating at frequencies so close in range that they interfere with each other. At the same time, radio and television frequencies, for instance, pass right through the wall and your hand as if they weren't even there. When you struck the wall you weren't hitting a solid object. Instead, two energy fields met and the information was transmitted to your brain, where it was interpreted by you, based on memory, as the experience of hitting a wall. And the sound that you hear? Let's assume it's music. But it really isn't music you are hearing directly. You are experiencing a vibrational wave pattern moving through the air which hits your eardrum and is translated into an electrical nerve impulse received by your brain. Your brain then gives out a signal that you interpret, based on memory again, as music. Finally, the objects that you see are only seen because light energy bounces off other energy fields toward your eyes, where the frequencies are translated into patterns that you interpret as objects. What appears to be external reality is really all in your head. Why, that sounds like a dream.

While you're still reeling from that, think about this. Have you ever had a dream at night that seemed just as real or even more real than your daily experience? If so, then you know the only way you could tell the difference was that *this* dream (or reality) had more memories you could hook into it. However, from the shaman point of view, memories are only other dreams. If you've not had such a realistic dream, you may have heard or read about people—mystics, drunks, schizophrenics, people taking drugs, who are sleep deprived, sick, the elderly, children, or shamans—who have had what psychologists and psychiatrists like to call "hallucinations" that for them were every bit as real, or more real, than the dream we call ordinary experience (*hallucination* means "your dream doesn't match my dream").

Think about the fact that the only test we use for the reality of such experiences is whether or not someone else experienced them. And even that isn't always enough. If you are angry about being left out or you don't like what others say they've experienced, you can always call it "mass hallucination." For the shamans, the experience we call ordinary everyday reality is a mass hallucination, or, to put it more politely, a shared dream. It is like we are all having our own individual dreams about life and the sharing occurs at points of agreement or consensus. If you were in my office right now we could both agree that I am working at my computer which has a carving of the word *love* and a jade carving of a Maori tiki from New Zealand in front of it. But you might not be able to feel or see the energy field around the jade and I might not be able to smell your perfume or after-shave lotion, nor hear the music coming from the earphones of your portable cassette player. Parts of our dreams would be shared and parts would not. Of course, you could always bend closer so I could smell you and put the earphones on me so I could hear the music, and I could teach you how to sense the jade's energy, but that doesn't prove anything about dreams and reality because we can learn how to share those other experiences usually called dreams as well.

Being practical, urban shamans know there is a point to this point of view. *If* this life is a dream, and *if* we can wake up fully within it, then we can change the dream by changing our dreaming. We will explore many ways to change the dream of life in this book, most of which will work for you whether you decide that life is a dream or not. But for those who dare to experiment with such an idea, a rich adventure filled with challenge and opportunity will open up for you.

Corollary: All systems are arbitrary

There is a story of a young man who embarked on a dangerous and time-consuming journey to find a wise old man and ask him the meaning of life. When at last he confronted the wise one and had asked his question, the old man replied, "Life is just a bowl of cherries." At first stunned speechless and then furiously angry, the young man said, "That's it? I've come all the way here, past oceans and mountains and deserts and jungles to find you and ask you the meaning of life, and all you have to say is that life is a bowl of cherries??!!" The old man smiled, shifted his robe, and replied, "All right, so life is not just a bowl of cherries."

For untold ages humans have sought to find the Ultimate Meaning and the Absolute Truth, something solid and eternal for their *lono*s to cling to. They have tried Mysticism, Religion, Science, Metaphysics, Art, and Philosophy in order to make sense of life so they can feel more secure within themselves, and often, to control life in order to feel more secure outside themselves.

Shamans have come up with their own solution to the problem of meaning by a logical extension of the ideas that everything is a dream and the world is what you think it is. If those are accepted as basic assumptions, then obviously all meanings are made up and the Absolute Truth is whatever you decide it is. The meaning of experience depends on your interpretation of it or your decision to accept someone else's interpretation, and the decision to accept a basic assumption is also arbitrary. Therefore, all systems that describe life and its workings are arbitrarily made up based on certain decisions to accept certain interpretations of experience. So what really matters is not whether a particular system is true (an arbitrary concept), but rather how well it works for you. The system known as *Huna*, with its seven principles, is acknowledged as being just as arbitrary and made up as any other system. So it isn't presented as Truth, but as a set of hypotheses that allow you to practice shamancraft more effectively. It's similar to learning the scales in music or the rules of perspective in painting so you can practice those crafts more effectively. The principles of any craft are useful for the practice of that craft, but they don't necessarily apply to a different craft or a different aspect of life. This is why the seven principles are not presented as dogma, and why they do not have to be defended. If they work for you, use them; if they don't, then use something else. A wise shaman feels free to change systems at will, according to the situation at hand. This corollary also allows a great deal of tolerance for other systems because they aren't seen as antagonistic or threatening, but simply as different points of view.

Exploring the Power of Thought

If the world is what you think it is, then you ought to be able to change your world by changing your thought. Sit up comfortably with your eyes open and turn your head as far as you can to the left and look straight ahead. Find something in your line of sight that you can remember as a marker and bring your head forward again. Now close your eyes, keep your head still, and *imagine* that you are slowly turning your head to the left very easily and loosely, without any strain, way past the marker until you are looking directly behind you without any problem at all. Imagine the sensation and the feeling as well as the sight. Then imagine bringing your head slowly back to the front. Now open your eyes and turn your head physically to the left. To the degree you were able to imagine the feeling in your mind you will now find that your head moves easily farther than it did before and your line of sight is well past the marker.

What you just did was change your body by changing your mind. You imagined being able to do something different, and your body responded to your thought by changing what was possible only moments before. It's a simple demonstration full of powerful implications.

The Second Principle: *KALA*—There Are No Limits

At first glance this seems absurd because we can experience limitations all around us. Our bodies can only grow so much, we can only see so far, we can only hear within a certain range, we can only live so long without breathing, the earth is only so big, and we have only so much money in the bank. No limits?

Yes, no limits. The universe is infinite, as it would have to be if the world is what we think it is and it's all a dream. How, then, to explain the limitations we experience? One way is to recognize two kinds of limitations: creative and filtered.

An infinite universe implies infinite experience, which is the same as no experience because there wouldn't be any differentiation, contrast, or sensation of change. The concept of creative limitation assumes the purposeful establishment of limits within an infinite universe in order to create particular experiences. Our realm of physical experience, for instance, is arbitrarily limited by our natural perceptual range of the frequencies of sight, sound, touch, gravity, distance, and time, to name the most prominent, plus the extensions of those that we can make with mechanical instruments and psychic abilities. Without these apparent limitations, however, we couldn't even experience this dimension. If you assume an infinite universe, there is no logical reason why there couldn't be other beings just as physically real to themselves as we are to ourselves who see in the frequency range of ultraviolet, hear in the range of ultrahigh frequency, and touch in the range of radio waves. For all we know, each of us experiences the others' slight intrusions into our "home ranges" as static. So this physical universe of our perception may be the effect of creative choices of limiting factors on the part of God or our own Higher Selves that enable us to experience life on Earth.

Let's bring this topic down to a more manageable scale. Life is like a game of checkers (if it can be a bowl of cherries, it can be a game of checkers). On a checkerboard, representing the physical dimension, there are sixty-four squares—half black and half red—and twenty-four checkers, twelve of each color. At the start of the game you have your pieces ranged on one side and your partner has his ranged on the other. The rules say that you can move forward and take your partner's pieces when you jump them, and double up or king your piece when you reach the other side, which gives you freedom to move in any direction. Now *actually* there is nothing really preventing you from kinging all your pieces before you start, grabbing your partner's pieces whenever you want to, or throwing his pieces across the room so he can't move them. You could do that, but you wouldn't be playing checkers anymore. The rules of the game are limitations created so you can play the game. That's how the shaman views life. Only the shaman's game is more like using the same board but changing the rules and the pieces so you can play chess, thereby expanding the possibilities of experience within the same dimension. Creative limitation allows us to improve our creative abilities by enforcing a focus on a certain range and interpretation of experience. Even in the limited game of chess, human minds have still not figured out all the possibilities.

In contrast, filtered limitation is used here to mean limitations imposed by ideas and beliefs that inhibit creativity rather than enhance it, like beliefs that engender helplessness and hopelessness, or revenge and cruelty. Recently I spoke with a person who expressed helpless rage at a world full of pain and suffering. And we were discussing this in a place full of love and peace and harmony. This person's obsession with suffering was filtering out contrary experiences and making it nearly impossible to do anything about the suffering. Filtered limitations generate focus without the potential for positive action.

Corollary: Everything is connected

In many traditional shamanic cultures the idea that everything is connected is usually represented by the symbol of a spider web. The shaman is the spider who weaves the web (of life) in a lucid dream out of fine threads that come from within. The web not only represents the dreaming of life, but also its interconnectedness. Every part of life is connected to every other part, and what affects one affects all to varying degrees. A single thought of love or hate affects the whole Universe, but your body will probably be more affected than the star Betelguese, just as a fly or a leaf will affect the part of the web it touches more than the rest, though the whole web may quiver. Although the web is a common traditional metaphor used to explain an actual metaphysical connection between everything, some people might find it easier to think of the connection in terms of an electromagnetic metaphor of fields within fields in infinite array.

By assuming such an interconnectedness, we can assume the possibility of influence at a distance, which the shamans do and which they use for many types of healing and manifesting.

Corollary: Anything is possible

If there are no limits, then of course anything is possible. All you have to do is believe it (which comes from the first principle). However, because you are not alone in the Universe, the degree to which something can be shared depends on the beliefs of others around you. You may be able to levitate in the privacy of your bedroom, but you might not be able to do so in the presence of others because of their disbelief. On the other hand, someone else's belief in levitation may be so strong that you can do it in their presence, but not when you are with others or by yourself. Travel between the stars is possible, but the only way it is expressible in our current culture is through movies or books (except for the claims of certain individuals who may or may not have had a physical experience).

According to Christian scripture, even Jesus had difficulty in his hometown doing miracles because the people didn't believe the carpenter's son could or should have such powers (as has been pointed out to me, however, other interpretations of this event are possible). At any rate, the more people who believe that the change you want to make is possible, the easier it will be to make it.

Corollary: Separation is a useful illusion

I have known people to get so caught up in the idea and experience of connections and relatedness that they are immobilized by the fear of unforeseen consequences springing from their slightest thought or action, or they drown in empathy with the pain and suffering of others. At such times it is healthy to inject a little creative separation in order to function better. Fear makes you lose sight of your role as the dreamweaver, and the assumption for a while of the independence of all things will help bring you back into balance. Likewise, pure empathy makes you as helpless as the one suffering. A solution is to add a dose of separation by switching to compassion, in which you are aware of the suffering while realizing it isn't happening to you. Then you can help the sufferer move out of it. The main point is that there really are no limits, so as an urban shaman you can feel free to create limits when it's useful to do so.

Exploring Energy Connections

With another person or several, put your hands out, palm to palm, a couple of inches apart. You may soon feel a sense of warmth, a coolness, or a tingling. If you move your hands toward your partner's very slightly, you may even feel a sense of pressure, as if you were pushing against a magnet or a very light balloon. Now move your hands even farther away and check for sensations again. How much you can feel as you move farther away will depend on your sensitivity. The most important thing is to realize that you have been touching that person directly. You were touching his or her energy, which is as intimately a part of a person as the body. We do not end at our skin. Our energy, or spirit, extends to the ends of the Universe. We are all connected to everything because there are no limits.

The Third Principle: *MAKIA*—Energy Flows Where Attention Goes

Two of the most successful and long-practiced techniques used by shamans are meditation and hypnosis, because both make use of the third principle. Meditation means a lot of different things to people using different systems. For some it conjures up thoughts of a lonely monk in the cell of a monastery dwelling on the presence of God; others think of yuppies sitting cross-legged in a circle chanting mantrams in a language they don't understand; and others think of sipping tea while watching the sun go down. All of these and others like them are techniques or styles of meditation. Meditation itself simply means to think deeply and continuously; in other words, sustained focused attention. The word comes from a Latin root *med*, meaning "to measure," which is shared with a word meaning "to heal" that leads to the word *medical*. You are meditating whenever you are engaged in sustained focused attention on anything, and according to this philosophy such attention channels the energy of the universe into manifesting the physical equivalent of the focus. However, the manifestation is not just the equivalent of what you are looking at, saying, listening to, or doing. It is the equivalent of the sum total of your entire attention, including habitual expectation, during the meditation. To put it another way, whenever *lono* is meditating, *ku* is meditating, too. Part of one's development as a shaman involves learning how to get *lono* and *ku* to meditate on the same thing at the same time. Then the magic happens.

Hypnosis is just another kind of meditation. There is no generally agreed on definition of hypnosis, because some people treat it as a process and others as a state. The process is of no interest here, but the state is. As a state, hypnosis is simply a condition of sustained focused attention, just like meditation. The major difference is that meditation is considered to be more spiritual and hypnosis to be more practical; meditation is used for clearing karma and reaching enlightenment, while hypnosis is used for stopping smoking and losing weight. The fact is, you could use either one for the same thing. Hypnosis used to be distinguished by the use of an assistant called a hypnotist who helped you into the focused state, but guided meditation has eliminated that distinction. And meditation always used to be a private thing, but self-hypnosis has removed that difference. As processes, both meditation and hypnosis are simply different techniques for doing the same thing—refocusing your attention toward more positive beliefs and expectations. As states, both are identical conditions of sustained focused attention. Any difference can be attributed to the object of focus.

Since energy flows where attention goes, those aspects of your present experience which seem enduring are the effect of habitual sustained focused attention carried on by your *ku*. If you like what you've got, that's great. If you don't, then you need to find some way to shift your *ku*'s attention into a new pattern. Meditation and hypnosis are good tools for that, and I'll give you some others later on.

Corollary: Attention goes where energy flows

Attention is quite naturally attracted to bright lights, shiny objects, and loud noises, but we may not realize that the common factor of all three is their energy intensity. Attention is attracted to any strong source of energy that stimulates any of our senses, even those subtle senses of which most people are unaware. Certain people, because of their emotional intensity or sensory focus, have such a strong aura or energy field that they automatically attract the attention of others whenever they come into view. On a larger scale, some geographical areas—usually areas of high earthquake activity or potential—have a higher energy intensity than others, thereby attracting greater populations, which increase the energy even more. Much is written nowadays about sacred power spots, but I think their power is a passive one that allows you to relax and destress from the really active power spots of urban centers. The tingling sensations and psychic phenomena experienced at such places occur as you begin to relax and your bottled-up energy from the more highly active place you came from begins to flow. Human beings are such energy generators themselves, however, that if a lot of them move to a nice, quiet, passive power spot they can soon turn it into an active, dynamic, and possibly stressful power spot.

Corollary: Everything is energy

It is not new to either physics or metaphysics to say that everything is energy, but the logical implications are interesting because they include the idea that thought is energy and that one kind of energy can be converted into another kind of energy. This happens when the pressure energy of steam pushes a turbine to convert magnetic energy into electrical energy, and it happens when electrical energy pushes through a resistant wire to produce heat for an iron. Heat is also generated when a group of human beings in a room get excited or do certain breathing or meditative exercises. This idea also provides a neat explanation of how thought can produce its physical equivalent, especially when amplified by emotion and/or confidence.

Exploring Energy Flow

To demonstrate how energy flows where attention goes, and how thought affects physical energy, pick up a chair by its seat and feel the weight of it. Then put it back down. Now focus your attention on the very top of the chair's back and pick it up by the seat again. If your focus is good the chair will feel lighter. Regardless of how you want to explain it, the practical fact is that if you have to lift anything you will find it easier to do if your attention is focused on the very top of the object or even in the air a foot above it.

One of my students, a rather short woman, very proudly told me that she went to a garden shop and bought a concrete statue for a pedestal she had in her yard. Two husky clerks carried it out to her station wagon and she went home. There she realized she had no one to help her move the heavy statue out of the car, up a slope to her gate, twenty feet farther into her yard, and up onto the pedestal. After crying somewhat in frustration, she remembered what she knew about focus and energy flow and used it, in short spurts, to do the whole job all by herself.

The Fourth Principle: MANAWA—Now Is The Moment Of Power

In some Eastern traditions (as well as some Western metaphysical ones) your present circumstances are the effect of decisions and actions in past lives. If those were good decisions and actions, you have good experiences now, but if they were bad ones you have pain, suffering, and sorrow now to the same degree you gave it out in one or more of those other lives. This is called *karma*, a Sanskrit word usually translated as "cause and effect" or "reward and debt," but which really means "action and reaction." The good actions you perform now create "good" karma and the bad actions you perform now create "bad" karma for your next lives. In these traditions karma isn't usually something you can change; all you can do is reap the rewards or work off the debts of the past.

One common Western tradition holds that you are rewarded in this life for obeying specific social or religious rules and punished in this life for breaking those rules, no matter how long ago you obeyed them or broke them, nor whether or not anyone was there to see you do it. Some people trained in this tradition may carry twenty years of guilt for having driven past a stop sign in the Arizona desert at 2 A.M. a hundred miles from any other human soul.

Another, more modern Western tradition lays the praise or blame for your present attitude, actions, and circumstances on heredity and your early social environment. The implication is that you were shaped by forces beyond your control and cannot be held responsible for what your genes, your parents, or society did to you.

The shamanic tradition, both warrior and adventurer versions, is in stark contrast to the above views. It says that the past did not give you what you have today, nor make you what you are today. It is your beliefs, decisions, and actions today about yourself and the world around you that give you what you have and make you what you are. Karma exists and operates only in the present moment. Your environment and circumstances in this moment are the direct reflections of your mental and physical behavior in this moment. Thanks to memory we may carry over habits of body and mind from day to day, but each day is a new creation and any habit can be changed in any present moment— although that doesn't mean it will be easy. Your genes do not determine what you are or what occurs in your body. Instead, as an effect of your beliefs, you select out of the immense resources of your gene pool those characteristics that best reflect your present beliefs and intentions. In the same way, your parents or social background have nothing to do with your present circumstances, but what you believe about them now and how you react to those beliefs now most certainly does. To the degree that you change yourself in the present moment—your thoughts and your behavior— you change your world.

Over and over again my students and I have witnessed dramatic changes in personality and circumstances the moment a person decided to make a dramatic change in thought and behavior. I will mention only one such change right now. It took place in Tahiti after I had done a training there. One of my students, a Tahitian woman, had had a long-standing feud with her sister over some property to the extent that her sister was taking her to court in a very nasty way. After mulling over the teaching the night I left, this woman decided to say a prayer of forgiveness for her sister, no matter what she had done or would do. The very next morning her sister called, said she had thought the whole matter over and decided to drop the lawsuit and not dispute the property anymore.

Corollary: Everything is relative

Now is the moment of power, but how do we define what now is? The easiest and most practical definition is: the area or range of present attention. So now might be this second, this minute, this hour, day, month, or year depending on your focus. But using this definition involves accepting as now elements of what we would ordinarily call past and future, as in the case of focusing our attention on the present day, month, or year. And that's exactly right. What we call the future is only the future relative to what we define as the present moment, and the same is true for the past. If our attention is broad enough, we can even bring awareness of past and future lives into the present moment (if you believe in them). When our attention and awareness bring aspects of the past and future into this present moment, they are within the range of our power to change them. Which means that from the present we can change the past and the future.

Corollary: Power increases with sensory attention

There are a lot of people living in the world today who aren't even here. Most of their attention is focused on memories of the past, projections into the future, fantasies of alternate worlds, or on themselves. To the degree they diminish their awareness of the present moment during such ruminations, their power and effectiveness in the present also decreases. When done occasionally or cyclically for relaxation, recreation, inspiration, planning, or self-development there can be great benefit in withdrawing from the present world, but there is a point of diminishing returns which varies with individuals if such focus is carried on for extended periods. Unfortunately, some people are obsessively locked into the past, future, or elsewhere because of great fear and anger. Guilt, resentment, and worry keep them out of the present and away from the joys of life. Much of the fear and anger can be dissipated by shifting focus to the sensory present, although people who have decided that the present moment is a dangerous place will have more difficulty doing that.

What does it mean to focus on the sensory present, and what are the effects of doing that? It means being more and more consciously aware of the input from your senses. So few people practice real sensory awareness that it is sometimes taught as a meditation technique, and some people do it so well quite unconsciously that they have a profound impact on others around them without even trying. The effects occur as a result of the third principle—energy flows where attention goes. As you place more and more attention on the input from your senses, you may progress through experiences of heightened sensory acuity, relaxation, awareness of energy flow in and around you, awareness of more happening around you than you usually notice . . . all the way to an increasing realization of the dreamlike quality of physical reality and an awareness of becoming lucid in the dream. Some of it may frighten you with its strangeness, and some of it may cause you to feel like bursting with joy. On the other hand, a halfhearted effort will probably just make you feel bored. An indication of the shamanic under-standing of this practice is contained in the meanings of the Hawaiian word for it, *ano* (and its variant, *'ano*): the present moment, seed, likeness, peacefulness, awe, holy, sacred, in-tensive fire (*a* plus *no*).

Exploring the Present Moment

Wherever you are, become aware of the colors in your environment, the whites, reds, or-anges, yellows, greens, blues, violets, and blacks; then look at all the straight and curved lines you can see, the shapes of objects and the spaces between them. Next listen to all the sounds you can hear from all directions. And then feel the position of your hands and feet, your body as a whole, the sensation of your clothing and whatever you are touching, the movement of your breathing, and, as best you can, the energy in and around you. Finally, add other senses like taste and smell, if you wish, and let your attention roam among all your senses seeking more and more awareness of each. Do this for as long as you like during any kind of activity and decide for yourself whether it is worth following up on. Just remember that this kind of focus is a skill that can be developed. The present moment is a very rich field for experience and adventure.

The Fifth Principle: *ALOHA*—To Love Is To Be Happy With

Love is a word that many people find hard to understand because its use in English has become quite sloppy. It is used to denote pleasure ("I love ice cream"), sexual desire ("I want to make love to you"), intention ("I'd love to get my hands on that"), as a measure of caring ("If you love me you'll do what I want"), and to express addictive need ("I'll die without your love"). The effects of love in contemporary song and story even sound like vitamin deficiencies (insomnia, upset stomach, loss of appetite, weak knees, heart palpitations, dizziness, sweaty hands, fever, chills, etc.).

In Hawaiian the meaning of *love* is very clear and it provides a useful guideline for loving and being loved. *Aloha* is the word for love. The root *alo* means "to be with, to share an experience, here and now." The root *oha* means "affection, joy." Thus the full translation of *aloha* becomes "to love is to be happy with." This means that love exists to the degree that you are happy with the object of your love. In any relationship with a person, place, or thing, the happy part comes from love and the unhappy part comes from fear, anger, and doubt. You don't get sweaty hands from being in love; you get them from fear. You don't get hurt from being in love; you get hurt from anger. What you get from being in love is happiness, the intensity of it depending on how deeply you are in love. To be deeply in love means to be deeply connected, and the depth and clarity of the connection increases as fear, anger, and doubt are removed.

Corollary: Love increases as judgment decreases

I once attended a workshop called "Actualizations" (known to some as "est with heart"), which basically consisted of a few meditative exercises and a lot of personal sharing. By the middle of the second day the love and affection among us was already getting thick, and by the third day there were a hundred people in love. The workshop facilitator was honest enough to admit that they didn't try to make that happen; they didn't even know how it happened, it just did. When you know how love works, however, it's easy enough to understand. A hundred strangers got together without any expectations or history other than what they chose to share, and all they got from sharing was acknowledgment and support without criticism or judgment. Fear, anger, and doubt were not present, and so love was. The love is actually always there. It's just that fear, anger, and doubt cover it up.

Fear, anger, and doubt give rise to negative criticism and judgment, which cause separation, which diminishes love. Criticism kills relationships. On the other hand, praise builds and rebuilds them, because praise is an act of love—being happy with—that clarifies and strengthens relationships. Because of the third principle, when you give praise you reinforce the good that you praise and it increases and grows. When you criticize you reinforce the bad that you don't like and it also increases and grows. A new relationship is usually full of fun, happiness, and excitement because the tendency at first is to notice and dwell only on what is good in each other. As doubt about yourself, each other, or the relationship in general is allowed to come out, then the tendency is toward criticizing perceived or imagined faults and failings. If this happens quickly and openly it's a short-lived relationship, and if it happens slowly and subtly it's a long, unhappy relationship that breaks when one partner can't stand it anymore. To be blunt, the relationship contains more pain than pleasure. A relationship in the process of falling apart because of criticism can be revived and made happy again by removing criticism and adding strong doses of praise and compliments. This is easier if both partners participate; it is possible but difficult if only one does it. The key to success here is simply to increase your appreciation of what you do like about your partner, and increase your tolerance of what you don't like. Telepathic praise is just as important as verbal praise, and is sometimes a better way to begin.

Corollary: Everything is alive, aware, and responsive

For the shaman, life is not limited to plants, animals, and humans, because life is defined as movement. Some things move very slowly, like rocks, and some things move very quickly, like light. For the shaman these are simply different kinds of life. Also, operating from the second principle, since

the Source of Life is infinite and the Source is self-aware,
everything must be self-aware and therefore responsive in
some degree to what happens around it. Therefore the shaman, especially the adventurer shaman, tries to act respectfully toward everything. This might be considered sweetly
quaint, except that it has a very practical purpose.

Your *ku* is alive, aware, and responsive. When you criticize
yourself your *ku* feels under attack and tries to defend itself
by clenching muscles, which causes stress and inhibits
awareness, memory, and energy flow, making you weaker
and more subject to illness and accident. One little criticism
isn't going to do that, but a habit of self-criticism will. Self-
appreciation, by contrast, relaxes muscles; increases awareness, energy flow, and strength; opens up skill memory and
makes you feel better.

When you criticize or praise any part of the world around
you, three things happen. First, because of the second principle your *ku* does not distinguish between you and your
dream, so whether you criticize another person, a rainy day,
your car, or the government, your *ku* takes it personally and
your body gets tense. And when you praise any of those
things your *ku* says thank you and your body relaxes. Second, because of the third principle, whatever characteristics
or conditions you focus on will tend to increase according
to the responsiveness of the object. If you criticize a person
who values your opinion, your criticism, even if well meant,
will tend to reinforce the behavior you criticized. If they
improve it will be in spite of your criticism, not because of
it. If the person couldn't care less about your opinion, however, your criticism will have virtually no effect on them,
but it will still affect you. Praising a person will help reinforce
the good that you like regardless of whether they care about
your opinion or not, because the *ku* always responds in some
way to love. Likewise, if you criticize the rain it will do what
you don't want and if you praise it, it will rain just enough;
if you criticize your car it will tend to break down more and
if you praise it, it will tend to run better (and if it must break
down it will be conveniently); and, pay attention now, the

more you criticize government actions you don't like the more the government will tend to do more of them, and the more you praise what you do like the more those activities will be increased. Third, because of this fifth principle, each criticism will increase your separation from and decrease your awareness of what you criticize, until you end up responding to a secondary creation of your own that may no longer bear any resemblance to the original. Each praise will bring you closer and closer to and increase your awareness of what you praise, thereby expanding your growth in many ways.

An important issue is what to do when you are criticized by someone else. There are a lot of good teachings out on this subject, so I will only present one here that is derived directly from the current principle. The example I'll use is an extreme one, but the application will be clear.

In old Hawaii there was a lot of fear of curses, which are just criticisms phrased like a threat, because of a prevailing belief in the power of words. Whenever the people had contact with shamans, however, there was no such fear, for the very same reason. The shamanic teaching was that the power of a curse could be neutralized and offset by the power of a blessing, which is just a compliment phrased like a promise. So if an angry man said to a farmer, "May your crops rot and wilt!" the farmer would look lovingly at his field and say, "May my crops grow and produce abundantly." The effect of the curse would be nil and the crops would get a good boost of energy. Applying the same idea personally would simply mean that whenever you are criticized, praise yourself aloud or silently and the criticism will have no effect on you as long as you don't fear it.

Exploring the Power of Love

I'm going to ask you to do something you may never have done before. For one full minute, sit quietly, close your eyes, and compliment yourself unceasingly for any good quality, characteristic, or behavior you can think of. It's okay to repeat yourself if you can't think of a lot to say. With practice it gets easier. If negative responses or self-criticisms arise spontaneously, don't give them any importance; just keep on complimenting (it's also okay to do this for more than a minute). When you've finished, be aware of your feelings and sensations. You will almost always feel a lot better. Next, for one full minute, sit with your eyes open and compliment any good quality, characteristic, or behavior you can be aware of in your immediate environment. Again, don't pay attention to criticisms and go longer if you like. Isn't that a great way to feel?

The Sixth Principle: *MANA*—All Power Comes From Within

Most philosophies teach that we are relatively powerless, that real power exists outside ourselves in the form of a god separate from his creation, gods and goddesses who act at their own whim, fate, past events, genes from our ancestors, society (which means other people), government (which also means other people), parents, a spiritual hierarchy of ascended masters, forces of evil, Nature . . . virtually anywhere but inside ourselves. In complete and, for some, shocking contrast, *Huna* philosophy teaches that *all* the power that creates your experience comes from your own body, mind, and spirit. Logically speaking, if there are no limits, then the Universe or Source of Life is infinite, and if it is infinite, then all of its power is at every point of it, including the point which you define as you. Keeping this discussion at a practical level, nothing ever happens to you without your participation. For every event that you experience you creatively attract it through your beliefs, desires, fears, and expectations, and then react to it habitually or respond to it consciously. At this point I am usually asked, "What about innocent babies?" From a spiritual point of view, there are no innocent babies. In fact, many babies are wiser than their parents. A baby born into an abusive family or with some disability may have chosen that as a life challenge (no limits presumes life before life as well as after death), and a baby who develops an illness or injury may be reflecting family conflicts that aren't being expressed.

Similarly, no one else makes you unhappy. You may make yourself unhappy because others don't act the way you want them to or the way you think they should. If you are the victim of some kind of abuse or injury, it is important to realize that something in you helped bring that about. This does *not* mean that you are to blame, because you were probably not consciously aware of the beliefs, attitudes, and expectations on your part that were involved. Also, it does not mean that the other person was innocent, because whatever they did came from their own beliefs, attitudes, and expectations, and to whatever degree they made conscious choices to do harm they are subject to the laws of society. Nevertheless, it is important to realize your part in the event so that you can change the factors in yourself that helped bring it about. If the power was in you to create it, then the power is in you to change it.

Corollary: Everything has power

When some people begin to play with the idea that they are the creators of their experience, they often get the strange idea that no one else has anything to do with it. From the extreme of having no power they leap to the other extreme of having all power. On the contrary, everyone has the power to create their own experience. In any situation or event, all the people involved are creating their own experience. Everyone has the same power.

And everything has the same power. The wind, trees, flowers, stars, mountains, seas, rain, clouds, and all the rest of the elements and objects of the natural Universe have the same power to create their own experience. A well-trained urban shaman wouldn't be surprised at the idea that computers are making use of humans to put themselves together. The wonderfully curious thing is, apart from the assumptions we choose to make about that, we really don't have any way of proving it isn't so. I know my computer, Jonathan, thinks it's true. In any case, by taking the point of view that everything in Nature has its own power, you learn to work respectfully with those powers, rather than trying to impose your will on dead matter. And, in true shamanic style, you become able to learn their powers for your own use. In traditional societies the shaman learns the invisible power of the wind, the movement power of the jaguar, the healing power of the tree, and so on. While we can still do that today, as urban shamans we can also learn the invisible power of electromagnetism, the movement power of machines, and the healing power of music. There is power everywhere, and all power can be useful.

Corollary: Power comes from authority

In psychology there is a concept of outer authority and inner authority. Outer authority is when you give decision-making power to someone else, and inner authority, considered much the healthier variety, is when you give it to yourself. This becomes more interesting when we learn that one of the basic meanings of *mana*, or power, is "authority." And even more interesting when we discover that the word *authority* is based on a word which means "to create" (from which we also get the word *author*, by the way).

Speaking with authority means speaking with confidence that your words will produce results, as in "Let there be light!" Herein lies the secret of the power of prayer, blessing, spells, and affirmations. They have power to the degree that they are spoken with authority. Read the Twenty-third Psalm or the Lord's Prayer if you haven't, or again if you have, and you'll find that they aren't just wimpy pleas for help. They are strong statements to be spoken with confidence and authority (or faith and trust, if you prefer). Put aside any prejudice and look through a book on occult spells and you will find that they, too, are strong, authoritative statements. Neither prayers nor spells nor affirmations will do much good if they are spoken with wistful hope or as if the words themselves held the magic. Confident authority is the key to conscious creation, whether used with words, visualizations, or feelings.

Exploring the Power of Authority

To develop a feeling of confident authority, look around you and begin to tell things and circumstances to be exactly as they are. Tell chairs and tables to place themselves where they are at, tell pictures to hang where they are hung, tell flowers and trees to grow where they are growing and clouds to move as they are moving. Tell your body to be the way it is, your bank account to be what it is, your relationships to be what they are, and world conditions to be what they are (doing your best to avoid any doubt or criticism). This exercise will help you on the road to such a state of confident authority that when you decree changes they will occur.

The Seventh Principle: *PONO*— Effectiveness Is The Measure Of Truth

Many people have trouble with this one at first because they think it says that the end justifies the means. Actually, it says just the opposite, that the means determines the end. Violent means will produce violent results, and peaceful means will produce peaceful results. Reaching success through ruthlessness will produce a state of success in which others will act ruthlessly toward you, and reaching success through helping others will produce a state of success in which others are helping you.

This principle also says that what is really important is what works. Shamans are neither theologians nor theoretical scientists. They are more like counselors and technicians. Absolute Truth and Ultimate Reality are dismissed as having no practical value. Shamans are such pragmatists that even though the powers of the mind are their special province, they will not hesitate to use whatever physical tools and processes help bring about a healing, and will even change systems if that will help. When I used to do a lot of private counseling I might, in the course of a single day, jump between Christianity, Buddhism, Spiritualism, Voodoo, Psychoanalysis, and Science, working within the belief systems of each individual to help them find ways to help themselves. Healing is the goal and effectiveness is the criteria, not the proving of a particular system or method.

Corollary: There is always another way to do anything

Every problem has more than one solution. In an infinite universe, how could you doubt it? Yet people so often get stuck in one method, process, technique, or plan for reaching their goals, and if that doesn't work they give up. If the goal is important, you should never give up, you just change your approach. If a chronic illness isn't clearing up then do something you haven't been doing, such as working more with the mind and emotions if your approach has been primarily physical or using more physical means if your approach has been primarily mental and emotional. If a confrontational approach hasn't worked in a relationship, use a more cooperative one, and vice versa. If your present plan for making money hasn't been working, change your plan or change your career. If peace on earth hasn't happened yet, then let's do more of what works and create more workable ways. Life, and the ways to improve life, exist in endless variety and potential. There is always another way.

Exploring the Power of Flexibility

I magine that you are walking on a road toward a city that has a central square with a treasure chest in the middle which symbolizes an important goal in your life (you don't have to decide what that goal is right now). At the edge of the city is a high, guarded wall, and where the road enters there is a huge, solid gate. Using whatever comes to mind in your imagination, get into the city and reach your treasure. When you've done that, replay the scene and get into the city by a different means. Then do it again, and again, at least half a dozen times, changing your method for entering each time. With your imagination you will be training your *ku* for great flexibility in reaching your goals.

The Seven Shaman Talents

The seven shaman talents are simply derived from the principles. They represent essential skills to develop, rather than specific techniques.

Seeing (from The World Is What You Think It Is)

This is the ability to operate in the world from the perspective of the principles, to "see" things from that viewpoint rather than in the ordinary way. We often call this operating at second level (*ike papalua*) instead of at first level (*ike papakahi*). In first-level thinking, the "ordinary" reality of most folk, the world is independent of your thinking, everything is separate, energy flows by physical mediums only, the past has more power than the present, to love is to risk unhappiness, power is outside of you, and effectiveness is a matter of genius, reward, strength, or luck. Operating at second level in a primarily first-level world is not easy, but it is the key to a shaman's success. What makes it especially challenging is that you also have to hold first level in awareness so you can communicate with others operating at that level.

Clearing (from There Are No Limits)

For the greatest effect this means using the best means at hand to keep the connections clear between all parts of yourself and the universe around you, mostly by continually releasing mental and physical stress and tension as well as remembering to bring other aspects of yourself and the world into conscious awareness.

Focusing (from Energy Flows Where Attention Goes)

The skill involved here is that of keeping your intentions, objectives, goals, and purpose in mind, which means frequent review of your motivations for doing whatever you do. This helps you maintain a high degree of efficiency and a low degree of frustration.

Presence (from Now Is the Moment of Power)

It is important to remain in the present moment as much as you can, especially when dealing with present-moment affairs. From hard experience I have learned that people I am talking to can sense a drop in my energy level if I let my mind wander, but not knowing what it is, they take it as aloofness or rejection on my part. I attended a special school once where the competition for grades was fierce. During a lecture I allowed myself a brief glance out the window that cost me the answer to a question on the next quiz. As it was I only got first place by three-hundredths of a percentage point. You may never need such extreme presence, but then again you may. The greater your presence, the greater your influence and effectiveness.

Blessing (from To Love Is to Be Happy With)

To bless is to reinforce actual or potential good by word, image, or deed. When you acknowledge beauty, admire skill, or appreciate kindness you are giving a blessing. What the shaman does that's extra is to bless potential. "May you have a safe journey," "I wish you success in your venture," "Let the wind be always at your back" are examples of this type of blessing. And remember that telepathic blessings can be effective, too.

Empowering (from All Power Comes from Within)

We empower something whenever we attribute any kind of power to it. People who attribute special powers to certain crystals are empowering them, and they will get more benefit from the crystals as long as they maintain the empowerment. Another way to empower is to personify, to attribute human qualities to nonhuman entities or objects. For instance, by empowering him, I enable my computer, Jonathan, and I to have a better relationship. The skill of empowering also implies the skill of disempowering. As an example, warrior shamans tend to empower evil by personifying it so they can learn to conquer it, while adventurer shamans tend to disempower evil by depersonifying it so they can learn to harmonize it. You can empower or disempower anything at all, including people, places, things, the past, the future, and endlessly on and on.

Dreamweaving (from Effectiveness Is the Measure of Truth)

As a weaver of dreams, the shaman weaves dreams for himself and helps others to do the same. This is also called "shamanic healing." A first-level masseur doing a massage is using his hands as tools to heal a physical body. A shaman masseur doing a massage is using the physical body as a tool to weave a new dream and heal the spirit. It might look the same, but it isn't. Dreamweaving doesn't depend on technique. It has to do with having a healer's attitude and taking healing action, mentally or physically, in every situation you encounter. At least, that's the goal.

THE FOURTH ADVENTURE:

CREATING HARMONY
IN THE BODY

*Mai ka piko o ke po'o a ka poli o ka
wawae, a la'a ma na kihi 'eha o ke kino*
(From the crown of the head to the
soles of the feet, and the four corners
of the body—*an expression used in
healing*)

Health is a state of peace and harmony, while sickness
is a state of war and conflict. An urban shaman
healer of the adventurer tradition doesn't try to stop war,
in the body or the world, but seeks instead to create harmony.

The Hawaiian concept of health and healing is a very
useful one for our modern world. It is based on the word
ola, which also means "life" and "the attainment of peace,"
with strong root connotations of abundant energy. The
opposite condition, sickness, is called *ma'i*, with the root
meaning of "a state of tension." Here we have a clear understanding of sickness as a condition related to stress.

The several words we use for unhealthiness—*illness, sickness*, and *disease*—each reflect a philosophical approach to
healing, though we usually aren't consciously aware of it.
Illness really means "evilness" and implies an effect of sinful

behavior and a malevolent force to be feared. Subconsciously, many people react to illness in just this way. Sickness comes from a root meaning "to be troubled or grieved," and implies an emotional basis for the condition. Disease really just means "discomfort," but it now carries a strong connotation of physicality, a *thing* that invades the body and has to be destroyed, cut out, neutralized, or endured. So if a person is mentally ill, we tend to fear him; if mentally sick, to be sorry for him; and if mentally diseased, to recommend surgery.

In contrast to the Western approach which tends to treat each manifestation of sickness as a separate entity—according to its symptoms, location, and reaction to treatment—and which places great importance on naming each one individually (often after the person who discovered that particular set of symptoms), the shaman approach derived from the principles and expressed in the Hawaiian language seems absurdly simple. The shaman approach is that all sickness (note that, *all*) is considered to be self-generated as an effect of stress. The location is simply where the stress is focused. All Hawaiian words related to healing carry connotations of causing energy to flow, implying the release of stress-related tension. Viruses certainly exist, but in the *Huna* view they are effects of stress not causes of sickness. And bacteria certainly exist, but they don't cause sickness, they just take advantage of it. I can already hear a lot of objections, so I will deal with the major ones as we continue. Please remember, though, that I am not trying to refute the traditional Western medical system. As stated before, I am just presenting a different system.

The Stress Effect

Virtually everything we do causes stress and that's quite natural. Thoughts, emotions, physical activity, food, environmental conditions—all of these naturally cause stress. What isn't natural, as opposed to normal, is sustained stress. The natural flow of life is a repeating cycle of stress-tension-

release-relaxation-stress and so on. The unnatural flow looks
something like this:

        stress-tension-release-relaxation-
        stress-tension-release-rela-
        stress-tension-relea-
        stress-tension-stress

   As the release and relaxation parts of the cycle are inhibited, the stress and tension continue to build. When the
tension from stress reaches a certain point, which varies with
individuals, the body functions begin to break down. While
we are primarily focused on the body here, keep in mind
that the same concepts apply to relationships, societies, and
Nature.
   When the body experiences stress, five things happen almost simultaneously:

1. Sugar is released into the bloodstream. The natural purpose is to provide energy for action and in the natural
   cycle just the right amount of energy is released to deal
   with the situation experienced. If the release and relaxation parts of the cycle are interrupted, more sugar is
   released than is needed, and disharmony occurs. A little
   bit of vigorous physical movement will help use up the
   extra sugar.
2. The thymus gland contracts. Related to growth in children, this large gland in the center of the chest behind
   the breastbone is related to the immune system in adults.
   A natural contraction and release is intended to stimulate
   the production of white blood cells, but sustained contraction inhibits them and adds to feelings of anxiety.
   Lightly tapping your chest with your fingers will help the
   thymus relax.
3. Muscles tense. The purpose is to strengthen and stimulate
   the cells in preparation for appropriate action. The relaxation part of the cycle allows them to recharge. Body-
   builders know that muscles are strengthened and

increased by repetitions of tension and relaxation. Sustained muscle tension will cause cells to break down,
toxins to accumulate, and oxygen and nutrient supplies
to diminish. Pain apparently is due not only to muscular
tension impinging on nerves, but also a lack of oxygen
at the cell level. Muscles, by the way, are not just those
big masses of flesh that move your body. Your nerves
and your internal organs are also sheathed in muscle
tissue. Stretching and brisk, self-applied massage will help
relieve muscular tension.

4. Capillaries dilate. Capillaries are the very small veins and
arteries that carry blood directly to and from your cells.
They are sort of like a tubular net that allows the oxygen
and nutrients of the bloodstream to seep through and
nourish the cells. Under stress the holes in the net expand
and plasma, the clear watery substance that carries the
blood and nutrients, pours through faster. The purpose,
when the relaxation part of the cycle is operating, is to
feed the cells faster and cleanse them quickly, washing
toxins into the lymph system where they can be carried
away and discharged. Under sustained tension, lymph
movement is slowed down and plasma and proteins accumulate between the cells, causing a buildup of toxins,
pressure, and swelling, as well as inhibiting the cells'
supplies of nutrients and oxygen. Under extreme stress,
such as injury or shock, the net opens so wide that blood
corpuscles spill out, causing black-and-blue marks and/
or pallor (unnatural paleness). Due to this effect, very
severe shock may even require blood transfusions as the
corpuscles continue to spill out of the stressed capillaries.
Gentle massage, except where there is injury, is also helpful for this condition.

5. Cells release toxins. Our cells are releasing toxins all the
time as a natural part of their regular activity. Under stress
their activity increases (as long as tension doesn't inhibit
it) and so does the amount of toxins they release. The
natural process is for these toxins to be washed clear by
the plasma and carted off by the lymph system to be

discharged through perspiration, respiration, and elimination. When sustained tension inhibits the cleansing of toxins they build up locally, poisoning the local cells and finding their way into the bloodstream through the dilated capillaries, where they can affect the brain and the glands. This is one reason why some people get dizzy or irritated when they are beginning to relax, through massage or some other means, after a long state of tension. Deep breathing, which stimulates the lymph system and discharges toxins itself, is very helpful.

The effects of stress described above occur all over the body to some degree, but most especially in those areas directly affected by the stress. Since all conditions of sickness in the body are stress related, according to Hawaiian shaman teaching, knowing the source of stress will be highly useful in helping to bring about a healing.

The Source of Stress

I won't waste any time. The source of stress is resistance, *ku'e* in Hawaiian, meaning "to stand apart." Natural resistance is like the friction that enables us to walk across the ground, the momentum that keeps a baseball on its course and not wandering all over the place, the tendency of habits to maintain themselves and of memories to hold their pattern. Natural resistance produces the healthy cycle of life in which things tend to hold their pattern, but are flexible enough to adapt and change.

Generally speaking, there are four kinds of resistance which will be discussed below. I'll describe the positive and negative aspects of each, along with what I call "quick-n-easys," brief techniques that can help greatly to relieve each kind of tension.

Physical Resistance

When your body experiences a punch, poke, slam, stab, cut, or burn, it reacts with the stress effects mentioned above, and we think that bruises, wounds, and blisters are also a natural effect. That's not necessarily so. There are people who can punch steel needles through their arms without bleeding or wounding, who can poke their hands right into another person's body without hurting them or leaving a hole, and who can walk on fire without getting burned. That might sound unnatural to you, but I'm convinced it's the most natural thing in the world, albeit pretty abnormal. Your body reacts stressfully as well to poisons, toxic substances, radiation, and positive ions, but there are people who can drink arsenic and wood alcohol without harm, not everyone who works around asbestos gets sick, some people can stand much higher levels of radiation than others, and many people find mental and physical stimulation from positive ions.

What distinguishes those who don't react stressfully to poisons and injury from those who do is that the former have a higher tolerance for those substances or conditions. What does a higher tolerance mean? It means that they can ingest or be exposed to a greater amount of the substance or condition than most people before resistance produces enough tension to cause a breakdown in the body. Now that means that they were either more relaxed to begin with, so it would take more stress to cause enough tension to produce the symptoms, or they had trained their bodies to respond differently in the first place, to reduce the resistance by changing the reaction pattern. We do know, for instance, that some people have trained their bodies by gradually drinking stronger and stronger doses of arsenic. Personally, I would rather practice deep relaxation.

In any case, maybe it is possible to change our physical reactions so that acute physical contact does not result in physical injury. In 1983 while on the island of Tahiti I slowly walked barefoot across a wide bed of red-hot lava rocks with a Tahitian *kahuna*, stepping firmly on each stone all the way. Neither my feet nor the hair on my legs was burned. I've seen a fair amount of fire-walking and I know of several ways to do it. The most common in the world is devotion, belief in the protection of a divinity, and it works well if the belief is strong enough. The second most common that I know of is distraction, a trancelike state of focused attention on something completely different than the fire. The third is motivation, an intensely energetic desire fully focused on getting to the other side. Each of these has in common the effect of moving the conscious mind's attention away from the fire, thereby reducing or removing the resistance to the heat and allowing the body to follow a natural instant-healing cycle. That, at least, was my theory before walking the lava rocks. I decided to test my theory by trying a different method in Tahiti. Instead of using devotion, distraction, or motivation, I focused all my attention on exactly what I was doing, without the slightest bit of comment, question, or analysis. The effect was a sense of oneness with my imme-diate environment to such a degree that there was absolutely no fear. Therefore, there was no resistance and no burning. My body went through the cycle of stress-tension-release-relaxation so quickly that cumulative tension effects could not occur.

Repatterning

A long time ago, so long that I can't remember the source, I learned that if you stub your toe, all you have to do is repeat the same action several times, *without quite stubbing your toe again*, and the pain will go away. I used that a lot unthinkingly, but in later years I studied the process in detail and began teaching it in my courses, suggesting that the students try out variations. The concept I developed was that by re-creating the pattern *and changing the ending*, you were, in effect, giving the *ku* a new memory of the event, requiring the *ku* to change the body state in conformity to the new version of what happened. The sooner you could do this after the event, the sooner the body would get back into harmony.

What the students did amazed and delighted me.

A man in California, one week after the training, was in his backyard building a fence. At one point he smashed his thumb hard with a hammer and then pulled the hammer back prior to dropping it and following the normal routine of jumping up and down while squeezing his thumb and cussing. At the high point of his swing away from his thumb he remembered my lesson about repeating the pattern and changing the ending, so he followed through with his swing without quite touching his thumb. He repeated that action about seventeen more times. By then his thumb barely tingled and he went on with his work. When he was through he looked at his thumb and there was neither bruising nor swelling nor pain.

A medical doctor in Texas reported that he was chopping up lettuce for salad with a knife and sliced deep into a finger. Professionally he knew it would require several stitches, but he decided to try out my crazy idea anyway. After a few repetitive passes with the knife his finger stopped bleeding and the pain went away so he forgot about it and finished the salad. Three days later he remembered the accident and looked at his finger. There was no sign it had been cut.

A woman in Minnesota burned her finger on a hot pot and quickly repeated the action with a different ending. There was no blister and no pain.

A woman in Canada slammed a car door on her fingers and, oblivious to the stares of passers-by, repeated the movement of the door toward her fingers until the pain went away. She had no bruises or cuts.

Perhaps most exciting of all, a woman in California decided to act on the assumption that the *ku* lives only in the present moment and doesn't distinguish between vivid imagination and physical experience. She'd received a bad burn on her leg from a motorcycle exhaust pipe some weeks before, and it had not been healing well. Vividly re-creating the accident in her mind, she gave it an ending change that left her leg clear of the pipe. She did this in her mind about forty times. The long-standing condition which had begun to fester cleared up in three days.

The possibilities of this simple process are fantastic and boundless, especially if we can use it to help the present effects of past events. As a guideline, we've found that the best results come from making as small a change in the pattern as possible.

Emotional Resistance

Resistance also comes from fear and anger. We resist what we fear, and we resist what angers us. Even though the resistance might originate with *lono* decisions, however, the *ku* still expresses emotional resistance with the physical stress cycle.

Natural fear is intended to warn you of impending danger, and in the natural process it will disappear as soon as you take action. With our creative imaginations, however, we often generate unnatural fear long after an event and frequently in spite of an event. Recently during a class at our center on Kauai a woman reported that she had just come from saving a child from drowning and was still traumatized by fear because of the event. I had her examine her thought patterns and she was able to realize that the fear and trauma were coming from imagining vividly what *might* have happened if she hadn't been there. Instead of rejoicing in the actual success of her rescue, she was scaring herself silly with fantasy. By dwelling on the fearful fantasy she was inducing a continuous increase of tension in her body. Symptoms of paralysis, hypofunction (lowered activity), rigidity, anxiety, nausea, and dizziness may have fear as an important factor.

Natural anger has the purpose of focusing energy to change something in your immediate situation, either by warning or direct action. It gets unnatural when we use memory to refuel it over and over again. Besides the fact that we end up being angry at the memory rather than the actual person or situation in the present, sustained anger plays real havoc with the body and is probably the primary factor in most sickness. Wherever you have swelling, infection, inflammation, fever, soreness, and sores or tumors, you have anger as an important factor. It is also a factor to take into account in conditions of rigidity and pain of any kind.

Now let's look at some "quick-n-easy" ways of dealing with each.

The expectation effect

It is helpful to know what fear really is. Fear is simply the expectation of pain, the result of projecting the imagination into the future, from a point in the present or in the past, and making up an experience of pain. Fear is never about the present, but only about the future. The problem is, the *ku* doesn't know that. Whatever you put in your mind is treated by the *ku* as a present-moment happening. Anticipating pain is the same as experiencing pain for the *ku*, and so it takes the body into a negative stress cycle.

Relaxation, of course, reduces fear, and so does knowledge in many cases. Fear is always accompanied by tension, so if you are completely relaxed you can't feel fear, and if you have certain knowledge that what you fear can't happen or won't cause pain, the fear will also go away. However, the fastest and simplest method I have found for getting rid of fear is to shift your focus to its opposite. Fear is the expectation of pain, so its opposite is the expectation of pleasure. I usually demonstrate this by having a class focus on the idea, "What if something terrible happens in the next five minutes?" After a few moments of letting them feel their body's reactions, I then say, "But think of this, what if something wonderful happens instead?" And then they feel the immediate shift toward pleasure that the positive expectation brings. Even if you are in a situation where you are absolutely certain that something painful is going to happen (as in a dentist's chair), go ahead and make the shift to an actual or fantastical positive expectation anyway. Once the fear has given you the warning you don't need it anymore, nor do you need the tension it causes.

The blanket forgiveness technique

Unnatural anger, the stress effects of which we want to change, is primarily a result of unnatural standards. All of us have standards of the way things should be and the way people, including ourselves, should act. These standards allow us to keep aligning with our ideals and to keep making changes to improve our world. An unnatural standard is one

which says, "Things and people shouldn't deviate from my
expectation, because if they do they are bad and should be
punished." That one causes a tremendous amount of anger
and stress, because things and people are going to deviate
whether you want them to or not simply out of creative
spontaneity if nothing else. Some people like to try to do
away with all *shoulds* to reduce the anger and stress, and
that's helpful up to a point. Others like to practice relaxation,
because anger is also associated with muscle tension and if
you are completely relaxed you can't be angry. But my preferred quick-n-easy method is blanket forgiveness.

Forgiveness is basically a process of deciding that whatever
happened is no longer important or doesn't matter anymore.
It is wonderful for all the conscious resentments and guilts
that many of us carry over from the past. Not all the sources
for the *ku*'s present reactions are readily available to the
conscious mind, however, partly because anger may be only
one of the factors involved in a current condition. But if you
can reduce whatever anger exists, the whole condition will
be relieved to some degree. So in practicing blanket forgiveness you first assume that in any current condition of
pain or discomfort there is some anger involved, even if you
don't know what it's about. Then you touch the area of your
body that is in pain or discomfort with the fingers of either
hand and say, "Whatever this is related to, I forgive it completely and it doesn't matter anymore." Most of the time
you will experience at least some instant relief, and often
complete relief, but if not keep doing it for one full minute
with the full focus of your attention. The slightest amount
of change is a relief from the anger part of the stress, and I
would continue these one-minute sessions every so often
along with whatever else you do. If there is no change whatsoever after one full minute, you either aren't dealing with
anger or aren't willing to give it up.

Mental Resistance

Whenever we resist anything we generate stress. Mental
resistance differs from emotional resistance in the same way

that evaluation differs from analysis. Emotional resistance comes from thinking of something as bad; mental resistance comes from thinking of it as wrong. By itself it doesn't have the devastating power of fear and anger, but it erodes confidence, self-esteem, and the health of the body the way a tiny stream erodes a mountain. Mental resistance takes the form of negative criticism, and each individual criticism, which the *ku* feels like a punch, causes a relatively small amount of negative stress. However, the same punch that you can handle easily when relaxed and healthy can hurt like blazes when you are tense and sore from previous blows. This kind of criticism is such a subtle thing when habitual that it can race across your mind before you notice, and please note that the tensing occurs whether or not the criticism is spoken aloud.

One of the craziest ideas modern society has is that criticism is good for you or that it helps you learn. All that criticism does is create stress and reinforce what you criticize. Noticing or remembering what we haven't done right just gets in the way of learning. When you learned to walk as a child you did it by forgetting what didn't work and remembering what did work. People who keep in mind what doesn't work tend to repeat it. If anyone learns under criticism it's in spite of it, not because of it. I often get asked about the value of "constructive criticism." It has no value because it's usually just an excuse to criticize. Pointing out faults is motivated more by a desire to put someone down and feel superior than a true desire to help. If you really wanted to help you would point out successes and ways to increase success. Now there is a highly developed skill called critical analysis, but it's rare to find a skilled practitioner. Constructive criticism usually goes like this: "No, no, that's wrong. Do it this way, stupid." Critical analysis goes like this: "What you just did doesn't give you the effect you want. Doing it this way does." It is recognition and recommendation without judgment. Of course, a person with very low self-esteem is likely to interpret even positive critical analysis as a personal negative criticism and get tensed up about it.

It has been my experience that the response to criticism is a major factor in asthma, allergies, colds, headaches, and, perhaps because the habit of it encourages rigid thinking, arthritis.

The Twister and the Sandwich

Some people are so stuck in the conditioned habit of criticism that they don't know any other way to help bring about change in themselves and others. If you are one of them, don't feel bad, because you are in the majority. The solution is to criticize if you must, but do it differently.

The Twister refers to twisting around the usual pattern of criticism, which is to acknowledge something good and then offer the criticism. As in, "That's a beautiful painting, but you put too much red in the sky." For better effect, twist it around so that it's like this: "I think you put too much red in the sky, but it's a beautiful painting." The reason for twisting is to finish with the compliment, because in terms of tension and relaxation in the body, a compliment neutralizes a criticism—especially in the body of the speaker, but also to a large degree in the body of the listener, who will be more open to assistance.

The Sandwich is similar, except that this time you start with a compliment, give the criticism, and end with a compliment, as in, "That's a beautiful painting, although it has too much red in the sky, but I really like the way you did the waves." Such an approach will encourage a more relaxed acceptance of the criticism and a greater inclination to change, besides helping to relieve stress.

Spiritual Resistance

Resistance, and the resulting tension, can come from pushing toward or away from a physical stimulus, from reactions of fear and anger, or from defending against negative criticism. It can also come from alienation. Remember that the Hawaiian word for resistance is ku'e, meaning "to stand apart." Resistance tension occurs when you separate yourself from something, or try to do so. In spiritual resistance you alienate yourself from a place, a group, or the entire world because you feel you don't belong. This is often because you don't feel accepted, but it can also be due to a sense that you belong somewhere else. There are so many possible combinations of beliefs that could give rise to these feelings that their source doesn't matter. What does matter is that the more severe the alienation, the greater the negative stress. Not participating in group activities or having no sense of connection with the area you live in causes a relatively low amount of stress (discounting fear, anger, and critical factors), but the extremes of extended daydreaming, extended meditation, and autism can cause a lot of physical problems. Extended daydreaming means spending most of your day with all of your conscious attention in dreams other than the one of this world (novelists generally maintain balance by the physical activities of writing, typing, or dictating). Extended meditation means spending most of your day in any kind of meditative focus that takes your attention away from this world and away from your body. Part of the reason for the increase of physical tension is simply the extended inactivity, which lowers oxygen intake and builds up toxins, but tension is also produced by separating your *lono* from your *ku*, or your mental awareness from your body awareness, for extended periods of time. The same thing can happen if you sleep too long, which is why sluggishness, aches, and pains can occur from oversleeping. People engaged in any of these alienating activities (extended sleeping, daydreaming, or meditation) often find that it is increasingly uncomfortable to come "back into the body" after extended periods away from it, which induces them to spend longer periods spaced out. The kicker is that it was the extended disengagement which caused the body to get uncomfortable in the first place.

I had a personal experience along these lines while backpacking with my sons in the High Sierras. I was finding it difficult to keep up with them at one point, so I used a technique of repeating a chant which disengaged my mind from my body so I could move at a faster pace without any

discomfort signals. I kept up with them beautifully until we
reached our campsite. As soon as I reengaged with my body
I collapsed from heat exhaustion. My disengaged *lono* had
been totally unaware of my *ku* screaming signals of increasing tension and dehydration. The boys had gone off to a
waterfall and it took me a half hour of carefully talking my
ku back toward recovery before I could even reach my can-
teen.

There are no hard and fast rules for how long you can
stay disengaged without undue tension, because we all differ
in metabolism and motivation. The best test is how you feel.
A healthy period of disengagement will produce a good feeling when you get back. If spiritual alienation has been a
problem, conscious engagement with physical activity, people, or the land will be very helpful, and the practice of
blessing will help you with that.

Autism is a special case because in this condition a person
has turned so far away from the world that he or she usually
needs outside help to get back. The symptoms usually range
from a refusal to speak or participate in activities, to a refusal
to even acknowledge people or surroundings, to a total ob-
liviousness of them. There may also be rhythmic, apparently
purposeless movement. The most productive solution seems
to be unconditional love, and I would recommend the books
of Barry Kaufman for anyone with concerns in this area. But
in some cases all it takes is a little bit of love. One of my
students was a grade-school teacher who had a student herself who might have been described as borderline autistic.
The girl didn't speak and didn't participate. She just sat quietly from the time she was delivered to school to the time
she was picked up and wouldn't even respond to the teacher's attention. Because of the limited amount of time the
teacher could spend with each student, I suggested that she
simply sit with the girl for two minutes out of every class,
duplicating the position, expression, and any movement the
girl made as best she could, and end each two-minute period
by touching the girl gently and saying, ''Thank you.'' By the

end of three weeks the girl was conversing, smiling, and beginning to participate in class.

Kahi—The Touch of Magic

Hawaiian tradition has a system of bodywork called *lomi-lomi*. It is usually considered a system of massage, but it has elements that resemble Swedish and Esalen massage, rolfing, acupressure, and polarity therapy, plus some things that don't resemble anything else. For the first time I am writing in detail about one of these other things, a rarely taught process that I have been sharing in my shaman courses for several years. I think it is one of the most useful things I have ever learned or that I teach.

The process is called *kahi*, which means "oneness" and also refers to a *lomi-lomi* technique using very light hand or finger pressure. Some of my Hawaiian friends learned it differently than I did, but the way I was taught, what the mind is doing during *kahi* is more important than what the hands are doing.

The Eight Centers and Four Corners of the Body

In traditional Hawaiian healing, the eight centers of the body are the crown, chest, navel, pubic bone, the palms of the hands, and the soles of the feet, while the four corners are the shoulders and hips. I was also given the seventh cervical vertebra (the bump at the bottom of the base of the neck) and the coccyx as additional centers, making fourteen in all. Each of these is considered in *kahi* as a "power center," or source of energy, somewhat like the oriental *chakra*.

To practice *kahi* you put the fingers or palm of one hand (it doesn't matter which) on a power center and those of the other hand on a "release point," an area of the body with tension, pain, injury, or some other condition of disharmony. In some cases this might even be another power center. So for a headache you might put the fingers of one hand lightly on the place of pain, and the fingers of the other hand on the navel or the base of the spine. Or for a stomach-ache you might put one hand gently over the stomach and the other hand on the back of the neck or on one of the person's palms. Then, and here is the important part, you focus your attention on both hands at once while you do deep breathing. Until you get practiced at such a dual focus you can shift attention quickly between hands or imagine something like a rainbow connecting them. To further help keep the attention focused I usually teach a Hawaiian chant in my course based on the seven principles, but since I can't help you now with pronunciation I'll give you the following chant in English, which is also based on the principles:

"Be aware, be free, be focused, be here, be loved, be strong, be healed."

Use whatever rhythm and tone you like. The chant will serve the dual purpose of helping your focus and giving sugges-tions to the *ku*. However, the main effect comes from the dual focus on both hands. In *kahi* you do not try to send your energy into the person's body, nor do you try to be a channel for energy with your breathing or your mind. *All* you do is hold the focus. Because of the third principle the focus itself intensifies and harmonizes the energy in the body you are working on. I can't emphasize this too strongly, because so many people want to control the process or the energy with their *lono*. You don't have to. The energy knows exactly what to do, and the *ku* knows how to respond. This is a technique that also teaches trust. Use your *lono* to hold the focus and let the rest happen by itself. When you have taken three or four complete deep breaths, check your body or that of the person you are helping for feedback. If the condition has changed for the better you are finished. If not, you have the option of continuing.

What happens in *kahi* is that the focus on the hands in-duces a flow of energy between them, much like the flow of electricity in a wire. The effect of this flow in *kahi* is twofold: first, it increases the intensity of your personal energy field, and second, it stimulates the release and relaxation portion of the stress cycle, resulting in an easing of tension and a harmonizing of the area at and between the hands. When you apply your hands to someone else's body the same thing happens to both of you. In line with the second principle, when you use *kahi* for someone else you are healing yourself at the same time. The specific effects are these:

1. Relaxation of muscle tension, an easing of pain, and stimulation of the body's healing process at the release point. This may be accompanied by sensations of warmth and/or tingling.
2. Sometimes an apparent shift of pain to a new site. Experience indicates that this is actually uncovering a new layer of pain that was masked by the first one. Continue on the new area as you did with the previous one.
3. Sometimes no change of condition at all, even after several rounds or sessions of *kahi* (a "round" is a *kahi* focus that lasts for three or four cycles of deep breathing; a "session" is any length of *kahi* application separated in time from another such application). This may happen when the source of stress is primarily resistance due to anger or fear. While a more intensified focus might break through such resistance, it is recommended to use a technique more directly related to changing the emotions or the memory patterns that generate them. Such techniques will be discussed later in the book.
4. Sometimes a recurrence of the condition after the *kahi* session. This is due to a renewal of the same thinking patterns that caused the condition in the first place. *Kahi* is only an aid to healing that works by changing the state of the body from tension to relaxation. Cures come from changing the mind.
5. Frequently sensations of movement, warmth, and/or tingling under the hands of the person doing the *kahi*. Also, it is common to feel more refreshed after doing *kahi*.

Because you are not trying to control or force energy, you don't get tired doing it.

As implied above, you can do *kahi* on yourself or someone else. I've found that the effects are best when you follow the general practice of using the farthest, most convenient power center from the release point. Thus, if working on someone's upper back I would use a palm center, the coccyx center, or the navel center (I don't suggest using the pubic center except with an intimate friend) rather than a shoulder, chest, or neck center. If the two areas of focus are too close, the flow is lessened, and if they are too far apart the strain of reaching will increase your own tension. This is not a rule, just a guideline, because there are times when you might want the two points to be close or far for some reason of your own.

You will also find that *kahi* is a wonderful alternative to acupressure and reflexology. Without diminishing the worth of those valuable systems, I must say it is a pleasure to do them painlessly. The way to do it is to combine the *kahi* power centers with any tender acupressure or reflexology points (on the feet you can work from the center of the sole of one foot to the tender point on the other foot). Press the points just enough to discover tenderness, and then ease off and keep a light touch while you focus. After one round, check the point again for tenderness.

Mutual *Kahi*

An excellent way to calm someone down, lift someone's spirits, do cooperative healing, or establish deep rapport is to do mutual *kahi*. When you are working one-on-one, two great variations are:

1. Face your partner with your left palm up and your right palm down. Touch palms with your partner and curl your fingers in so you are lightly gripping each other's fingers. Then both begin *kahi* by focusing on your own hands while silently chanting.

2. Place your right palm or fingers on your own navel and your left palm or fingers on the chest or forehead of your partner, while your partner does the same, touching his or her navel and your chest or forehead. Focus on your own hands and chant while you breathe.

Among other things you may notice, after several rounds, is a tendency to lose track of where you physically end and your partner begins. This doesn't happen to everyone right away, but it's a sign of the blending of personal energy fields, of moving into "oneness." If you do this a lot with someone you will find yourself developing a deep friendship and considerable telepathic rapport.

Group *Kahi*

Just as electrical power can be increased by placing batteries in a series, healing power can be increased by placing people in a series. The following two variations work very well.

1. Sit or stand in a circle with whomever wants to be worked on included as part of the circle. Hold hands and all do *kahi* together. Sometimes there's a greater group effect if you do the chant out loud. If you want to add a bit of ritual you can have everyone hold hands with the left palm up and the right palm down. It isn't necessary, but some people like it.
2. Everyone in the group stands in a line, curved if you like, with one hand on their own navel and the other hand lightly touching the neck center of the person in front of them, and they all do *kahi* together. The first person in the line applies *kahi* in the normal way to someone who wants help.

Mental *Kahi*

Suffice to say that using the hands for *kahi* isn't absolutely necessary, since it's the focus that does the work. What the hands mainly do is help you focus, but a lot of people need that help and a lot of people heal better when they are touched. Nevertheless, there may be times when knowing that a clear and sharp mental focus may work just as well will be very useful, such as:

1. When the release point of a person you are working with is too sensitive to touch or is in a delicate area of the anatomy. You can hold your hand a few inches above the point or just use your mind to focus on that point.
2. When you want to work on yourself and both hands are occupied. I had to do this once when I got a charley horse while driving a car.
3. When you want to help someone else nearby, but doing *kahi* openly is not practical or advisable.

Distant work will be discussed in the next chapter.

Kaulike—Another Magic Touch

Kaulike means "balance or harmony" and refers to an extremely simple way to help someone feel good. It's possible to do it on yourself, but it always works better when someone else does it because it's a way of sharing love and friendship. Essentially, it consists of lightly touching a person's body while they are standing, sitting, or lying down. When done with the right attitude on the part of both giver and receiver, it feels amazingly nice. The right attitude is simply one of willingly giving and receiving. The beauty of *kaulike* is that it requires no thinking by *lono* at all, not even the focus of *kahi*.

First, stand in front of the receiver and touch him or her with the fingers of alternating hands for about the length of two heartbeats on the crown, throat, chest, solar plexus, and navel. Then use both hands on either side of the body and touch in turn the jaws, shoulders, elbows, wrists, hips, knees, ankles, and toes. Finish by raising your arms out to your sides and above your head, and sweeping your hands palm-outward down in front of the receiver to about hip level. That's it. There isn't any second step. You don't have to think, or chant, or breathe deeply, or do anything except touch and sweep.

Now we'll go on to working more with the mind, but always in partnership with the body.

THE FIFTH ADVENTURE:

INITIATING CHANGE THROUGH INTUITION

Ka po nui ho'olakolako, ke ao nui ho'ohemahema
(The inner world provides, the outer world ignores)

Shamans do not teach intuition, they assume it. It's a function as natural as breathing, and it follows logically from the first three principles. Intuition is one important way in which the world becomes what we think it is; it is one of the ways in which everything is connected; and it is carried by the energy that flows where attention goes. However, just as breathing can be developed into a refined skill, so can intuition.

Let me explain here at the beginning that I am using the word *intuition* in both an active and a passive sense, and as an alternative to the words *telepathy* and *clairvoyance*. First of all, intuition generally refers to information or knowledge gained through any of the inner senses of seeing, hearing, and feeling (plus, sometimes, smelling, and rarely, tasting), whereas telepathy has the usual connotation of something active and verbal, and clairvoyance usually means something passive and visual. Secondly, just as in the outer world, inner knowledge and information can be given as well as received.

So how does intuition work? For an explanation we have to use a metaphor, because we are not describing a physical thing that can be separated into pieces with its parts all named. This is what drives first-level scientists batty. The evidence for intuition—the exchange of data without physical intervention or proximity—is unquestionable, if you don't choose to ignore it, yet it doesn't seem to have a physical basis. Since the physical world is a product of the nonphysical world, according to shaman thinking, a physical basis may or may not ever be found. To such researchers I recommend an observation of C. W. Leadbeater: "It is the commonest of mistakes to consider that the limit of our power to perceive is also the limit of all there is to perceive."

On to the metaphor. One good, often-used, and previously mentioned metaphor is the web, also called the *aka* web. *Aka* is a Hawaiian word meaning "essence" or "shadow," and also refers to the idea of a nonphysical web of threads connecting everything in the universe. Frequently made connections with emotional content are sometimes referred to as cords or even cables. One could say that, whereas most people are bound by cords to their outer life on the planet Earth until the moment of death, shamans seek to be connected by threads to everything all the time. Using the web metaphor, we can say that the connections of the web always exist, but specific threads are only activated by conscious attention. That is, intuition occurs—information is transferred—whenever you think of or become aware of something. In a typical example, you think of a friend and that friend calls you soon after. Now the thought of the friend might have carried a suggestion or desire that he or she responded to, or the friend might have been thinking of you prior to the call and you perceived it. Either way, it could be explained by information transfer along the web.

Another useful metaphor suitable for modern, urban shamans is the signal effect. In this one, everything in the universe is broadcasting its own signal, much like a television station, and everything is also a receiver. Each signal is a combination of frequencies that broadcasts all the information there is about the signal source, but each receiver is only designed to pick up a certain range of frequencies, like a radio that can pick up audio signals from a television station but cannot pick up the visual, or a TV that only receives certain channels. Metaphorically speaking, your perception of another person's broadcast signal is limited by your attunement with that person. The closer the attunement, the more you pick up; the less attunement, the more you miss. Attunement is done on purpose with conscious awareness or attention, either passively to receive information or actively to send it; and by default through similarities of beliefs held in *ku* memory. Specific sending to or receiving from an individual is like a communication between a transmitter and receiver set in a specific and narrow range of frequencies. Static can occur externally from other signals near the same range, or internally from slippage and interference (read that as losing focus or having doubt and/or receiving criticism). This is a great metaphor because it can explain so many intuitive phenomena.

A third metaphor, useful for the mystically inclined, is the field effect. In this case, since the universe is infinite, you are infinite. If you are infinite, you are everywhere. If you are everywhere, then you can be aware of anything and influence anything by putting your attention on it. The key to this one, then, is purity of intent and clarity of focus.

Should anyone ask what intuition really is, it's what you think it is.

Shamans use intuition for gathering information about the past, present, or future in preparation for healing activity, or for healing itself. We'll be discussing a number of tools and techniques for doing this, but a little more discussion is necessary so you can use it effectively.

Most important of all is the idea that, following the fourth principle, you cannot tune into the past or future even if you want to, because the present moment is the only reality. If you go to a professional psychic and ask for a reading, he or she will usually start by telling you about your past, then about your present, and then about your future. According to the point of view presented here, the psychic is not really tuning in to your past, but only to your memories (conscious or not) of the past which you are presently broadcasting (to use that metaphor). Likewise, he or she is picking up memories and thoughts about your current concerns when telling you about your present, and is tuning in to a logical projection of your current patterns and inclinations when telling you about your future. Note that I am not saying this is a conscious effort on the part of the psychic. Most are simply turning the matter over to *ku* and *kane*, with an internal process that goes, in effect, like this: "Okay, fellas, give me some information about this person's past, present, and future." Then the psychic waits for words, pictures or symbols, and feelings to arise, interprets them consciously if necessary, and gives the information to you.

A good psychic is usually pretty accurate about the past, reasonably accurate about your present, and woefully inaccurate about your future. This is partly because the information has to be filtered through the psychic's own system, and partly because you are constantly changing your mind about your own past, present, and future, and you also probably have some memory blocks and conflicting ideas. Assuming the shaman concept that we are creating our future as we go along, you can imagine the difficulty a psychic has in sorting out a meaningful assessment from the mass of frequently conflicting and muddled information that you and those presently or potentially connected to you are broadcasting. It's amazing that they do as well as they do.

Admittedly, psychics sometimes come up with information about the future that actually turns out that way, but that is usually when they tune into a present pattern of strong habits, strong suggestibility, or strong determination. Most of the time, because we change so much, they are either completely inaccurate or only partially accurate. I once visited a highly reputed psychic in southern California for a reading. Her reading of my past was quite insightful, her reading of my present brought several things to my conscious attention that I hadn't noticed, and her reading of my future was very mixed. She tuned in well to my plan for public speaking, which I hadn't begun at that time, and she accurately timed the meeting and described the appearance of a man I didn't physically connect with for six more months. However, she also described him as one who would be an important teacher in my life. As it turned out we became good friends and shared some knowledge, but he never played a teacher role for me. If my state at the time of the reading hadn't changed, though, he might very well have played such a role. Finally, she delighted me by saying I would eventually move to the French Riviera and live there six months and travel six months. That never happened, of course, but that reading may have been a mixed expression of my past experience in the French-speaking African city of Dakar, which resembles the Riviera a lot, and my desire to live in Hawaii and travel the world from there.

In spite of promotional hype, psychics are rarely more than 30 percent accurate in their overall predictions, and 50 percent is guessing. The problem has to do with static from the psychic's own desires and stresses, as well as from the fact that people change their minds. The Earth changes its mind even more often, apparently, because the one thing psychics are worst at predicting (not counting alien encounters) is earthquakes. I have only run across one "psychic" whose predictive percentage ranged consistently from 90 to 98 percent. However, this was because of the infrequency and the method of his predictions. The "psychic" in question was Jack Smith, a columnist for the *Los Angeles Times*. His method was to wait for the *National Enquirer*'s annual issue of predictions by famous psychics for the coming year. Then, next to each of the famous psychics' predictions he would write "This won't happen." He was outstandingly accurate.

If we're not really tuning in to the past or the future and what we do pick up is only memories or possibilities, why bother to turn our intuition in those directions at all? Why not just work on extending it into the present? Precisely because intuition of the extended present can give us valuable information about inhibiting ideas we still hold about the past, as well as present patterns that may lead to a future we don't want. We can use intuition to understand ourselves and others better; to change our ideas and therefore the effects of the past; and to change the future by changing current patterns.

Hailona—Creative Intuition

Hailona refers to the art of casting for divination, which is an old word for tuning in to intuition. Casting itself is a technique for making intuitive information available to the conscious mind. The basic process is one of consciously focusing on a question and then letting the inner self (the *ku/ kane* combo) give you the answer through some kind of arrangement of signs and symbols. In most cases the meanings of the signs, symbols, and arrangement pattern have been worked out beforehand. Some commonly used casting methods are the tossing of coins for the I Ching and the dealing out of tarot cards. The concept taught in the shaman system is that the inner self gathers the information desired through the web, broadcast, or field and manipulates the signs and symbols in such a way that the arrangement pattern gives you the closest answer possible for the method chosen. In an I Ching reading, you could say that the *ku* gathers the information desired through intuition and then, taking into account gravity, air resistance, muscle strength, and surface friction, releases the coins in a way that gives a meaningful pattern.

In the next few sections I will describe an old Hawaiian casting method, a modified African method, and a highly flexible method of my own invention built on ancient models.

'Oi-pahu
The name of this method used in old Hawaii means "odd-even" or "successful-unsuccessful." It is used when you

want to determine the outcome of an event or a venture. First you lay out two pieces of cloth—handkerchiefs will do—or two bowls, and designate one as representing yourself and the other as representing the person, place, event, or venture you are concerned with. Then you relax your body, focus on the question of success, and out of a pile of stones or marbles you take a random handful with each hand and place them under the cloths or in the bowls. Finally, you count the stones or marbles out by twos. Count yours out first to save time, because if you end up with an even amount, forget it. No matter what's in the other pile, this is a sign of failure. If your pile has one left over (odd) and the other pile is also odd, this is also supposed to be a sign of failure. However, I think this is overly pessimistic. The original thinking was that you both couldn't win (*'oi*, odd, also means "successful"), that two odds canceled each other out. On the other hand, if you accept a "win-win" philosophy, this outcome could mean success for both sides. The last result, in which your pile is odd and the other is even, is a definite sign of your success. Remember always, though, that the information you receive has nothing to do with the future. It is a reading of the probable outcome of your present attitudes and plans. Change those and you can change the result.

The Sixteen Eyes of Fa

Ages ago among the Fon people of Dahomey (now called Benin) in West Africa, where I lived for two and a half years, a system of divination based on legend was developed that is still in use today. The legend had to do with the god Fa, creator of mankind and messenger of the great gods, who had sixteen eyes in the form of palm nuts that opened every morning so he could look out and prophesy. Doing this divination is called "opening the eyes of Fa." It is an odd-even method, but the original process has been simplified by me for easier modern use. It now consists of relaxing and focusing on your question, then tossing a coin (heads = even, tails = odd) or a die four times and noting the odds and evens.

Then you simply refer to the chart below for your answer. An "odd" toss is represented in the chart by one dot, and an "even" toss by two dots. It helps develop your intuition because you have to think of different ways in which the single-word answer can apply to your question, and then choose the interpretation that *feels* right. As an example, if you asked whether you and your lover would still be together next year and got four odds in a row, the answer would be Union, which would be rather obvious. But if you got two odds, an even, and an odd, giving the answer Weakness, you'd have to think about the strength of your relationship, or the strength of your desire, or the motivation behind your question.

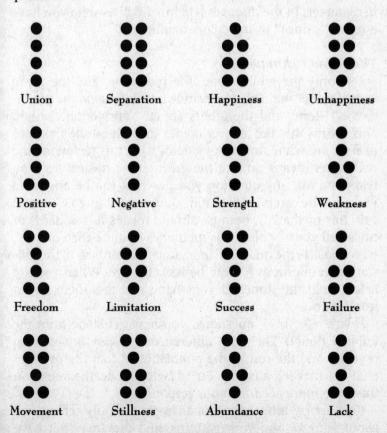

Shaman Stones

This method, which is in three parts, is what I teach in my courses. It uses a total of seven "stones," which don't have to be stones at all. I generally give out seven plastic beads, colored white, red, orange, yellow, green, blue, and violet. Students who like the method often buy or make a more personal set afterward. Semiprecious gemstones are popular, as are waterworn basalt stones dabbed with colored paint, and for my blind students I have recommended brace-let charms. If you like crystals a nice set can be made from clear quartz, rhodochrosite or rose quartz, carnelian, citrine, malachite or aventurine, turquoise or sodalite, and amethyst or purple fluorite. The best size is not more than a half inch in diameter. In the discussion below I will assume you have a set of "stones" in the colors mentioned.

The yes/no technique

Use only the white stone, the red stone, and the green stone for this one. The white stone is called *kumu*, the "foun-dation" stone, and the others are *eo*, "answering" stones. This means that the answer comes from the stone that falls nearest the white, on either side of it. In this technique the red stones means no and the green stone means yes. You relax and ask any question you like that can be answered yes or no. Be careful of "should" questions, though ("Should I do this or that?"), because should relates to standards or rules and your *ku* often has memories of more than one set, which makes the question ambiguous. Regardless of the rea-son, such questions tend to be less effective. When you are ready, hold the stones in your hand and toss them out in front of you.

If you ask "test" questions, you may get static from the implied doubt. The only difference between professional psychics and the rest of the population is that the psychics tend to trust their answers. Stress factors aside, the more you trust, the more accurate your responses.

Remember, too, that your answers are only telling you about your *ku* and your patterns, and they may not have anything to do with the situation as others perceive it or as it may actually turn out. You may ask about anything you like, but this technique is particularly good for discovering attitudes and beliefs at the *ku* level and for getting information on your subconscious perceptions of other people and situations.

In asking questions about matters that really concern you, you may find a desire to immediately toss again when you don't like the answer. I suggest that you don't, because that tends to stimulate fear and suppression. Instead, I recommend the following process:

The Secret Shaman Process for Getting the Answer You Want

1. Get an answer from the stones that you don't like.
2. Acknowledge the answer as representing a current pattern.
3. *Forcefully* grab the two answering stones and reverse their position, *shouting* as you do, "This is the new pattern, *ku!* Remember it!" The forcefulness, the shout, and the physical movement will make a strong sensory impression on the *ku* and help to establish a new pattern with better results.

The advice technique

Use all seven stones for this. The white is still the *kumu,* although it is presented in the list of meanings below with the *eo* stones.

> White = First principle, key word *awareness*
> Red = Second principle, key word *freedom*
> Orange = Third principle, key word *focus*
> Yellow = Fourth principle, key word *persistence*
> Green = Fifth principle, key word *love*
> Blue = Sixth principle, key word *confidence*
> Violet = Seventh principle, key word *flexibility*

When you are ready, relax and focus on a request for advice, like "What's the best way for me to get what I want?"

Or "What's the best thing for me to do in this situation?"
Remember that this technique does not answer yes or no.
Then toss the stones and read the one closest to the white.
Use a combination of the principle and the key word to derive
an answer to your question. It is in the nature of divination
for the answers to require as much intuition as the questions.

In a variation, instead of advice on a particular matter,
ask for a plan of action, deciding beforehand the number of
stones you wish to be part of your answer. For instance, if
you asked, "Give me a three-step plan of action for increasing
my income" and you got the orange, red, and green stones
in that order nearest the white, the answer could be read as,
"Clarify your goals, get rid of guilt, and do what you love."
That's simplified, of course, because in actuality you would
probably get a lot more ideas around each one.

Or instead of asking for advice or a plan, ask, "What's in
the way of achieving my goal?" Toss the stones and read
the answer from the one nearest the white, only this time
read it in its opposite sense:

Red = mental or physical stress
Orange = lack of focus
Yellow = procrastination
Green = anger
Blue = fear or doubt
Violet = rigid thinking

Picture-casting

This is one of the greatest secrets of shamanic divination
there is. Imagine an anthropologist on a tropical island
watching the village shaman toss out shells and bones and
stones and then give a long reading. Time after time the
scientist watches the shaman cast, and still he can't figure
out the meaning of the objects or the structure of the pattern.
And he doesn't believe it when the shaman tells him there
isn't any, unless he finally dismisses the shaman as a fraud.

What is the shaman doing? He's looking at pictures. In
my opinion this is the highest form of the divining art because

it stimulates the deepest intuition through symbols and associations.

To use it with your stones, relax and ask for a picture to represent the current or future state of a person, place, thing, situation, or condition. Then toss all seven stones, without regard to which is *kumu* or *eo*. When the stones are cast, look at the stones without any effort. What does the pattern look like or remind you of? You might imagine the stones are like dots in a children's book, and try to connect them in different ways with imaginary lines. Although we call it a picture, sometimes the main sense comes from feeling. You might just gaze at it and be aware of what associations or memories come to mind. If it feels appropriate, you can take into account the meanings of the stones that were given in the last technique. For some people this technique will be a snap, but others will have to practice it for a while before the barriers to this kind of perception fall down. If, no matter what you try, the pattern still doesn't tell you anything, thank your *ku* for trying, tell it to give you a different picture about the same thing, and toss again.

You can also use the pattern-changing process given in the first technique for this one, if you don't like the picture. This can even work as a distant healing process if you ask for a picture of someone else's condition. In this case you forcefully improve or change the picture by moving the stones around.

La'a kea — The Light of Love

Because of the web, the broadcast, or the field, take your pick, everything influences everything else, but not to the same degree. A valid observation we can make is that the *ku* is influenced most by the strongest, nearest, most resonant field.

A field is an area of influence (like a magnetic field) or perception (like a visual field). Here we are mostly concerned with influence, and mostly with the human energy field, also called the aura, or *hoaka* in Hawaiian. The human energy field has both physical and nonphysical components, but for the moment we'll treat it as a single entity. It will also be helpful to note that energy itself is properly defined as influential movement or activity; that is, movement or activity that creates change. It could also be called influential vibration. Another thing to note is that energy is not a tangible thing, but tangible things have energy. Therefore, a reduction or lessening of energy is equivalent to slowing the rate of vibration, not taking away anything tangible; and an increase of energy is equivalent to speeding up the rate of vibration, not adding anything tangible. Increasing energy is not like adding a cup of water to a cake mix. It's like increasing the speed of the mixer.

Resonance has two meanings applicable to the human energy field. One, related to electricity, is "the condition of adjustment of a circuit that allows the greatest flow of current of a certain frequency." In human terms this means that the state of the mind and body determines what kind of energies will most influence it. Simply put, whatever fear you have will resonate to, or be influenced by, additional fear around you; and whatever confidence you have will be more resonant to additional confidence. This is why the most important first step in any healing by an urban shaman is to build up a person's confidence. Of course, because of the third and sixth principles, you can consciously choose to shift your own attention to whatever confidence you possess and thus tune in more to the influence of confidence around you and diminish the influence of fear. The other meaning of resonance, from physics, is "the reinforced vibration of a body exposed to the vibration, at about the same frequency, of another body." Speaking in human terms, this means that your fear will tend to increase the fear of those around you and your confidence will tend to increase the confidence of those around you.

Proximity and strength of human energy fields are closely related because, generally speaking, the closer you are to the source of the field, the stronger—more energized—it usually is. Your aura extends infinitely, but your mental and sensory attention usually do not. Due to the third principle, then, your effective field might be quite different from your actual field. Also, frequency considerations aside, human beings tend to be more influenced by physical energies perceived through the physical senses (sight, sound, touch, etc.) than by mental energies perceived through the mental senses. So proximity is an important influential factor.

Strength of a field has to do with energy intensity, which has to do with vibration. The quality of vibration has two components, frequency and amplitude, or put another way, rate and intensity. Using ocean waves as an example, the number of waves in a hundred-yard stretch would determine the frequency of the waves; the size of each wave would determine the amplitude. Obviously there would be more energy in six-foot waves than in two-foot waves of the same frequency. Likewise, a C struck on a piano vibrates at a specific frequency; and the same C played on a tuba vibrates at the same frequency, but with a much higher volume (the musical equivalent of amplitude). In the human aura, frequency is determined by focus and amplitude by emotion. The focus comes from the attention of *kane*, *ku*, and *lono*, and the emotion comes from intentional responses and habitual reactions to your inner and outer environments.

Putting this all together, it means that the *ku* is influenced by the strongest, nearest, most resonant field. If you walk into a room of people in a state of potential anger (meaning there are things in your life that anger you, but you are not presently feeling that anger), and there is a person in the room who is currently very angry but not showing it openly, it is likely that you will start feeling increasingly irritated and angry without knowing why. If the other person is angry about something which would also make you angry, the effect on you will probably be greater. This is field strength, nearness, and resonance at work. If you have a subconscious habit of avoiding anger, then the field effect will probably influence you to subconsciously suppress your emotions by tightening your muscles, and the longer you stay in the room the more ill or drained you will feel. It is *important* to realize that the other person did not drain you or make you ill, your reactions did. No one can drain you of energy because energy is infinite and so are you. If you feel drained in someone's presence, your *ku* is just reacting to something about them you don't like. In the same situation, if you were to enter the room in a strong state of happiness, you would have a softening, healing effect on the angry person.

It is not just people who can influence your emotions. Physical environments can, too. A little bit of stress carried into a highly energetic environment like an air-conditioned office or a great pyramid can be amplified into a large amount of stress accompanied by anger or fear, depending on your habitual reactions to stress. And memories stored in the *ku* of the place could add to your reaction even more. In Egypt once I visited a small temple of Isis on an island in the Nile at the end of a long, tiring day. As our party approached the inner sanctum one of the women, a very sensitive type not given to freely expressing her emotions, fainted dead away at the entrance. Later she said she felt overwhelmed by a sense of anger. The closer I got the more angry I began to feel, so that by the time I reached the entrance I felt outraged and memories not my own were coming up about desecrations in the temple. With great effort I went inside the chamber and tried to harmonize it, but I was no longer in a suitable state to do that. Curiously, after taking care of the woman, no one else went into the chamber. It looked like they weren't interested in it, but it was probably a *ku* response. Just before getting back into the boat to leave I found a four-inch quartz crystal in the sand and realized the island must have an abundance of them, which would also add to the energy. Even so, it took a lot of conscious destressing and reprogramming before I could get back to my normal state. If I had come to the island in a happy, relaxed state my experience would have been amplified in a different way. Either I would have actively explored the place with increasing interest, or I might have become euphoric and tuned in to whatever happy memories the place had.

The practical knowledge to be gained from this story is

that, while you do create all of your own emotions, the intensity of those emotions may be influenced by someone or something in your environment. Rather than waste time trying to figure out why you are having the emotion, then, the smart thing is to go ahead and do something about it. If you like the experience, enjoy it. If you don't, here are some techniques to consider.

The White Light of Protection

Where fear reigns, conflict follows. In a world governed by so much fear it is not surprising that even metaphysical techniques arise that are based on defense and attack. Perhaps the most common one found around the world is the "White Light of Protection," as it is often called. It's a beautiful concept, but its application leaves a lot to be desired.

In its simplest form it consists of imagining yourself surrounded by a white or clear light that protects you from all harm, either emanating from your own spirit or given to you by a spiritual being. I was told of a good application of this by one of my students. He was living in New York City in the Sixties, and one of his friends was a lovely young woman who usually wore just a thin cotton shift and wandered around the roughest parts of town free as a bird. He and others tried to warn her of the dangers, but she just smiled and said her Light would protect her. One time he followed her, just in case, and was amazed to see hardened men of the street consistently treat her with courtesy and kindness. The Light removed her fear, and they responded to the lack of fear and the presence of love.

All too often, however, the use of the White Light reinforces fear and worse. When this happens it comes from the emphasis on protection rather than trust. In such cases it is used like a fence or a barrier that keeps the source of fear away and apart, and therefore it doesn't get rid of the fear at all. Actually, each time it is used this way it reinforces the fear by creating a habit of fearing. If you put a White Light of Protection around yourself, your family and friends, your house and your car, and then trust that everything is taken care of, it will work well for you. But if you use the same Light with a focus on what it is protecting you from, you will wear yourself out with making the Light stronger and stronger, and will start attracting that which you fear.

The worst and most abominable use of the Light is sometimes even taught by well-meaning metaphysical teachers who are too steeped in fear to know what they are doing. In these instances the Light is used not just as a shield of protection, but as a reflector or mirror to send negativity back to its source. The assumption is that any negativity you feel has been purposely sent to you by a meanie who deserves to get back what they sent. While psychic battles are not impossible, they are extremely rare because so few people in the world are smart enough to know how to really engage in them *and* stupid enough at the same time to do it (remember that the *ku* takes everything personally). The assumption in this system is that any negativity you feel is your reaction to your spiritual and physical environment, regardless of whether any particular person is angry at you or wishes you harm. To use the Light to send harm to another, even if you think you are just reflecting what has come your way, is to engage in black magic.

The White Light of Protection is most useful as a first-aid mindshield for someone so stuck in fear that nothing else will make them feel safer. Once a minimum state of confidence has been reached, however, it's time to move on to something more advanced and beneficial.

The Lovelight of *La'a Kea*

La'a kea is a Hawaiian idiom meaning "sacred light," referring to the good things represented by daylight, such as sunshine, knowledge, and happiness. It is also used in shaman practice to mean an aura charged with sunshine, knowledge, and happiness. The technique is similar to that of the White Light described above, except that it is used for healing and harmony. To clarify the distinction we'll call it the Lovelight. Drawing on the power within you, you use your own mind to imagine yourself surrounded by and filled with the Lovelight. We call this "turning on the Light." Don't let the emphasis on light bother you, though. You can imagine colors, sounds, and feelings, if you prefer. My own Lovelight is usually filled with colors, symbols, patterns, music, and soft or tingly sensations, depending on the effect I want. As you turn on the Light you also "charge the Light" by generating a positive emotion. A simple appreciation of something beautiful will do this, or you could go for a stronger emotion.

The first assumption is that the Lovelight exists. The second one is that it will extend outward or beam toward any area of your focus. The third assumption is that it will follow your instructions. Here are some suggestions for using it:

1. Start each day by turning on the Lovelight and extending it throughout your immediate environment. Speak to the Lovelight (everything is alive, aware, and responsive) and give it the instruction, mentally or aloud, "Harmonize this place."
2. Use the Lovelight throughout the day with different people, places, and situations in the same way as above.
3. Whenever you experience physical or emotional distress, turn on the Lovelight and say, "Harmonize the energies around me."
4. If you are having a difficult relationship with someone, extend the Lovelight to include that person, no matter where they are, and say, "Harmonize the energies between us," or "Harmonize our fields."
5. If you want to protect family, friends, or property, imagine them surrounded by the Lovelight and say to it, "Keep this (person, place, or thing) in peace and harmony."
6. If you want to use the Lovelight for distant healing, practice surrounding yourself with the Light in different colors (or symbols for the colors), with a different instruction for each. If you already have a color system you like, use it, but here is the one we use:

    White/clear—"Enlighten!" (used in healing to help increase self-knowledge and connection with the Higher Self; also when no other color seems appropriate)

Red/pink—"Clear!" (used to help remove mental and physical tension and limitations; good for increasing group rapport)

Orange/peach—"Focus!" (helps to focus attention and energy)

Yellow—"Center!" (helps to relieve worry, resentment, and guilt; helps remove procrastination, increase persistence, and stimulate enjoyment of the present moment)

Green—"Bless!" (helps to increase self-esteem, appreciation, friendship, love, and happiness)

Blue—"Empower!" (helps to increase spiritual and physical strength, self-confidence, and inner authority)

Violet—"Assist!" (helps to establish spiritual and physical harmony, attunement with purpose and prosperity, alignment with others for common goals)

In addition, if you wish, black ("Absorb!") can be used to absorb and transform negativity, gray ("Neutralize!") can be used to neutralize excess of any kind, and a rainbow can be used as an alternative to white. After you've practiced with the colors on yourself and gotten the feel of them, use them with other people, places, and things you care for as in number 5 above.

7. For an especially intensive form of distant healing with the Lovelight, select a small object—perhaps a coin, a crystal, or a pebble—to represent a person or place you want to assist with a healing. Place this in your left hand. Next, take one of the shaman stones or another object of a color from the list in number 6 above, and place that in your right hand. Then surround yourself with the Lovelight of the same color as the object in your right hand, and do *kahi* on both hands with deep breathing as you give the appropriate instruction. Here your focus is threefold: on both hands and on the Lovelight. You don't have to focus on an image of the person, because the symbol for the person is in your hand. The physical objects help to involve the energies and attention of the *ku* in the

process. At some point you will get a signal to stop. This may come as a deep sigh, as an internal impulse, or a physical sensation such as tingling or tiredness. When it comes it's like a signal from the other person's *ku* that it has received enough for the time being. Complete the process by finishing with a word or phrase like "It is done," "Thank you," or the Hawaiian *"Amama,"* roughly equivalent to "So be it."

May you always bless and be blessed by the Light of Love.

THE SIXTH ADVENTURE:

CHANGING THE WORLD WITH SHAMAN DREAMING

Aia ke ola i Kahiki
(Health and prosperity are in *Kahiki*,
a place in the inner world)

This chapter is going to introduce you to the power of shamanic dreaming for changing the world. It's going to start out with ways to use dreams very close to our outer world, and then move gradually into deeper and deeper dreaming until you will be able to understand and use the ultimate shaman dream—the vision quest.

In traditional Hawaiian culture the universe is divided into *Po* and *Ao*. *Po* is the inner dream, the unseen realities which give birth to this outer dream of *Ao*. Because *Po* refers to that which is unseen, the realm of experience which Westerners might call mind or spirit, the same word is used to mean "night," the time of darkness. For the poetic Hawaiians of old, nighttime, or *po*, became a symbol of the inner world, and daytime, *ao*, became a symbol for the outer expression of the inner world, which is why *ao* also means "teaching and learning." The moment of sunset was the beginning of a new day and dawn was the beginning of the manifestation of all the creativity that had taken place during the night. The West itself became a symbol for *Po*, which confused a lot of early explorers and continues to confuse anthropologists. Whenever Polynesians said they came from the West, they didn't mean Asia, they meant *Po*, the realm of spirit. The significance of all this is to emphasize the shamanic idea that what we experience as outer reality is the expression or reflection of an inner reality, and that one of the most effective ways to change the outer reality, the dream of life, is to change the inner reality, or dream of Spirit.

The Three Regions of *Po*

Just as this outer world has its three regions of land, sea, and sky, so does the inner world have its three regions, at least in Hawaiian shamanic thought. These are *Lanikeha*, *Kahiki*, and *Milu*.

Lanikeha is the Upper World in the unseen realm. It is where God, angels, and saints exist; where gods and goddesses live and play; where great heroes, heroines, and myths abound. In your own night dreams you may have been there on occasion when you experienced big, important, or super-real dreams. Shamans go there primarily for inspiration, as Maui did to find the secrets of fire and cultivation.

Kahiki, the Middle World, is the inner region that is most like this outer reality. Most of your night dreams and daydreams take place in *Kahiki*. If this word sounds a lot like "Tahiti" it's because they are the same word in different dialects. It was quite common in Polynesia to name outer world places after inner world places. *Kahiki* in Hawaiian means "foreign" as well as "the power to do something." In Tahitian, the word *tahiti* means "to transplant" and "to cross over." In addition to anything else, these meanings have to do with using the dreams of *Kahiki* to make changes in this world.

The third region is *Milu*, the Underworld. This is the place of nightmares and challenges, and the place where shamans often go on a vision quest for recovering lost power.

We'll start our process by working in *Kahiki* with the dreams you have at night.

Mo'ike—The Art of Interpreting Dreams

This is going to be short, sweet, and simple. You are the best interpreter of your dreams, and with the method I'm about to share you can bypass books with interpretation lists, time-consuming association processes, and thematic analyses. You can go straight to the real meaning of your dreams because of the corollary to the fifth principle that says, "Everything is alive, aware, and responsive." Everything includes all of the characters and objects in your dreams, as well as the dreams themselves.

The way to interpret a dream is to recall it while you are relaxed and awake and speak directly to any of the characters and objects in the dream, asking, "What are you doing here? What do you represent or symbolize?" In most cases the person, animal, or object will talk back to you and give you the information you want. To speak to the dream as a whole, imagine it as a ball or globe. If you have a bit of subconscious stress about the matter, there may be some resistance to answering you and you may have to be extra nice and persuasive, or highly assertive, depending on your own personality. Should there be no response at all, you then apply the technique of "inventive interpretation." This means you ask the question and then consciously make up the response as if you were speaking for the character or object. Sounds weird, I know, but it works because *you cannot make up a response in that moment that isn't valid*, due to the second principle corollary, "Everything is connected." After a few applications of inventive interpretation you will find spontaneous responses coming easier.

As a note of interest, memories of outer world experiences can be treated just like dreams for interpretation. Once while in Malibu I was having lunch with a friend, talking about our transformative work. A man at the next table overheard us and invited us to a presentation he said would be of great interest to both of us. My friend couldn't make it, but I went and quickly wondered what on earth I was doing there. It was so flaky that I left early, even though another friend was there whom I hadn't seen in a long time. The presentation was about a project to create a center that would cost $22 million! Part of the money was for an immense dome to be partly sunk in the earth for some obscure reason. Another part was to fund an intelligent computer system, relying on technology that hadn't been invented yet. And still another part was for supporting inventions like a device to fit around your nose and automatically blow gusts of air in alternate nostrils to simulate a yogic practice. And those were the best parts. After I left I was confused and upset because I trust my intuition and guidance to lead me to situations that serve my intended purposes, and this experience didn't seem to fit. My choice was to start doubting myself, or to trust more. So I trusted more and treated the experience like a dream, asking the participants for interpretations. As it turned out, part of the reason for my being there was to stimulate the other friend in a positive way, and part of it was to make me aware—through exaggeration—of my concerns for the possibly flaky appearance of my own projects at the time. Since all life is a dream, all memories can be treated as dreams.

Dreamchange

One of the most powerfully effective ways to use night dreams is to change them with your imagination. Dreams are real experiences in another dimension, but like all real experiences they are the effects of belief structures or habit patterns. In that way they are like languages, which are based on structures and patterns. Even with the most flexible grammatical structure and abundant vocabulary, a language can only express what the mind that produces it has to say. So, too, the inner and outer dream environments can only express what the mind that produces them thinks. And just as changing language by saying something a different way can change one's mind and thereby one's experience, so changing the dream environment can change all the dream experiences produced by a particular mind. In practical terms this means that if you change a dream, you also restructure the patterns that gave rise to it, and you automatically change any other dreams that arose from the same patterns. You can heal the outer world by healing the inner world.

While it is possible, with enough motivation, to learn how to wake up within an ongoing dream, that isn't necessary in order to get the benefits of dreamchange. This is because memories retain the same patterns as the original dream, modified by any changes of mind you may have had since having the dream. So for healing purposes, changing the memory of the dream is as good as changing a dream in progress.

Three ways to change a dream—or the memory of a dream—are by changing your reaction in the dream, allowing the dream to continue, or changing the events of the dream. Each of these is most beneficial for recurring or single dreams of fear, anger, injury, or frustration. These changes are done in the realm of *Kahiki*.

Changing your reaction means to consciously choose to respond differently to what's happening. In one of my workshops a woman recalled a recurring dream in which she was being chased by a fire-breathing dragon. In the original dream she ran as if in slow motion and the dragon was always just about to pounce on her when she woke up. In class she put her attention on a moment just before the usual wake-up point and imagined herself stopping, turning around, and shouting, "Why are you chasing me?" To her surprise the dragon stopped, looked confused, and said, "I'm not chasing you, I'm following you!" The result in her life was a reduction of fear and an increase in self-confidence.

Allowing the dream to continue means recalling the dream and keeping your conscious attention focused on it past the usual wake-up point. Some dreams are more suitable for this than others, but there will always be a positive resolution if this change technique is followed long enough. In an early workshop a student recalled a recurring dream in which he drove a car into a parking garage where another car was waiting for him (driven by his mother, as he found out through the interpretive process). Then both cars raced up the spiral ramps of the garage to the top floor, where his mother's car stopped and his shot off into space. This was the point at which he always used to wake up in fear. In class he reexperienced the whole dream again (with feelings of fear, he said later) until his car flew off the top ramp. Then he stayed with the dream and let it continue by itself. His car kept on flying over the city and gently landed on a freeway at the other end. As the car drove off he could see the license plate, which said, "Life goes on." His effect was an improvement in his relationship with his mother and a lessening of his fear of death.

Changing the events of a dream is a form of direct, creative intervention which tends to instill a strong sense of self-confidence and self-esteem. If these are quite low to begin with, this process may have to be repeated with different parts of a dream over a period of time. One woman who was helped a lot by this technique worked on the same dream for about six months. Usually, however, a one-time intervention is all that is needed. To give an example of how creative intervention can also lead to spontaneous change, I'll relate my helicopter dream. This one started out with me as a passenger in a helicopter (already unusual for me) which took off, but couldn't go very high because there were power lines in the way (I don't need any interpretation for that, thank you). The rest of the dream was a frustrating ride of ineffective hopping until I woke up. Right after waking up I went back into the dream at the beginning, where I stopped the pilot before the helicopter took off, went around to the other side, and sat in the pilot's seat myself. Taking the controls, I lifted the copter, found a space between two power lines, and zoomed straight up. It felt wonderful. Then I found myself, without intending it, flying over the United

States, with all the states nicely bordered. Next, to my delight
and astonishment, the sky was suddenly filled with helicop-
ters being flown by all the other shamans I had trained, and
they began dumping copies of my booklet, *The Aloha Spirit*,
all over the country. This was followed in the outer dream
of life by a rapid increase in the number of people I was
reaching.

Almost invariably after I teach how to do dreamchange,
someone will express concern over changing the dream before you know what it means or what the "lesson" is, and
sometimes concern that such change is tantamount to sup-
pressing what the dream is intended to convey. To any of
you with these fears let me say this: The inner world isn't
that much different from the outer world. If you break your
arm in the outer world you don't sit there and agonize over
the meaning of the event, or leave the arm broken so you'll
be sure to remember the lesson involved. You fix it fast. The
first message is very clear. It's "Hey! Your arm's broken!"
And the second message, given by the pain and discomfort,
is just as clear. It's "Do something about it now!" Of course,
you can also look for other meanings or examine what kind
of thinking led to your injury, if that seems important (it
might be, if this were the third time you'd broken your arm
in the past year), but the time to do that is after you've taken
steps to heal it. The same applies to inner dreams of fear and
anger, pain and hurt. Heal them first. As for suppression, I
always recommend full conscious acknowledgment of the
dream as it is before you change it. Then you can heal out
of love with full, conscious sensory involvement. If you try
to quickly change anything you don't like without really
paying attention to it, you are probably acting out of fear,
and the results won't be as good.

Daydreaming Your Cares Away

It is a little-known or -appreciated fact that we dream inner
dreams twenty-four hours a day. It is not just at night that
inner dreams happen. Dreams happen all the time, and we
just tune in to them from time to time. In our society tuning

into dreams is highly discouraged among both children and adults—although it is tolerated, barely, among poets, novelists, and people on vacation, as long as they don't do it too much. Passive daydreamers, those who just allow their minds to drift to whatever comes up, are considered idlers, and active daydreamers, those who creatively fantasize, are considered escapists unless they get paid for it. I want to teach you to use both passive and active daydreaming for healing yourself and others. The process we'll use takes place in *Kahiki* and is a logical extension of all seven shaman principles.

We begin by assuming that everything dreams, not just people. Then we assume that we can tune in to these dreams (at least our translated version of them) by focusing our attention on a particular object with the intent to know its dream. We next assume that whatever comes into our mind from that moment until we stop focusing is the dream of what we are focusing on. Finally, we assume that by changing such a dream in the same way that we change night dreams, we can get the same kind of healing results, sometimes immediately. In my workshops people have had many immediate healings, from the disappearance of flu symptoms to pain relief and reductions in tumor size. Complete healings aren't always immediate, but there are almost always some immediate benefits.

Let me give some examples that will make the process more clear. In one case I was in a restaurant having coffee. The waitress was in a foul mood, not speaking to anyone, not refilling their cups, and spilling food when she served it. I tuned in to her current dream, which I imagined was occurring right over her head. What I saw was a bleak landscape with gray clouds above it. So, in creative fantasy, I caused the clouds to rain and then part to let the sun through, caused flowers to sprout up, and caused birds, bees, and butterflies to enter the picture. I was having a great time when she suddenly left and went into the kitchen where she stayed for five full minutes. When she came back out she was completely changed. She smiled at everyone and filled their cups carefully, said hello to a new customer, and generally seemed happier. Now what I did didn't cause the change, it just helped it happen. Changing her dream as I perceived it was like sending her *ku* a new idea by intuition, and the new idea was so nice that her *ku* decided to use it to make a change of its own. Note also that there was no invasion of her mind or her privacy. I only picked up what she was broadcasting, translated it into a form I could understand, and beamed back a healing message for her to use or not use.

We can do this for other people, and we can also do this for ourselves. Using the assumptions given, try saying that every part of your body is now having its own dream, in addition to any dreams you as a whole may be having. You can make practical use of this technique by tuning in (putting your attention on) a part of your body which may be sick, weak, or not functioning as well as you'd like. Most people find that it helps to close your eyes, but you can do it with your eyes open if you prefer. The body part can be anything you can name as a body part, like your heart, a hand, or a shoulder. First, be passive and let the dream form on its own. It may be expressed as sight, sound, feelings, or any combination, and it may be wild and fantastic or very mundane and ordinary. Even if the only thing that comes to mind is housework or work at the office you still have to do, treat that as the dream. Once the dream has formed, go in consciously and change it in some way. If the dream is scary and unpleasant it won't be hard to think of something to do, but even if the dream seems perfect in every way, *change it for the better*. If the body part isn't as healthy as you'd like it to be, perfection can be a mask and any change will start a healing. In making your changes, you'll get the best results if you use all your senses. Continue as long as you like, or until you can feel a physical response in your body.

Since everything is dreaming, you can tune in to and change the dream of a tree, a home, a machine, a group, a nation, or a planet, if you wish. The key to success is dreaming a new dream so pleasurable to the *ku* of the object of your attention that it will want to change. That is where the development of your dreaming skill as an urban shaman comes in.

Haipule—Bringing a New Dream Into Being

One way to change the dream of the outer world is to create a new dream in *Kahiki* to replace it. *Haipule* is a very ancient tried-and-true process for doing that. It can take many forms, and the form given here is designed for the purpose of this book. A brief examination of this very important word can give us a greater understanding of the process.

Hai is a root meaning "desire or need," "to present an offering," "to declare," and "to pursue." *Pule* is generally translated as "prayer, blessing, magical spell." Its related roots are *pua*, "to appear"; *pu'u*, "to desire"; *lele*, "to burst forth"; and *le'a*, "to succeed." Each syllable has a meaning for the process as well: *ha* means "to energize by deep breathing and remembering"; *i* means "to affirm what you want"; *pu* means "to imagine what you want"; and *le* means "to perform an action." *Haipule* is therefore a process for using affirmation, imagination, and action to create a new dream. When the new dream has enough energy it becomes reality (that is, in shaman terms, it replaces the current dream).

First, as always, you decide what it is that you want to dream into existence. Is it better health? A new relationship or the improvement of an old one? More money? A new car or home? Dolphins protected and respected by all nations? Peace on Earth? Just remember that the more people who will be involved in the experience of your new dream, the more energy it will take to manifest it. Getting others to do the same *haipule* will make it more effective. Deciding what you want is what you do before doing *haipule*.

The process itself is divided here into short *haipule* and long *haipule*. Short *haipule* is what you do all day every day until the dream is real enough to manifest itself. This is what really creates the dream. Long *haipule* is like a meditative practice that serves to reinforce the short *haipule*. Here is the practice of short *haipule:*

Ha—Remember your dream frequently while breathing deeply and building up positive emotions about it.

I—Speak positive words and affirmations about your dream all the time, mentally and out loud. Don't force people to hear about it and don't argue about it, but don't try to keep it a secret, either. If your motivation is so weak that somebody's skepticism will destroy your confidence, you better work on motivation and confidence first. The exact words you use don't matter, but using the present tense (*I am, it is,* etc.) about your dream is helpful. Keep in mind that your affirmations are not describing the outer world as it is, they are describing the new dream you are bringing into being.

Pu—Vividly imagine with every sense all the pleasures, benefits, and changes that the new dream will bring, as if they were happening right now. With a little practice you'll be able to do this often for a few seconds at a time. A hundred ten-second imaginings throughout the day are better than a single twenty-minute session in the morning or evening.

Le—Do something physical as often as you can to reinforce the dream. This might be an action directly related to the manifestation of your dream, like drawing up plans or meeting with pertinent people, or it could be symbolic, like making a special gesture or touching a symbol of the dream (e.g., a lucky coin, a charm that symbolizes the outcome, or a picture that represents the realization). *Touch,* don't just look.

Negative thoughts, memories, and reactions from yourself and the people around you definitely have to be dealt with immediately so you can keep your new dream alive and well. The solution is an ancient variation of short *haipule* that I call "The Triple Whammy." It consists of instantly applying positive words, positive images, and a positive posture in response to any expression of negativity regarding your new dream. If you think, speak, or hear negative words about your dream, immediately, as soon as you can be aware of it, say the positive opposite aloud or silently. What you say may not be true about the current dream, which doesn't matter at all. The words are about the new dream. So if the negative thought is "It can't happen," immediately come back with "It can happen"; if you think "How is this ever going to work?" come back with "I don't know, but it is going to work." A phrase used by many shamans in response to doubt is EWOP! (an acronym for Everything's Working Out Perfectly and a reminder to turn over the tough problems to the High Self). Positive opposite images will be useful with imaginings of your own fears and doubts based on past experience and future projections (both of which are just dreams anyway). If you imagine yourself being rejected, immediately imagine yourself being accepted; if you imagine yourself failing, immediately imagine yourself succeeding. This may feel very odd at times because you will be changing energy patterns of old dreams. Finally, use a positive posture whenever negative emotions arise, like fear, anger, and depression. Every emotion is associated with a particular body posture that reinforces that emotion. Basically, fear is tense and pulled back, anger is tense and pushed forward, and depression is tense and pulled inward. So for fear take a relaxed posture of courage and confidence, for anger use happiness and playfulness, and for depression use enthusiastic expectation. As you change your posture the feelings will change too. Watch other people, especially actors, if you need a model for the emotional stance you want. Of course, you may not "feel" like making the change, but then ask yourself how important the new dream is.

Long *haipule* is when you can spend more time clarifying, strengthening, and reinforcing your new dream. You go through the same process of energizing, affirming, imagining, and posturing in a comfortable place, perhaps with your eyes closed, for as long as you like. It's good to end your long session with a definite close. A good way is to make a physical gesture of completion (a clenched fist, a hand over your heart) and speak an ending, like the Hawaiian *amama*.

Structured Dreaming

The more deeply you enter into *Po*, the more difficult it is to keep your focus. Frequently the result is you wander away from your intended purpose or lose conscious awareness. One of the oldest shamanic solutions to this difficulty is structured dreaming. In a structured dream certain basic elements of the inner world are preprogrammed, so to speak. Thus, in the Egyptian Book of the Dead there is a river to cross, a certain being to meet, and a weighing of the soul on a scale; and in many shaman cultures there are holes to enter and trees to climb. Within the structure there is free choice, though guidelines are often given, so that each experience in the inner world may be quite different even if the structure becomes familiar. It's something like going to Hawaii for your holidays. The basic geography will remain the same and the tourist magazines will give your guidelines for what to do and see, but every time you go the experience will be different. A Polynesian name for such inner structures is *tiki*. Ordinarily we think of a *tiki* as a wooden statue, but the word really refers to the idea behind the form.

The Garden *Tiki*

In my book *Mastering Your Hidden Self*, I give a detailed description of the nature and use of a type of *tiki* called "the Garden," so I won't be as detailed here. But I will give an introduction and some other uses for it.

The Garden is in *Kahiki*, only farther in than the kind of dreams we've dealt with so far. It's essentially a private place that you create with your imagination out of memory or desire and to which you go in your dream body for various purposes such as rest, healing, insight, and adventure. As part of its structure the Garden has Helpers who work under your direction (aspects of yourself in the form of servants, elves, fairies, or whatever), a Master Gardener who assists with advice and tools, and a source of water. Of course there will be plants, and perhaps trees and walkways and other things. Because it is your creation, everything in it is a reflection of your conscious and subconscious beliefs, attitudes, and expectations at any given moment. As with other dreams, changing the Garden changes you, which changes your life experience.

One good way to use the Garden is to go there and ask for a symbol of some present challenge in your life to appear, speak to it for interpretation if you wish, and then direct your Helpers to improve it, transform it, or replace it. You might also use it for inner meetings with people you want to talk to but can't reach or deal with physically. However, our emphasis here will be on making the Garden into a place of stability in the inner world, a familiar location from which you can explore more distant areas of *Po*.

I suggest you start with the creation of a dream body, which is simply imagining that you have another body that can leave your physical body when you want it to and that can change form as you desire. This happens automatically whenever you dream, but conscious intent and attention will give your dream body more power and flexibility. And the more sensory awareness you can give your dream body, the more conscious focus you will have in *Po*. Then, with eyes open or closed according to your preference, imagine that you enter a cave which leads to another place, your Garden. Once you are there, increase your focus by seeing the detail of an object like a leaf or a flower; hearing the clarity of a sound like a bird's call, the breeze, or flowing water; and feeling the texture of an object like a rock or the bark of a tree. Learn the arrangement and contents of your Garden or fill in details if you have already planned how the Garden will be. You can even put a hut, cabin, or house there if you like, an ideal place of your own for solitude or receiving guests. Some people like to draw maps or pictures of their Garden to fix it in their memory and make it easier to focus on when they go there. Whatever you do, allow for growth, change, and new discoveries in your Garden. Each time you go there you will increase its "reality" as part of your experience.

A Shaman Journey to a Special Place

Around the world the legends of many cultures include stories about a magical village, city, or gathering place of some kind. The legends usually speak about these places in such realistic terms that explorers and adventurers have frequently gone searching for them in the physical world. Sometimes the legends have turned out to be about actual geographical locations, such as Lhasa, Troy, and Cuzco. We are concerned now, however, with the ones that aren't physical, but are nonetheless very real, such as Agartha, Shamballah, and Cibola. I'm referring to the concept that there is a place in *Po* that is just as real to those who live and visit there as our physical Earth is to us. Being in *Po,* however, where the laws of nature are different, the appearance of this inner place can differ according to the beliefs, attitudes, and expectations of the visitor. Mystics and shamans know it very well and have different names for it according to their cultures. You may have been there yourself in your night dreams and experienced it as a busy city, a university, a many-roomed palace, a temple, or a fair. In spontaneous dreams it often appears to me as a shopping center. In Hawaiian tradition this place is called *Pali Uli,* "deep-green cliffs," but I prefer the more well-known Samoan name, *Bali Hai.* Although it can take many forms, the model I use in my workshops is of a village on a tropical volcanic island surrounded by a lagoon, much like Bora Bora. It is a place to go to learn, to heal, and to discover. On their first trip I usually have my students learn something from another shaman, help someone in need, and give and receive a gift. You start the journey by entering your Garden, as explained above. Following is the experience of one of my students, which is typical of the process.

"I closed my eyes, entered my dream body, and went through the crystal cave to my Garden as usual. I checked on my little waterfall and the lilies in the pool, and took some dead leaves off my chrysanthemums, then found the path leading off from the Garden and down to the beach. As Serge said there was a sailboat pulled up on the beach and a crew of two good-looking Hawaiians waiting for me. Serge said it would be an outrigger sailing canoe, but to me it looked like a Hobie Cat. The Hawaiians and I pushed the boat out into the ocean and climbed aboard. I handled the jib while one guy took the tiller and the other held the mainsail. We sailed very fast over the ocean until we spotted a cloud on the horizon and steered toward it. Pretty soon we could see the island of Bali Hai with its emerald green volcano and a white ring of surf surrounding it. Just then a white bird flew out, circled our boat, and guided us in through a channel in the reef. Right ahead was the village, which looked to me like a small town I saw in Maine when I was a kid. We docked the boat and I left the crew to take care of it.

"Waiting for me at the end of the pier was the Master Shaman who was going to help me. She wore a circlet of flowers around her head and a long white dress, and she had the most dazzling smile. I went up to her and we hugged and I asked her to help me with my anxiety attacks. She taught me how to weave a ball of light with my fingers and to blow love into it, and then to sort of screw it into my chest where it could glow and relieve the attacks (I've done that ever since and it really works). Then I looked around for the person I was supposed to help and found a young boy sitting on a boulder and looking very sad. I asked him why he was sad and he said it was because he had died and didn't know where to go. I remembered that Serge had said that a shaman sometimes helps people to cross over after death, but at first I couldn't think of how to help. Finally I just wished really hard that he would find his way and an angel came down out of the sky and said, 'Thank you, I've been looking all over for this boy,' and took him away.

"Then I went beyond the village to look for the sacred place where Serge said shamans left gifts for other shamans. I found a grove of trees with all kinds of things hanging from the branches. I left a crystal flower to increase love and picked up a bamboo flute that played songs of happiness. Then I went back to the boat, sailed back to the beach, thanked the crew, returned to my Garden where I put the flute away, and came back out here. I'm looking forward to going again and meeting another shaman who will take me on a journey beyond Bali Hai."

Lanikeha and the Power Animals

The Upper World is a place to get inspiration and divine assistance from the *akua,* those personified forces of transformation which can take many forms and play many roles. It is entered by going into the Garden and looking for a hole in the sky, which you then reach by climbing a tree, a ladder, or a rope; by jumping; or by flying. Then you grab the edges of the hole and pull yourself up and through and look around at a beautiful and wondrous place. The first reason I give my students for visiting *Lanikeha* is to meet their Power Animals.

A Power Animal is an *akua* in animal form, a spirit being who can teach you and assist you in your journeys through various dreams. In the way my Hawaiian uncle taught me I received two sets of seven Power Animals, one for the sea and one for the land. Each of these had the name and the power of one of the principles, as indicated below:

NAME	SEA	LAND
IKE	DOLPHIN	LANDBIRD
KALA	SQUID	SEABIRD
MAKIA	SHARK	LIZARD
MANAWA	TURTLE	RAT
ALOHA	FISH	PIG
MANA	WHALE	BAT
PONO	EEL	DOG

Not surprisingly most of my students, being mainland Westerners, found it rather difficult to establish strong friendships with some of these animals, so I modified the list to suit the culture of modern urban shamans as follows:

NAME	POWER	ANIMAL
IKE	AWARENESS	DOLPHIN

KALA	FREEDOM	BIRD
MAKIA	FOCUS	CAT (any kind)
MANAWA	PERSISTENCE	OX (or Buffalo)
ALOHA	LOVE	HORSE
MANA	CONFIDENCE	BEAR
PONO	WISDOM	WOLF
		(or fox/coyote/dog)

Animals can be added or exchanged to suit personal tastes, of course.

Once in the Upper World a good place to meet the Power Animals is in a meadow (with a pool for the dolphin) or on an island. In this system you turn into the same form as the Power Animal and make friends with it. You always finish by going back into your Garden through the hole in the sky and then coming back to awareness of the physical world. The only reason for doing that, and it is a good reason, is to establish a habit pattern for your *ku* that will make future journeys easier, and to keep increasing the stability of your Garden. If for any reason you come back to physical awareness without doing that, don't worry about it; it's no big deal. Just do it by the regular route the next time if you can.

The Vision Quest to *Milu*

There is some confusion today about what a vision quest is and how to do one. Part of the confusion comes from the fact that there are two types of vision quests. There is a quest for a vision, which, in cultures that have used it, is generally done by all the young men of a tribe at a certain age in order to discover their divine purpose; and there is the use of vision (inner sight) for a quest, which is usually done by a shaman or the equivalent. Another part of the confusion comes from traditional techniques used for such quests which have been limited by technology.

In traditional cultures it was mostly the young men who went on quests for a vision, not because a woman couldn't do it, but because it was not part of her role. Since having

visions, even by the men, wasn't a normal part of life and
cultural rules were often very fixed, exceptional measures
were necessary to help the men break out of the boundaries
of ordinary thinking to receive a special revelation from the
gods or the Great Spirit. Among the measures used were
extreme privation (being sent into the wilderness away from
society with little food for an extended period), extreme
isolation (being tied in a blanket and stuck in a deep hole
for three days), and drugs (such as peyote and others). As
any psychiatrist might tell you, each of these practices is
inclined to produce hallucinations, which are the visions
these people were after. The visions themselves, while extraordinary, were still based on cultural elements in the
men's memories.

The vision quest for the shaman, on the other hand, became easier and easier as he built up experience in the spirit
world, until he could enter it at will without extreme privation, isolation, or drugs. Even though in some cultures it
became traditional for the shaman to fast, to go sit in a cave,
or to take a drug for a vision quest, it still did not require
the extreme measures used for an initial vision. And his use
of it was different. Instead of seeking a vision outside himself,
he used his own inner vision to seek healing power. Sometimes he would do this on his own account, so he could gain
the power to heal a particular sickness or condition, and
sometimes he would do it on behalf of another, seeking a
power that the person had lost or, in metaphorical terms,
had been stolen from him by a spirit. Very often the power
would take the form of a magical object which the shaman
would bring back and symbolically transfer into an equivalent physical object and keep it on hand or give it to the
person who needed it.

In spite of what many people think, the shaman used the
vision quest sparingly. He would first try the simpler means
of healing like intuition, practical psychology, and placebos.
Then he would go on to the laying on of hands or ritual,
and finally, if nothing else worked, he would enter the shamanic vision quest.

Urban shamans doing a shamanic vision quest today do not require a lot of special preparation or conditions, because we are part of a unique society that has already, though unknowingly, prepared us well. The wilderness is not an essential aspect of the vision quest, nor is a high degree of isolation. The vision quest is not dependent on outside conditions because it takes place in your mind, and our minds have had a lot of training. In a New York workshop I had twenty people doing a vision quest in a building in the garment district. It was summer and the windows were open. During the quest the air was shattered by the sound of police and fire engine sirens going by on the street right outside the window, *and not one person heard them*.

Ever since you started reading about Dick and Jane and Spot you were in training to be a shaman. Radio, television, and movies have all helped to reinforce your skill. The development of intentional inner vision took a long time in traditional societies, because it wasn't reinforced by the whole society. Exceptional people like poets, storytellers, and shamans seemed to be using magic when they evoked waking visions in the minds of listeners to their tales, legends, and inner experiences. Without that guided imagery, most people kept their attention on the outer world with its relative sameness from day to day and year to year. Even apprentices to poets, storytellers, and shamans who spent a great deal of time listening and remembering were limited to the memories of their teachers. You, now, have the skill of reading, a rare skill in the history of mankind, which trains you to focus your attention and evoke internal experience on your own at will. And you have access through books and magazines to most of the greatest storytellers of humanity. In addition, you have stored in your memory an incredibly rich treasure of human experience and imagination from radio, TV, and movies. Don't pass this off as unimportant. As I tell my students, it is because of this knowledge that you can immediately begin to apply the shaman skills that I teach. You've already done most of the work.

Milu, the Underworld, in Hawaiian shamanism is a place of challenge where obstacles or difficulties in the form of monsters, magic, and natural elements stand between you and that which you seek. The quest consists of getting past them, reaching your goal (usually a Power Object of some kind), and bringing the object back. The quest to *Milu* is not done for understanding. You can get understanding in the Garden. It is done to change the fundamental idea structures that are in the way of a healing, represented by the challenges. As each challenge is passed through in full sensory experience, its structure as an inhibiting factor is changed. I emphasize "full sensory experience." Only when the inner experience is as "real" as possible will it be fully effective.

In some warrior shaman traditions it is said that if you are in the Underworld and you meet an animal that bares its teeth at you, back out and try again another time. In the adventurer tradition we don't do that. If you meet an animal that bares its teeth, smile back. If that doesn't work and nothing else does either, let it eat you, be transformed, come out the other side, and keep going. Even the inner world is your dream, and you are the dreamweaver. Don't let anything stop you in your quest.

My tradition teaches that there are seven basic challenges in *Milu*, any of which may or may not be present in a particular quest. Each challenge is the opposite of an equivalent positive power of a principle. They are *pouli* (ignorance), *haiki* (limitation), *hokai* (confusion), *napa* (procrastination), *inaina* (anger), *weli* (fear), and *kanalua* (doubt). *Milu* is entered by a hole in the ground, and the shaman is usually accompanied by a Power Animal. As with *Bali Hai*, I think the experience is best presented in the form of a student's actual quest. The process is the same as that used for the Garden and *Bali Hai*.

"I closed my eyes and took a number of deep breaths to charge myself with energy for the quest. Then I went to my Garden and looked for the hole in the ground that would be the entrance to *Milu*. I knew it might be a whirlpool, a gopher hole, a cave, or a hole at the base of a tree and that's what I looked for at first, but what I finally found was a six-inch hole lined with stone, like a miniature well. I called on a Power Animal to come with me and my hawk suddenly appeared on my right. We made ourselves smaller and then we jumped into the hole. After a long time of falling we suddenly came flying out of the hole and landed on a path leading into a weird kind of forest, like one of those enchanted forests in Disney films. I knew that the path would lead to the Power Object I was after, so I started walking with my hawk sitting on my right arm. The forest got darker and darker until soon it was pitch-black and I couldn't see anything. Before I could think of anything to do my hawk screeched and light came out of its mouth. So I screeched, too, and between us both we made it light again. Then we kept going for a while, and suddenly a whole mass of trees and branches fell down in front of us, completely blocking the path. Everything was so thick we couldn't go around it or over it, so we made ourselves very, very small and slipped through the cracks and crevices, then made ourselves big again on the other side. Next we came to a place where the path forked off in all kinds of directions and I didn't know which way to go. Even the hawk didn't know. I tried to toss a stick and have it tell which path to take, but it just kept spinning around. Finally, the idea came to me like a voice speaking that any of the paths would work, so I picked the one closest to the middle and kept going.

"The next obstacle, or challenge, was a bridge going over a big ravine, but it only went halfway, like the builders had taken off for lunch and hadn't come back. There were even tools still lying around. I made a length of rope with bark fiber and held one end while the hawk carried it across to the other side and tied it to a big tree (I don't know how he did that). Then I made some more rope, and with some branches we finished the bridge and I walked across. Later I thought the hawk might have flown me across, but I didn't think of it at the time. Continuing through the woods we came to a clearing where we were attacked by angry savages with spears. The hawk flew up out of reach, and my first reaction was to take a karate stance and get ready to fight, but then I remembered I was supposed to act like an adventurer if possible, so I imagined that I had a bag of laughing dust and I threw it into the air. In a moment all the savages had dropped their spears and were lying on the ground laughing like crazy, so we went on. As I was crossing another clearing a huge grizzly came charging at me, so I just stood there, expecting it to stop or change into something else, but instead it came right up and swung at me with its claws. What stunned me was that I could see the cuts and blood and feel the pain in my arm when it hit me. Hey, I thought, this isn't supposed to happen. It struck me again in the chest and I fell backward on the ground. Now I was really scared. The bear stood over me and roared, and I could smell its breath and feel saliva dripping on my face. Just as I began to truly panic and the bear was bringing its head down to bite me, my hawk flew by and threw something in the bear's mouth with its talons. Immediately the bear closed its mouth, smiled, and fell over. While I was bandaging my wounds the hawk told me it had tossed a Valium in the bear's mouth. After the quest was over I understood that fear was something I would have to do more work on. The last challenge was a small table, almost like an altar, set up next to a cliff where the path ended. On the table were two beautifully carved and painted eggs, like the ones the Russians used to make as works of art. There was also a sign that said, 'Take only one, but take the right one.' I smiled because it seemed so obvious and reached out for the one on the right. But then I wondered if it was so obvious because it was a trick. The correct one could be the left one. I asked the hawk, but he was silent, and so were the eggs when I asked them. I was stuck until I asked the altar, and all it said was, 'Who dreams the dream?' At last I understood and tore the sign in half and took both the eggs. In one was a moon that represented Love, and in the other was a sun that represented Power. I brought them back to my Garden, put them away, and thanked my hawk and sent him back to *Lanikeha*. Finally, I came back to my normal awareness and symbolically placed a spiritual form of the eggs into each half of my brain so I would remember to use Love and Power together.''

THE SEVENTH ADVENTURE

SHAPECHANGING AND COMMUNITY SERVICE

Kino lau
(Many bodied, *said of one who is able to assume other forms*)

Shapechanging, sometimes called shapeshifting, is one of the most natural and strange things that humans can do. Those names refer to the extreme development of a talent that all human beings share, the talent of *kulike*, which means "to be like the *ku*." In other words, to take on the characteristics or pattern of another *ku*, whether human or not. The minimal development of this talent is the ability to mimic.

Many animals also have this ability, which implies changing one's pattern of appearance or behavior, rather than just using what you already have. A tiger blends in with its surroundings because of its natural coloring, but a chameleon changes its color to blend in with its surroundings. That's active mimicry. There are insects that act like sticks, fish that act like rocks, healthy birds that act as if they have broken wings, and chimpanzees that act like people. There are also people who act like animals, birds, fish, and insects. I read a review once about a play in which Zero Mostel was supposed to turn into a rhinoceros and charge across the stage, without using a costume. The reviewer said that it was not Zero Mostel acting the part of a rhinoceros charging across the stage, *it was a rhinoceros* charging across the stage. In the movies, an actor took on the role of a bird in *Birdy!*, and Don Knotts even played the role of a fish once. In a play called *The Metamorphosis* Mikhail Baryshnikov did an excellent job of portraying a beetle. There is almost nothing in the known universe which humans have not tried to mimic.

People can mimic anything, with greater or lesser skill. It's probably the secret to our incredible learning capacity, and it's so natural that many people don't even realize they are doing it. I have a friend from New Jersey who has lived in New Mexico for a number of years. In New Mexico he still sounds like he's from New Jersey, but when he returns home his family says he sounds like he's from the Southwest. Once I took a bus trip and shared a seat with a woman from Canada for several hours. After an hour and a half of conversation she said, in a British-type Canadian accent, that I spoke more clearly than any other American she'd met. In the same accent I thanked her, only then realizing that I'd begun to copy her style of speech. A blond, blue-eyed, very fair woman friend of mine was dating a black man during one period of her life, and she spent a lot of time in his neighborhood with his friends. One day they were sitting in a restaurant in a black neighborhood and some white people walked in. When a black friend of this woman nudged her and pointed out how funny the white folks looked, she realized that she had unconsciously assumed the speech and behavior patterns of the blacks to such an extent that her black friends didn't even think of her as white anymore.

It is one thing to mimic unconsciously, or for the purpose of learning how to do something that someone else can do, or for the purpose of blending in with your social or physical environment, and quite a step up to do it for the purpose of influencing others and gaining powers. This was the shamanic innovation, and the first stage of it is called acting. Our whole acting industry comes from a shaman tradition. Makeup, costumes, staging, musical scores designed for the performance, and even special effects were invented by shamans. All of these were, and still are, used to influence an audience, but the shamanic idea went farther than that. In many traditional societies shamans acted out the parts of gods, demons, heroes, villains, and animals not only for teaching and entertainment, but for magical influence.

In traditional American Indian tribes, a shaman of the dry Southwest might have donned the garb of the thunderbird and danced a special dance in order to bring rain to his people; or a shaman of the Plains might have put on the horns and pelt of a buffalo and performed a ritual to find or attract the herds for his people. In Africa I have seen shamans act out archetypal roles of gods and animals to remove evil spirits and bring about healings.

Our modern conditioning makes us scoff at the idea that the behavior of a person, costumed or not, filled with belief or not, can actually influence the environment. And it's a valid attitude if you accept the first-level ideas that reality is outside of us, everything is separate, and energy acts according to its own laws. But if you accept the second-level shamanic ideas that the world is what you think it is, that everything is connected, and that energy flows where attention goes, then of course the behavior of a person can influence the environment. The only constraining factor then is the degree of belief, connection, and energy. Shamans have specialized in ways to increase the amounts of each of those. In this chapter we'll be mostly concerned with increasing the degree of connection.

First though, let's talk a little about the extreme end of *kulike*, the art of changing from one form to another. This is an ancient idea that has never ceased to fascinate human beings. Gods, of course, are expected to be able to do it. Zeus became a bull to woo Europa, Odin became a serpent and an eagle to win the mead of inspiration, and Pele became a beautiful woman to seduce Chief Lohiau. Our own modern literature gives this power to certain human beings, either as a curse or a blessing. So we have Count Dracula who turns into a vampire bat, Dr. Jekyll who turns into Mr. Hyde, a scientist who turns into the Hulk, and Billy Batson who turns into Captain Marvel, to name only a very few. Shamans, also, are expected to partake of this power. Tales abound of shamans who change into various animals for different purposes, and in Hawaii the skill was supposed to include changing into rocks and ropes. The president of an African country I lived in was reputed to be a shaman who visited the northern areas in the form of an antelope.

No doubt many such tales are of experiences in *Po* (the inner world) rather than in *Ao* (the outer world), but not necessarily all of them. Think a bit. If everything is broadcasting its own pattern *and* if you could match and rebroadcast the same pattern, then you would take on the appearance and qualities of the thing you were matching. It's theoretically possible within the system we are studying, and many shamans believe it can be done. If this were an extension of the talent under discussion that could actually be developed, it would be very dependent on the skill of concentration. It really isn't any different from the intention of certain mystics who meditate on God so they can become one with God. I'll let you take it from there.

Grokking

Of greater interest to us right now is using *kulike* for practical healing purposes. We can define four different stages of *kulike*:

1. Copying—unconsciously adopting patterns in your environment
2. Imitating—consciously adopting patterns in your environment for personal safety and development
3. Role-playing—consciously adopting patterns in your environment or in your mind for influencing other people
4. Becoming—consciously adopting patterns in your envi-

ronment or in your mind to change what you are (as a mystic might do)

For our purposes we want to find and use a position somewhere between 3 and 4. That is, we want to adopt the pattern of a thing so well that we can think of ourselves as being that thing and have such resonance with it that changing our behavior will change its behavior, yet at the same time we want to remember our original pattern so we can return to it at will. The name I've chosen to represent this delicate position is *grokking*. This is a word from a book by Robert Heinlein, *Stranger in a Strange Land*, in which the hero has the ability to merge with the pattern of something, know it from the inside, and change it from the inside by directed intent.

Grokking implies the ability to remember your original pattern and your purpose in grokking. I also call this "keeping the 1 percent shaman." This means retaining at least 1 percent (an arbitrary metaphor) of your own self-awareness no matter how deeply you grok. Our purpose in grokking is to bring about healing and harmony. If you were to grok a sick tree 100 percent, you would simply feel like you were the tree and forget to do any healing. You wouldn't turn into a tree, however. Most of the time you would just snap back into your original self-awareness without having accomplished anything, or you might fall asleep and wake up later. A complete change of pattern requires consciously applied skill of a level that most humans will never reach.

The process of grokking is very simple.

1. Close your eyes.
2. Energize.
3. Enter a spirit body.
4. Merge with the grokee.
5. Check for appropriateness of action.
6. Change your behavior.

7. Ungrok by remerging with your spirit body and returning to your physical body.

Here I've suggested closing your eyes to diminish distractions from your immediate environment, but you can learn to grok with your eyes open. Energizing can be done by using the Lovelight from the Fifth Adventure along with deep breathing. Entering a spirit body is like entering a dream body, but the spirit body is more like a borderless ball of pure light or energy that you create with your imagination. To enter it you just imagine that you have a formless energy body rather than a physical one. As usual, feeling is more important than seeing. Using the spirit body makes it easier to go in and out of the grok at will. Merging is done by imagining that your spirit body is merging with the spiritual, mental, emotional, and/or physical pattern of the grokee, with feeling again being the most important sensation because you want to imagine what it feels like to be what you are grokking. This is the most important part, since its success depends on a kind of unconditional love. The degree of merging is limited by any negative attitudes you may have toward what you are grokking. The more fear, anger, or criticism you have toward it, the more separation and the less grokking. That also translates into less influence. While merged you check for appropriateness of action by feeling whether it's right to go ahead and make a change. This has nothing to do with fear that it might be wrong. When the grok is good it's a simple *knowing* that it's right or not right to do something. When you have merged to the greatest degree possible while still retaining a bit of self-awareness, you change your behavior as the *grokee* in a fashion conforming to your healing intent. Most of the time this would be in your imagination, but some people are able to involve their physical body in the change without losing the sense of being the grokee. Finally, separate from the grokee by imagining yourself back in your spirit body, and then back in your physical body.

The following sections will deal with grokking for healing

and for your personal development as an urban shaman. We'll cover the subject by working with seven elements of the earth: water, stone, fire, wind, plants, animals, and humans.

Grokking Water

Shamans grok water mostly for rain, but it can be grokked for many other reasons as well. Once I was on the mainland and received a call from Kauai asking our shamans to help with a tidal wave that was heading for the Hawaiian islands from Alaska. Satellites were tracking it and it was known exactly when it was due to hit. Evacuation procedures were being carried out on Kauai and emergency systems were in readiness. A number of us grokked the tidal wave and, as the wave, decided to flatten out and dissipate our energy sideways. People of that curious breed who like to be on hand when disaster strikes were on the beach when the tidal wave was supposed to hit, and they reported that the surf receded as is common in such cases, but then just came gently back in as if nothing unusual were happening. Headlines the next day proclaimed "The Tidal Wave That Wasn't."

This is a good place to clear up some more matters about grokking and shamancraft. First, those of us who worked on the wave did not exert control over Nature. Second, grokking was not the only thing being used. And third, we did not neutralize the wave all by ourselves.

Nature can only be influenced to do what it might do anyway; it cannot be controlled. This conforms to the sixth principle. In any activity of Nature there are ongoing courses of action, potential courses of action, and improbable courses of action. Shamans work with ongoing and potential courses of action, leaving improbable courses of action alone because they require more energy than they are worth. In the tidal wave example, dissipating the energy of the wave laterally was a potential inherent in water and that particular wave, as was the forming of another wave from a different direction to cancel some of its effects. But stopping the wave dead in its tracks or making it go backward were so improbable in terms of water behavior and energy requirements that they weren't even considered.

With regard to the second consideration, grokking is only one technique in the shaman repertoire. Not all shamans use it or gain great skill at it. So in dealing with the tidal wave some shamans were using intuition to talk to the wave, and others were working with its dream. Shamans will use whatever techniques they feel are effective in any given situation, which reminds us of the seventh principle.

With respect to the third consideration, a shaman would be very foolish to take full credit for changing any event or condition, not only because of the power innate in everything, but because of the influence of thoughts from other people, shamans or not. In the Kauai experience, for example, there were enough people praying, hoping, and wishing that the tidal wave would do no harm that all the shamans had to do was help focus all that positive energy. On the other hand, if enough people wanted, needed, expected, or feared that tidal wave for some reason, shamans, no matter how powerful, would have had little effect on it.

In recent years the state of Texas (and surrounding areas) suffered from a long-term severe drought. We received a number of requests for help, but nothing we did made any difference for a long time because the potentials for the drought were so much greater than the potentials for ending the drought. Finally, one of our shamans in southern Texas stopped trying to work on the whole state and concentrated instead on her little valley. She worked intensely one night with her husband (who was tolerant enough to go along with her) and the next day was the first of three days of abundant rain for her valley, but not for the rest of the state.

Crazy as it seems, human beings can influence the rain. Not just to bring it, but to keep it away. It doesn't have to be shaman work that does it, either. Pasadena, California, has had a Rose Bowl parade and football game on January first for almost a hundred years running. Even though it is in the middle of the area's rainy season, to my knowledge it has only rained twice on Rose Bowl day. I myself have watched it pour buckets on New Year's Eve, be bright and clear on New Year's Day, and pour buckets again on January second. I think it's the combined energies of the float makers, the visitors, the spectators, and the chamber of commerce that does it.

When the potential energies are right, shaman grokking can perform what seem to be miracles, but which are only a wise use of available resources and natural patterns. Rain can be brought to drought-stricken areas or moved away from flooded areas, wave patterns can be altered, oil slicks can be dissipated, and pollution can be neutralized or precipitated out. The possibilities are wide open, but some changes will require a lot of shamans acting in concert.

Practice—Grokking Water

Following the process already given, grok water by becoming the spirit of water, and then the specific water you want to influence. For a drought, what works well is to become the spirit of water in the drought area and call water to you, becoming that water as it gathers until you are heavy and thick enough to rain.

You can also grok for the purpose of learning what water has to teach you about flowing and adapting.

Grokking Stone

A lot of my students have difficulty with grokking stone because it seems so solid. I find that in their minds they are often trying to merge their physical bodies with it rather than their spirits, and that, of course, feels suffocating and rigid, if not impossible. I remind them that stone is alive and that its form is only an energy pattern. The intent is not to move their bodies into the stone, but to have their energy body take on the energy pattern of the stone. This seems to work much better.

Everything is connected. The natural phenomena of the Earth do not operate independent of humanity. Nature does its own thing whether humans are around or not, but when humans are around they are always part of what Nature is doing. The interchange comes from the energy of human emotions. Human emotions, positive or negative, do not cause natural phenomena, but they can trigger them or delay them, amplify or diminish them, and attract or repulse them. If a human being is affected, a human being is involved. Because of this relationship, when a shaman is changing a natural event, he is also changing the human emotions involved in the event. This kind of indirect healing is often easier to do and more effective than trying to work with human beings themselves, especially in a grouping like a village, city, or region.

Earthquakes make an interesting study. In areas inhabited by human beings they are directly related to social pressures. Where there is sufficient social pressure in an earthquake-prone area, any sudden change in the society or the environment can trigger an earthquake, even if the change is positive. The summer before the death of Mao Ze-dong, in keeping with an ancient tradition which foretold the death of an emperor, China was racked with devastating earthquakes. When the Shah of Iran was deposed, ending a very oppressive regime, Iran was racked with devastating earthquakes. The night that Queen Liliuokalani of Hawaii was deposed, Honolulu was shaken by an unusual earthquake. A terrible earthquake in Armenia occurred just as the Soviet premier was speaking of social change in the U.N. And in 1987, after a summer of severe drought, an autumn of severe forest fires, and an early winter of freeway shootings, Los Angeles suffered a harsh earthquake. In the future, perhaps, social engineers will be able to predict earthquakes more accurately than any other group.

As shamans, we can work to ease the pressure in unstable areas before a quake, and we can ease the pressure after a quake to diminish the effects of aftershocks. To do this with grokking, we enter the spirit of stone, merge with the bedrock under a specific location, and *gently* relax and stretch and calm ourselves down.

Volcanic eruptions can be worked with in a similar way. In merging with molten lava you can either change the direction of its flow or slow down, cool off, and solidify. By the way, we have not been working with the relatively peaceful eruption of Kilauea on the Big Island of Hawaii because, apart from destroying and threatening some roads, homes, and buildings that were constructed on a known lava-flow site in the first place, and causing some "vog" (volcanic smog), the only other effect has been to increase the size of the island.

As an element, "stone" includes any material that we consider solid and inanimate—such as metal, plastic, cut wood, and glass—even when put together as a machine. By grokking and changing the pattern to one that feels harmonious I have had many good healing results with motors and computers.

Practice—Grokking Stone

Grok some of the physically unstable areas of the world like Beijing, Tokyo, Los Angeles, San Francisco, Mexico City, Cairo, and Teheran and ease the pressure under them.

Grok an object (perhaps a sculpture), a tool, or a machine and heal it or learn from it.

Grokking stone can also teach your *ku* the nature of strength and stability, and help you learn more about geology and crystals.

Grokking Fire

Nature has its own reasons for having fires. It can be to replenish the soil with the nutrients in ash, to germinate seeds that need the fire's heat before they can sprout, or to thin out old vegetation so that new plants may live. It can also be used to thin out animal populations and feed animals in need. In Africa I have seen birds of prey and other animals gather at the edge of a fire to catch the smaller animals as they come running out.

Fires that occur near human habitations, though, even those of natural origin, are expressions of human emotion, whatever other purpose they may serve. That emotion is usually anger, but not always. The fire that serves a purpose in Nature also serves a purpose in human lives. Just as we may say that every sickness is a *ku* attempt to solve a problem that the *lono* hasn't dealt with, so may we say that every disaster is an attempt to solve a problem that the *lono* hasn't dealt with. In Malibu a plant nursery on the coast that had been in operation for thirty years was burned to the ground during a brush fire that left the neighbors on either side untouched. Everyone felt very sorry for the owner until he gave an interview in the local paper. He said he had been planning for a long time to sell the place and move overseas, but could never make the decision to do so. Now the decision had been made for him, and with the insurance money he was going to follow his dream.

In the above story I mentioned that the neighbors were untouched. A curious thing about fires in human-inhabited areas is that they will often jump over or bypass some buildings and find their way to places that were thought safe. A shaman explanation is that the emotions of the people involved either repulsed or attracted the fire. Again in Malibu, my oldest son was living in a trailer on a hill in the middle of the mountains, a place called Decker Canyon. When a fire swept through the area I received calls of condolence because I had lost my son, who could not possibly have survived such a fire. I tuned in, however, and knew that my son was fine. As soon as the roads were clear I went in and found that the fire had swept up the hill to within fifty feet of his trailer, jumped over the trailer, and swept down the hill on the other side, leaving him and his property safe and sound.

Fires are very responsive to human thought and emotion, which means that calming down a fire will tend to calm down the thoughts and emotions that feed it. Grokking is a powerful way to do that. In India among the fakirs, a group of people who make a living specializing in certain yogic practices, it was not uncommon to take a seven-year-old child and set him before a fire with the instruction to make friends with its spirit. Day after day the child was set before the fire for however long it took until the child—perhaps by then a young man—had achieved such a state of fearlessness and oneness with the fire that he could touch it, walk on it, and roll in it without harm. Fortunately most of us are not out to make a living at it, so we don't have to grok fire to that degree, but we may have to practice until we have gotten over any fear of it.

Some people have a good rapport with fire the first time they try to grok it. Usually they feel excitement, tingling, and high energy. When a group of such people is working together the temperature of the room will actually rise. The challenge these natural "fire shamans" have is to keep enough separation so that they can do some healing work. Often they are enjoying the experience of being fire so much they don't want to calm down. In guiding people through their first fire grok I generally suggest that, as fire, they stand still, calm down, get smaller and smaller, and become embers and then warmth. Usually this works fine, but on occasion someone will "humanize" the fire too much and think that this process is killing the fire or going against its wishes. I have to remind them that fire is not human and remains itself no matter what its size or form. Fire is just happy to be and doesn't feel diminished by change. If you wonder how I know this, I've done a lot of fire grokking.

People who have the most difficulty are those who have had unpleasant experiences with fire in the past. The moment they begin a fire grok it stimulates the memories of those experiences, which can produce enough fear and anger to abort the grok. One solution is to change the reaction to those experiences; another is to strongly distinguish the present fire from any other fire; and still another is to practice until the fear and anger no longer occur.

Practice—Grokking Fire

Grok a fire that you see or hear about in the news. Feel that it is all right to change it. As the fire, decide to stop your progress, decide to calm down, to get smaller and smaller, to become embers, to become warmth, and to feel good as warmth. Bless the spirit of fire and come out of the grok.

Grok any fire and feel its energy, movement, light, and warmth. With your 1 percent of self-awareness tell your *ku* to remember this pattern, then ungrok. At other times practice evoking those qualities when you want them.

Grokking Wind

Wind is sometimes called "the mother of weather" because of its critical role in the formation and experience of weather. It has so many important connections with our lives (not the least of which is the fact that we breathe it) that wind grokking is an extremely useful skill.

One of the most powerful forms of wind is the hurricane, which is a circular wind pattern with speeds of more than 74 miles per hour at the outside edge of the hurricane proper. They can be seen by satellite and their path tracked, but they are very unpredictable in their direction. One of the reasons for this is their responsiveness to human emotion.

A number of years ago my shaman group was asked to help with a hurricane in the Gulf of Mexico that was headed for the coast of Texas. We tuned in, felt it was appropriate, and guided it back out into the Gulf. This turning away from Texas was shown on the evening news. We felt quite pleased with ourselves until we learned the next day that the hurricane had slammed into Louisiana! Where did that come from? It never even entered our heads that it might do that. So we plunged in and worked to pull it back out. It was interesting to watch the news over the next few days as the tug-of-war played itself out. The hurricane would head inland, then it would back out to sea, then it would head for the land, then it would back out again. Finally we realized that we had not paid attention to appropriateness. On tuning in for this we felt that there was a greater purpose for the hurricane in Louisiana, so we let go and the next newscast showed that it had stormed deep into Louisiana where it caused a great deal of property damage but no loss of lives. Eventually it dissipated at the northern end of the state. The whole area was declared a federal disaster area. National attention was on a place that had been ignored and was stagnating. Money and people poured in, lives were changed, and new connections were made. Destructive as it was, the hurricane had a very positive purpose in that place at that time. In Louisiana it was a healing experience because it was attracted by a desire for change. In Texas it would not have been because the attraction there was fear and anger.

When I say attraction I mean that literally. When you grok a hurricane you can feel a kind of magnetic attraction toward a human population center and sometimes it takes a definite effort of will to move away from it. You needn't be concerned about interfering with destiny, however. If there is a positive purpose for the hurricane—or for any event—it will take place regardless of what you do. You may delay it, but you won't prevent it unless your shaman work involves an even better solution for carrying out the event's purpose. In most cases you simply won't be aware until after the fact that there was anything to work on. If someone doesn't want your help, you won't even think of helping them.

Tornadoes are a lot like hurricanes. Full of great destructive potential, they occur naturally in certain areas at certain times of the year, yet they are also highly responsive to human thought and emotion. Like fires, tornadoes have a knack for skipping over or around some places and apparently seeking out others that were presumed safe. The experience of grokking a tornado can be thrilling, but the excitement of destruction can seem like such fun that it may be difficult to remember you are intending to guide the tornado away from a place.

Grokking can be used to raise a wind, to diminish a wind, or to turn a wind. It can also be used to have a wind affect another element. In good old Malibu again, we once had a very bad fire that destroyed forty homes in our neighborhood. The whole neighborhood was in danger, and I barely made it home in time to help my family water down our roof and others and put out some spark fires that were threatening homes whose owners were away. One of the great problems was that we lived in a canyon where the fire generated a wind that in turn whipped up the flames, and the smoke was so thick that the fire fighters couldn't get in to work on the fire. As soon as our immediate situation was taken care of, I climbed up on our roof with my oldest son who had trained with me for some time. Together we grokked the wind to calm it down. The momentum of the pattern made it difficult, but after twenty minutes of continuous focus the wind calmed down, the smoke cleared, and the ring of fire stopped its progress. Then the fire fighters could get in and finish it up. I might point out that there was no first-level reason for the wind to stop in that situation.

Practice—Grokking Wind

Start out by practicing in the area where you live, grokking the wind to feel how it moves, and changing its movement and direction. Pay attention to the news and grok the wind for healing and harmony in situations that seem to call for it. Remember to check for appropriateness.

Grok the wind to learn lightness, freedom, and playfulness, as well as for the feeling of influencing the movement of other beings.

Grokking Plants

I have a friend who groks plants. Her goal is to be able to induce plants to flower and fruit in one day, as some masters can do in India. I don't know if she'll reach that goal, but she already has an emerald-green thumb. I saw her plant fresh pumpkin seeds and two days later the shoots were standing four inches tall with big leaves.

One way to work with plants is to grok them, know what their state, condition, or needs are, then ungrok and take care of them. If you grok a plant and discover it's thirsty, you can then ungrok and give it some water. Or you can, as the plant, extend your roots to find water or call for the rain spirit to come and help you. For other needs you can spread your leaves to get more sun, move your sap to give more life to different parts of your plant body, and give forth new shoots to expand yourself. Nursery people know that plants can get stressed by both too much change and lack of change in the environment, as well as by poisons and toxins, and that such stress leads to sickness and the attraction of insects and fungus. In grokking a plant, then, the best thing is sometimes just to help it relax. But if you want it to grow more, assuming it's relatively unstressed to begin with, the best thing is to get it excited. Excitement stirs up energy, which stirs up activity, which stirs up the operation of natural or learned patterns—a good thing to remember when working with any of the seven elements.

A great deal of research has documented the fact that plants are influenced by human thoughts and emotions. In the simplest way, plants will grow better if you praise them and their growth will be retarded if you criticize them. In a more complex way, with the right kind of attunement they will perform miracles for you and reveal incredible secrets to you. Two men who had this kind of attunement were Luther Burbank and George Washington Carver.

Burbank worked with Nature to create over a thousand plants that had never before existed, including giant daisies, better potatoes, nectarines, thornless cacti, and fast-growing hardwoods. The 1906 earthquake that devastated San Francisco and leveled his hometown of Santa Rosa left his enormous greenhouse intact, and Burbank himself attributed that to his harmonious connection with Nature. Although he admitted to talking to his plants with love and coaxing them to do what he wanted, his rapport went much deeper than an intuitive contact. There's no doubt that he was grokking in his own fashion when he would walk down rows of thousands of plants—seedlings or mature ones—and without slowing down pick out the ones that would succeed and the ones that wouldn't. A farm agent following him said that he couldn't tell any difference even up close, but Burbank seemed to have such an instinct that he only needed to glance at them. The closest he came to explaining what he did was during a talk entitled "How to Produce New Fruits and Flowers."

Listen patiently, quietly and reverently to the lessons, one by one, which Mother Nature has to teach, shedding light on that which was before a mystery, so that all who will, may see and know. She conveys her truths only to those who are passive and receptive.

George Washington Carver was another man who did incredible things with plants, primarily the peanut and sweet potato. He derived hundreds of separate, economically important products from the plants he worked with, not by scientific study, analysis, or experimentation, but by deep communication. When asked how he performed his miracles he said that all plants and living things talked to him, and that "I learn what I know by watching and loving everything." Much of his work was done in a private laboratory in which no books were allowed, where he would spend hours communing with plants to learn what they had to teach. Not long before his death he said that in touching a flower, "I am touching infinity. Through the flower I talk to the Infinite. It is that still small voice that calls up the fairies."

Practice—Grokking Plants

Grok the plants around your home to learn how they think, feel, and experience life. If you want to go farther, plant some seeds or seedlings and grok them as they grow, adding your own intent for them to grow faster or larger. Grok plants you know that may need help, such as trees suffering from blight or those of the Brazilian rain forests.

Grok plants also to learn about cycles of life and death, light and darkness, growth and reproduction, lunar and solar seasons, energy use, and transformation. Try grokking herbs and plant-based remedies for their healing qualities rather than taking them into your body, just as an experiment.

Grokking Animals

In every shaman culture I know of, animals are treated, at least in part, as teachers and guides for how to live harmoniously with the Spirit and Nature. The normal Western reaction to this is that of course we can learn a lot about Nature by observing the behavior of animals. That's not what I mean, as you can probably guess. To learn the most we can, we must learn to communicate with animals, and even go farther and grok them. Then we'll be on our way to learning more than we've ever known about Nature.

All the oldest shamanic cultures tell of a time when humans and animals could talk freely with each other, and some have stories of how that ceased to be. Our own culture has many accounts of intuitive rapport between humans and animals, mostly with dogs and horses, so the talent isn't dead. But most of this rapport has to do with love, friendship, and mutual assistance, and maybe learning on the part of the animal from the human. The best modern account I know of about learning from an animal was given by J. Allen Boone when he told of his relationship with Strongheart, a German shepherd who starred in the movies. Assigned as a part-time caretaker for the dog, Boone first started out with the common humans-are-superior attitude, but that changed dramatically as he learned how to engage in silent talk and be receptive.

> When I was willing and ready to be taught by a dog, Strongheart shared precious wisdom with me, wonderful secrets having to do with the great dog art of living abundantly and happily in the present tense regardless of circumstances.

Though he didn't use the word, what he had learned how to do was grok, for the state that Strongheart taught him to reach was one in which each, "without sacrificing the uniqueness of his own individuality, harmonizes himself with the other so that they seem to function as a single unit."

The way to grok animals and learn from them is to be aware of and imitate their behavior in an open, egalitarian, receptive way. Being aware means more than just looking at them; it includes using all of your inner as well as outer senses. And imitating their behavior means more than just copying their movements. It also means practicing their sounds, moods, attitudes, and characteristics. One fascinating thing Boone did was carry a dictionary and book of synonyms around and note the characteristics that Strongheart displayed, as if he were a universal being who just happened to be in a dog's form. So besides sniffing, running, and barking, there were courage, confidence, compassion, and a host of others.

Every thing an animal does has a purpose, and every purpose has to do with the present moment. Animals don't dwell on the past or the future. If a dog performs a task that was taught in the past, it is always in response to a stimulus in the present. When a squirrel stores nuts, it isn't planning for the future, it is responding appropriately to signals in the present environment that indicate it's time to store nuts. Until you have grokked animals enough to share their experience of life, you really don't know what the present moment is. I'm not saying that reflecting on the past or planning for the future is bad. I'm saying that experiencing the present is good. Very good.

Practice—Grokking Animals

Grok an animal just for the experience, using a pet, animals at the zoo or around your home, or the Power Animals as patterns. Grok a sick or stressed animal and use the shaman techniques you know to ease your pain and heal yourself as the animal.

Grok an animal to learn more about life and living, or for special characteristics that the animal has.

Grokking Humans

Grokking a human is perhaps the most difficult because they are so much like us. You might think it would be easier, but the hard part is not carrying our own patterns into the grok. As with animals and all else, you need to be open, receptive, and unconditional. The more closed, rejecting, and conditional we are with ourselves, the harder it will be to grok other humans. Grokking humans can also lead to unusual insights. I once taught a woman how to grok her husband in order to improve their relationship. She began speaking and walking and thinking like him, and as she did he began to open up and develop a more and more friendly attitude toward her. However, at the same time she began to realize that she actually didn't like him.

In grokking humans for healing it is both easier than other elements and more difficult. It is easier because we are more familiar with the human body, but more difficult because of fear of sickness. When you are grokking a human who is sick you have to be able to feel what that human is feeling without identifying yourself (that 1 percent) with it. If you do identify you may mimic some of the same pattern when you ungrok and feel it in your own body as your own feeling. You can change that by telling your *ku* firmly, "Stop that this instant! That's not mine! Change back to normal now!" And then be sure to relax. If for any reason that doesn't work, use one of your healing skills on yourself. But back to the grokking. There you also use the healing skills on yourself, *acting as the person you are grokking*. So you could talk to your *ku*, use *kahi* on yourself, dream and change your body's dream, or do anything else you've learned. One friend of mine, on receiving a healing request, groks the person thoroughly and then, as that person, goes out and has a great time partying. Because of the rapport and resonance established during the grok, the grokee receives the benefit at a *ku* level.

One of the greatest things about grokking a human is that the grokee doesn't have to be alive. Or even human. When you grok, you are merging with an energy pattern, not the physical being. Well, the energy patterns of humans no longer alive, those of accomplished men and women and spiritual masters of the past, still exist for you to grok and learn from. All you have to do is put your conscious attention on them and let your *ku* do the grokking. By "not even human" I mean that the energy patterns of fictional characters also exist for you to grok. Superman and Wonder Woman are out there waiting for you.

Practice—Grokking Humans

Grok a friend who is sick, get a sense of the factors, and use what you know to heal "yourself."

Grok someone who is well and who expresses some quality or characteristic you would like to have, and in deep grok tell your *ku* to remember the pattern.

With your mind create a spirit form of an ideal Master Shaman who has abundant love, abundant power, and abundant skill, and then grok that being to learn that pattern.

As a final word, the more you grok the more skillful you become at it, and the more often you grok a pattern you want to learn the better you will learn it.

THE EIGHTH ADVENTURE:

INCREASING YOUR CREATIVE ENERGY

*'Ike no i ka la o ka 'ike; mana no i ka la
o ka mana*
(There is a time for knowledge; and a
time for power)

Everything is energy. And energy, as we have seen, is influential movement or activity, activity that creates change. In order to create change, there must be something to change. That is, there must be something for the energy to act upon, something different in some way from the energy doing the acting. If heat energy is brought into contact with ice, the ice changes its form or pattern and becomes water. If no more heat is added the original heat energy is incorporated into the water and becomes water energy. That sounds a little odd because we usually only think of water as energy if it's moving to create pressure. Water just lying as quietly as it can is still in rapid motion at a molecular and atomic level, however, and that energetic movement in a particular pattern is required to keep water from becoming anything but water. If more heat energy is applied to the water, more than its own heat potential (i.e., of a higher temperature than it already is), then the water begins to vibrate faster and starts to change its pattern (form). At a mild level of additional heat energy this is called evaporation. If a lot more heat energy is used the water turns to steam, which moves very fast compared to water and extremely fast compared to ice. What we've done here is to increase the energy of the water in a particular way, by getting it to take on more and more of the qualities of another energy pattern. Note that we didn't really add anything to the water. We brought a heat source in contact with the water, and the water began to resonate with the heat, becoming as much like it as it could. As it did so it changed form or pattern, trying to become more and more like the pattern of heat. Metal also resonates with heat, but it can do so while maintaining its own primary pattern for a lot longer than water can as the heat increases. It changes, too, but not as noticeably until a much higher intensity of energy. Propane gas, on the other hand, already vibrating at a very high frequency, doesn't need much extra heat to resonate with before it explodes in a very dramatic change of form.

What I want to do here is to get you, as an urban shaman, to think of energy differently from the way you usually do. Since everything is energy, there are obviously a great many different energy patterns in and around us, all influencing each other to various degrees. According to our philosophy, everything has a *ku*, and the *ku* is influenced most by the strongest, nearest, most resonant field, the field or pattern of energy that is most like it (or some part of it). Water, for example, already has some heat even in its ice form, or it couldn't resonate with heat. But all energy is potentially influential, not just heat. Water, and everything else, can be changed—its pattern altered—by a wide range of different kinds of energies, including the energies of thought.

Energy flows where attention goes, therefore thought influences change whenever the thought resonates well enough with the focus of attention. As we saw with heat, however, if the energy level can be increased, then the influence is greater. Heat energy greater than the heat energy pattern already in a given amount of ice can induce the ice to change into water. An even greater amount or amplitude of heat energy can induce the water to change into steam. Similarly, if we can increase the amplitude of thought energy in some way, then our thoughts will be more effective in creating change.

All change occurs by induction, by influencing a pattern already inherent in the thing to be changed with something else that has a similar pattern. And we are not necessarily talking about the complete pattern of a thing, because any major pattern has within it many minor patterns. You are unique as an individual. Your pattern of "youness" is not like that of any other person, even if you are an identical twin. Yet within your unique body, mind, and spirit are myriad different patterns in operation at any given moment. There are the different patterns of the chemical components and physical structures of your body, the patterns of your organs, the patterns of your memories, and the patterns of your potentials, just to name a few. Energies of different kinds can affect particular patterns within the whole, thereby changing the whole by changing a part. Changing the pattern of a headache alone can make you feel good all over.

The Power of *Kimana*

For many years I have done extensive research and written several books and articles on unusual energies and their application. Like a host of other researchers I have found abundant evidence for a kind of pervasive energy that can be experienced, amplified, directed, generated, and converted so as to influence and change mind and matter, yet which has so far defied all attempts at independent instrumental measurement. That it exists there is no doubt, but so far it can only be demonstrated by experiencing its effects through many different means. It may also be that the effects come from a multitude of different energies. But since the effects are the same no matter how the energy is brought into awareness, we are going to simplify things by assuming that the energy is both real and singular. Following a long tradition of everyone giving it a different name, I will call it *kimana*, roughly translated as "intense power."

We have some very practical reasons for working with this energy. As you will find out for yourself if you use what is given here, *kimana* will amplify the spiritual energy and inspiration you get from *kane*, intensify the focus and imagination of *lono*, and enhance the learning, memory, and physical energy of *ku*. The aim as a shaman is to use the tools presented below as well as others to raise your normal energy capacity. In other words, you want to develop the learned habit of operating at a higher level of energy all the time. *Kimana* can be used to help you change the world, and it can also be used to help you change yourself. Using outside energy in this way is like practicing a skill with the help of a book until you have memorized it so well you no longer need the book, even though you might go back and refresh your memory with it once in a while. As your *ku* gets used to operating at an amplified energy level it will tend to keep on doing so, because both you and the tools are using energy from the same source. Remember that the tools aren't giving you energy, they are stimulating your own energy.

In the following sections I will present some of the more simple and useful ways in which you can tap into *kimana* for enriching your life, empowering your thoughts, and increasing your energy capacity.

Linear *Kimana*

All frequencies are energy patterns, and as we have learned already, frequencies of one rate will tend to induce a resonance—will have an energetic influence—on frequencies of a similar rate. One way to get this effect is to use a linear measurement of wavelength. A friend of mine familiar with radios told me that in order to pick up a radio frequency with a wavelength of twenty-seven feet, he needed an antenna twenty-seven feet long. The antenna could be coiled, but it had to be the right length.

Kimana, apparently, can be tuned in to by antennae that are the right length as well.

A number of years ago I was introduced to something called a "cubit wand." This was a wooden stick twenty-five inches long. It isn't necessary to discuss here why that length was originally chosen. What's important is that that particular length produced the same energy effects that I had achieved by very different means (some of which will be discussed below). To be brief, when you hold such a stick, depending on your sensitivity, you will tend to get more relaxed if you are tense and more energized if you are relaxed. As you continue to hold it you may feel tingling in your hands or your body, and your mind will become clearer and your imagination sharper. If you were to test yourself you would also find your physical strength and endurance increased. Using a cubit wand while hiking or doing a long workshop helps me stay relaxed and full of energy. On another level your aura will intensify and therefore the power of your thoughts and your charisma will also increase. There may be a clue here to the influence of magic wands and military batons.

A length of twenty-five inches works, but neither twenty-four nor twenty-six inches gives the same effect. I have also made wands out of wood, plastic, copper, string, and rope. The material doesn't seem to matter, but I have to say that I got better effects from the string and rope when they were taut then when they were loose.

Ever curious, I experimented to find out just how critical that twenty-five-inch length was. First I doubled it to make a staff of fifty inches. The first time I tried it out, on the Kalalau Trail of northern Kauai, it took someone else to make me realize how effective it was. I was hiking with my wife and a friend, and before I knew it I was far ahead, walking at what I thought was a normal pace. At one point some hikers coming the other way looked at me and said, "Now that's the way to hike!" At first I just thought they meant using a staff, but suddenly I realized I was walking an uphill slope as if it were level ground. I got my wife and friend, neither of whom liked to hike with a staff, to try it and both of them had the same experience, getting far ahead of the others without effort. Fifty-inch staves are now a regular part of our hiking gear.

Still curious, I experimented further and discovered that the critical figure was not twenty-five. Doubling twenty-five to fifty had worked, but halving it to twelve and a half did not. The critical figure turned out to be five. I don't know why because I don't know yet what a five-inch length is resonating with, but a wand of five, ten, fifteen, or twenty inches works about as well as one of twenty-five. I say about as well because the best effects are still with five, twenty-five, and fifty, as far as I can tell. I haven't worked with lengths beyond fifty. And I have not yet worked with centimeters enough to present any conclusions about metric lengths.

A five-inch rod of wood, plastic, or metal is handy to carry around and put in a pocket or purse, and good to hold to empower your thoughts and your presence when you are thinking and speaking. Because of the third principle, keeping some of your attention on the rod increases its energizing effect. For meditation or long *haipule,* holding a twenty-five-inch wand with both hands will energize the whole experience and keep you energized for a while after. And you can get nicely charged with *kimana* by lying down between two fifty-inch staves laid on the floor. It's as if the staves have radiating, intersecting fields that amplify each other. Lying between two staves gives you a greater effect than lying next to a single staff.

Rotational *Kimana*

Early in the 1970s a man named Charles Sherburne displayed something really radical at various places in Los Angeles. It was an object shaped like a kayak made of either wood or plastic. Because of its form and polish it was beautiful to look at and pleasant to handle. The radical part had to do with its behavior. When placed on a flat, smooth surface and spun clockwise, it would spin smoothly for what

seemed to be longer than it should. When spun counterclockwise, it would spin for a while, then start wobbling up
and down, finally stop its forward motion, and actually spin
backward for a while. It looked as if it were actually resisting
movement in a counterclockwise direction. Much attention
was given to the apparent fact that at least one of Newton's
laws of motion was being badly violated by this innocent
object ("an object in motion tends to stay in motion unless
acted upon by an outside force"). Friction and gravity as
outside forces could slow down and stop a spin, but what
in heaven's name was causing the wobble, the stoppage of
the spin before friction and gravity could play their role, and
the reverse motion? Three extra phenomena with nothing
to account for them. Sherburne got a lot of people excited
and made a lot of other people unhappy. Part of that reaction
was caused by the behavior of the object, and part was because he said he got the proportional dimensions of it from
the description of Noah's Ark as given in Genesis (300 cubits
long by 50 cubits wide by 30 cubits high). In fact, he called
his object the Ark.

I used the model I bought from him for a long time to
demonstrate the existence of more aspects to the universe
than we've yet uncovered and also to freak out physicists
and other scientific types. I even had a neat theory going
about spiral energies to explain why the counterclockwise
effect occurred. To show that it had nothing to do with
Coriolis force (the effect of the earth's rotation that makes
cyclones in the Northern Hemisphere rotate counterclockwise and cyclones in the Southern Hemisphere rotate clockwise) I took my Ark to Tahiti and demonstrated that it
operated the same way south of the equator as north. My
neat theory was blown, however, by one of my students
who sent me two Ark models he had carved out of the same
branch of a pecan tree. One worked the same as my Ark;
the other did the exact opposite. When spun counterclockwise it would go smoothly, and when spun clockwise it
would wobble, stop, and reverse. I, who had freaked others,
was freaked myself.

Then in the late seventies an article appeared in *Scientific American* dealing with objects that exhibited the same phenomena as Sherburne's Ark. Objects made of stone that showed the same spin characteristics had been found in old Irish tombs and were called "celts" by archeologists or "rattlebacks" by physicists. No one has any idea what purpose they served. Some archeologists thought they were used by chiefs or shamans to impress the natives, but unless it flashed lightning or changed the weather I don't think people without an emotional tie to Newton's laws would be very impressed. Some scientific study showed that the effect basically had to do with the shape and the relationship between upper and lower axes, and lots of models were made that worked, but that still didn't explain the phenomenon or relate it to Newton's laws. Now you can get inexpensive models from the Emporium in San Francisco that spin either way, depending on their construction. But so what?

As I said, like many others I treated it as only a curiosity to amuse my students and stretch their thinking. Then, during a break in a workshop I was giving in Texas, I discovered something new about the "rattleback." While talking to a student I suddenly felt a wave of energy flow through my body from behind. I turned and saw nothing except another student fooling with the rattleback, so I turned back. Once again I felt the energy and turned in time to see the rattleback still spinning. That set off a chain of ideas and a number of experiments which eventually showed that the spinning rattleback was generating a strong wave of *kimana* which lasted during the spin and a short time after. In one experiment we used a bottle of cheap Chablis wine and spun a rattleback next to it for five seconds. In that short time the whole bottle was altered so that the wine tasted aged and smoother. Even more practical (although the wine experiment wasn't bad), was the discovery that keeping your attention on a spinning rattleback would give your aura a healthy charge along with the other energy effects mentioned above. Since then we have obtained the same effects from a gyroscope.

I can see it now. When this gets out there will be courses

all over the country teaching you how to "Spin Your Way To Success."

Geometric *Kimana*

Everything is energy vibrating in a pattern. The pattern, or combination of patterns, determines how the energy manifests itself, whether as wind or a bird or a human. It would seem logical, then, that the most basic patterns would be resonating with the most basic energies.

One way to describe our physical universe is as a combination of curved and straight lines. It is not the lines themselves that create patterns, but the joining of them. The most basic pattern of a curved line that we can make is a circle, and the most basic pattern of a straight line that we can make is a triangle. That's nice, you might say. It's more than nice, really, it's very useful. It means that we can use simple circles and triangles to relax our muscles, to stimulate our senses, to empower our bodies and minds, and to increase our energy capacity. How? By looking at them, by sitting in them, and by hanging them up around the house. Many ancient people have used such patterns as mandalas to gaze at or prayer rugs to sit on or wall hangings and paintings to energize the environment. Often they have modified the basic design into more complicated forms, but circles and triangles are still the foundation.

Circles generate an energy that tends to be more relaxing and more conducive to thinking and meditating. You can use circles made of any material, even printed or painted on a surface. Believe it or not, a Hula Hoop makes a great meditation device. Sitting within it is very relaxing and beneficial, especially as a break from busy activity. A piece of string or rope could be used, but it's not always easy to form a circle with one. Having a circle nearby to look at is also very helpful to counterbalance high activity and focus. I use a round coaster on my computer desk, but a hoop like you find in a hobby shop can be used, too, either lying down or hung up. You might try hanging a larger circle in a window so you can look through it. It changes the whole experience of gazing out the window. For a real treat, draw or print a black circle at least six inches in diameter on white paper, and gaze at it for a while. Once you relax enough you will start to feel a higher energy level and you will see many unusual visual effects.

The triangle tends to induce a more stimulating energy effect, good for active meditations and more outgoing mental and physical activity. A good, portable energizing center can be made from three fifty-inch staves simply formed into a triangle on the floor or ground. You can stand or sit in it as you will. Having a triangle to stand on or look at when you get up will help you wake up faster, and having some triangles around your work area will sharpen your mind and increase your endurance. But be sure to have some circles to turn to before you get too stressed out. Also, a point to remember: just having circular or triangular objects or drawings around isn't enough for the full effect. You have to put your attention on them to get the most benefit.

Trigonometric *Kimana*

The beginning of the seventies saw the beginning of a fad that swept the United States like wildfire for a few years. I imagine there are closets and attics and basements all over the country in which unused pyramids are taking up space. Having lived through the heat of it and written a book about it, it surprises me that so few of my students nowadays are familiar with pyramid energy at all.

To keep it short and simple, a pyramid form, especially a form based on the model of the Great Pyramid in Egypt, or one having all sides with equal lengths and angles, has energy properties that might be called peculiar except that the same unusual properties are shown by so many other things. After all, what is a pyramid but a bunch of triangles hung together? Still, among the pyramid's documented unusual properties are the apparent sharpening of razor blades, the preservation of food, and the stimulation of psychic and physical energy. In my opinion, the pyramid acts like a capacitor or condenser, intensifying local energy. Regardless of the explanation, it does have energy effects. The two best ways to use a pyramid for our purposes of enhancing our abilities and increasing our own capacities are to hang one over a place of work, play, rest, or sleep and/or to sit in one on a regular basis.

If you don't have access to one of the few remaining suppliers of pyramids for personal use, you can make one yourself quite easily. For a hanging pyramid, cut four equal-sided triangles out of posterboard or anything else with a little stiffness. I suggest using a base of ten or twelve inches. Then lay them side by side with the outside down and tape the touching edges together. You'll have to assemble it to get the last two edges together. String a button on some thread, push the thread through the top of the pyramid from underneath, and it's ready to hang. Since the pyramid works best—its energy intensity is greatest—when one side is facing magnetic north, you may want to add another thread to a corner to keep it in place. As long as there's no breeze you will often see that the pyramid will find its own way to north. For a pyramid you can sit in, get eight equal pieces of pipe or wood dowel about a half inch in diameter. You will need to make a square to form the base on the ground, fastening the ends any way you like, and then take the remaining four pieces and attach them to the corners of the square and to each other in the middle. For a pyramid that stands four feet high the pieces will have to be six feet each. Again, it works better when one side is toward magnetic north. As you may have guessed by now, a pyramid framework is just as good for energy as a solid-panel pyramid.

My favorite variation on the pyramid is a tetrahedron. Sometimes called a three-sided pyramid, it's really made of four triangles when you count the bottom. It's cheaper and faster to make because it only requires three triangular panels for a small hanging device and six pieces of pipe or dowel for a larger sit-in model. And because of the fewer sides the base can be smaller to get the same height. So using four-feet-long five-sixteenths-of-an-inch dowels (available precut at most building supply stores) and using the same basic method as above, you can build a nice meditation hut about four feet high. The final advantage is that a tetrahedron doesn't have to be oriented to the north. It's at its optimum in any direction. Some people, myself included, think that it is even more energizing than the pyramid.

Pyramids and tetrahedrons are three-dimensional expressions of the triangle. The circle equivalents are the cylinder, the dome, and the cone. Cones can be made by cutting out a circle from some flexible material, cutting through from the edge to the center, and then overlapping the ends till you get the exact shape you want. Experiments indicate that the greatest energy effects come from a cone whose peak is the corner of a right angle. Instead of suspending the cone it can be worn as a cap, as long as you don't mind the connotations. Actually, the dunce cap may originally have been designed to make its wearer smarter. The pyramid can be worn, too, but the cone is more comfortable and doesn't have to be oriented. Try it and you will get some interesting energy sensations. Domes are more expensive, but good to live and play in. (I think it's fascinating that domes can be made from triangles, as in geodesic domes. That's a great area for energy research.) Cylinders channel considerable energy. I have found that a grouping of four-inch diameter cylinders does a fine job of charging as long as you don't mind having what looks like cannons pointed at you. It might be interesting to have the cylinders twenty-five inches long.

Crystal *Kimana*

Crystals have always been objects of fascination for the human race. In large part this must be due to their durability and color. Many animals, including some birds, seem to have an instinctive desire to collect hard and shiny objects even when they appear to serve no useful purpose. Partly also, there is an attraction to the beauty and mystery of their structure, which arouses our human imagination and curiosity. More subtly, there is frequently a recognition that, somehow, crystals seem to radiate a mysterious force or energy.

According to one authoritative source, the definition of a crystal is "a solid composed of atoms arranged in an orderly repetitive array." Seven such geometrical arrays or arrangements are recognized by crystallographers: triclinic, monoclinic, orthorhombic, tetragonal, trigonal, hexagonal, and cubic. The arrangements of atoms determine what the eventual shape of the fully formed crystal will be. The atoms of sodium chloride have a cubic array, and with a magnifying glass you can see that salt crystals look like little cubes.

Another property of crystals is that the angle of the crystal faces is always the same for the same type of crystal. As an example, the angle of the upper face of a quartz crystal is always about fifty-two degrees, the same angle, by the way, as that formed by the base and sides of the Great Pyramid of Egypt.

Crystals are not all formed in the same way. Some, such as diamonds, are formed as a result of intense heat and pressure. Others, like quartz, are the result of the slow seepage and hardening of materials in solution. Because of the accumulation of material the latter may grow to a very large size, but no one yet knows what forces cause them to grow in different directions. A group of quartz crystals growing out of a matrix (the source rock) has the appearance of a frozen explosion.

One of the most attractive aspects of crystals is their color, and the possible variations are endless. The color in crystals is caused by tiny amounts of "impurities," substances other than the one of which the crystal is mainly composed. Chromium, titanium oxide, nickel oxide, iron, and manganese are some of the impurities which give color to crystals. It is important to note that the color we give to a crystal is the one that is reflected away from it. The colors we do not see have been absorbed by the crystal, apparently as a result of the impurities. Keep this in mind. Because impurities produce color, many times we give different names to crystals that are made of the same substance. For instance, ruby, sapphire, and topaz are all made of aluminum oxide, and opal, agate, amethyst, citrine, and clear quartz are all made of silicon dioxide.

An interesting and important property of some crystals is that, under certain conditions, they can actually generate their own light. For some this happens when they are stimulated by ultraviolet light, and the property is called "fluorescence." It also occurs when such crystals are exposed to ordinary daylight, which contains ultraviolet rays too, but the stimulated light is so faint compared to normal reflected light that it usually can't be seen. In the dark, when exposed to artificially generated ultraviolet rays, crystals that may look gray and dull in daylight can turn to brilliant reds, greens, blues, etc., and crystals that have one bright color in daylight can change dramatically to another under ultraviolet. These colors are caused by tiny amounts of impurities called "activators." Some of the more common activators are chromium, copper, gold, lead, manganese, silver, strontium, and zinc. The bright colors that are seen are not caused by a reflection of the ultraviolet light, which is invisible to our eyes. Instead, the ultraviolet light stimulates the activators so that they emit their own light. With most fluorescent crystals this stimulated emission of light occurs only as long as the activators are bombarded by ultraviolet rays. When the bombardment stops, so does the fluorescence. Some crystals, however, have a property called "phosphorescence," which means that they continue to emit their own light for a short period even after the ultraviolet source has been removed. Among these are diamonds, rubies, and gypsum. A diamond stimulated with ultraviolet light and then placed on a piece of photographic film will produce an image of the radiant energy field that surrounds it as a result of the stimulation.

Being very dense and structured solid objects, crystals can be charged to a considerable degree with heat energy, which they can then radiate for a fairly long time. This is why heated stones have been used since ancient times for comfort, healing, and cooking. A traditional Hawaiian feast of meat and vegetables is still cooked this way. Light energy may also be transformed into heat energy by dark crystals and stones which absorb the light and radiate it as heat.

Some crystals have electrical properties. Quartz and tourmaline, for instance, have what is called a "piezoelectric" effect. When they are squeezed and twisted in a particular way they give off an electric current. The pressure energy has been transformed into electrical energy. In quartz, pressure energy can also be transformed into light and fire. Rub a couple of clear quartz crystals together rapidly in the dark and they will fill and glow with light. They will probably also give off sparks, which is not surprising since flint is also a form of quartz. Furthermore, quartz, silicon dioxide, is frequently used in thin sheets for solar cells, where light is transformed directly into electricity. Some metallic crystals, such as copper, silver, and gold, are particularly good at transferring or "reflecting" electrical energy, some of which is converted into heat and magnetism.

Lodestone or magnetite, which has an octohedron (double pyramid) shape in crystal form, is an iron-based material that mysteriously radiates magnetic energy unceasingly. Other forms of iron, such as hematite, do not have this property, but they can be magnetized—that is, charged with magnetic energy for various periods of time. Copper radiates magnetism only as long as there is electrical energy passing through it, and in this it resembles the fluorescent materials stimulated by ultraviolet light.

So don't let anyone tell you that crystals don't have energy. They can absorb it, reflect it, generate it, radiate it, and convert it into other forms of energy. *Kimana*, which seems to be present when any other energy is present, is also part of the crystal energy complex.

Now for some practical information on using crystals in shaman work (use whatever kind of crystal you like):

1. Crystals have their own energy and can be charged with your energy. A potent way to charge a crystal is to do *kahi* with it. I suggest putting one hand (left would be

nice, but not necessary) on your crown or navel and holding the crystal in the other hand, and then focus on both hands for a while. You can keep your mind on a certain quality or characteristic at the same time to "program" the crystal. The length of time a charge will last depends on too many factors to give a set answer (your degree of focus, the kind of crystal and its origin, the environment, etc.). You could do two crystals at once by holding one in each hand. The nice thing about charging a crystal in this way is that you get charged, too.

2. Several other good ways to charge yourself with a crystal are: just gaze at a crystal like you would a flame; tape a crystal to your forehead while sleeping, meditating, or working (if you don't mind stares or you work alone); rest or meditate in a triangle or circle (eight crystals makes a good circle) of crystals; hold a crystal with awareness of its feel. Wearing a crystal won't charge you much unless you put your attention on it.

3. Be aware that you can get overcharged with crystal energy. The symptoms are those of any high-stress or tense condition. Once at a conference a friend of mine had a crystal booth and she came to see me all stressed out. I did *kahi* and relaxed her, but she came back again in a short while all stressed out again. This time I went to her booth and found that she had neatly lined up all her crystals to face her in the booth. Along with all the other energy of the conference it was too much for her. I scattered the crystals in random directions and her symptoms went away. If you get "crystal nerves" try a massage, a bath, a shower, or a negative ion generator. When you get more skilled as a shaman, you can just change the pattern.

4. Your *kahi* or other healing work can be enhanced by holding crystals in your hands as you focus, or by having crystals noticeably around you as you do your healing.

5. Forget about having to "clear" or "cleanse" crystals after healing or if someone else handles them, unless you just like to do it. Any cleansing ritual is done for your own

benefit, not because someone else's "impure" aura has come in contact with it. Because of the second principle, everyone in the universe is touching your crystal right now, including some weird beings on Arcturus, whether you like it or not and no matter what you do. For a simple ritual to make your *ku* feel better, bless some water, dip your crystal into it, and dry it off.

Orgone *Kimana*

"Orgone" is the name given by Wilhelm Reich to the fundamental energy we have been discussing. Reich had been a colleague of Freud until they had a falling out, and he did most of his life energy research in the forties and fifties.

When I came back to the States in 1971 from my long stay in West Africa, I came across the latest information on pyramid energy and began an extended research project. In 1972, as part of a completely different project, I was studying the works of Wilhelm Reich. It soon became clear that Reich's orgone energy had a lot in common with pyramid energy, and that both had a lot in common with *kimana*. One of the first things that attracted my attention was Reich's report of the dehydration effect of orgone, because I had been achieving the same effect with pyramids. But the first actual experiment had to do with razor blades.

The fact that pyramids could induce a sharpening effect on razor blades was well known and easily demonstrated by that time, so I reasoned that if orgone energy was the same as pyramid energy, an orgone device ought to be able to sharpen them, too. This is precisely what occurred when I made my first orgone device—a plastic soap dish lined with aluminum foil in which I kept a razor. Afterward, with myriad devices, I demonstrated that pyramid energy and orgone energy were identical, in that devices using the principles of each could produce identical effects. From then on it was just a case of refinement and learning how to increase the effects.

Reich's first orgone device—also called an accumulator or

"oraccu"—was a simple metal box. Later he found that the intensity of the energy could be increased by lining the outside of the box with some organic material such as cellotex. From this he derived the theory that orgone was slowly absorbed by the organic material, then quickly absorbed and expelled by the metal. Still later he found that the energy could be intensified further by adding layers of organic and inorganic material. His most powerful device was a box with twenty layers on all six sides, but for most purposes he used only three layers. His preferred metal was steel, in the form of plates or steel wool, but he did experiment with copper and aluminum. As organic material he preferred cellotex or wool, but strangely enough, he also found that glass would work. And in one of his books he mentioned the possibility that plastic might also be good.

I decided to use plastic as the organic material because it was cheap and available in great variety. Following Reich's theory I began using plastic boxes lined with aluminum or copper, and they were quite successful. Through experimentation I found that the energy passed right through a plastic cover, and so my first commercial device, The Amazing Manabox, was born—a small acrylic plastic box lined on five sides with copper. This was convenient to carry and had the advantage of allowing one to place containers for charging on top of it. At that time I still thought that the energy had to be absorbed by the plastic and expelled outward by the metal. However, one day my youngest son pointed out that he felt more energy from the bottom of the box, where the plastic was lined with copper. When this was confirmed I had a revelation. Having had some background in electronics, I now realized that what we had was a form of capacitor, and we were dealing with electric and dielectric effects, not organic and inorganic. The most important consideration for the materials was their conducting and insulating qualities, not their origin. That's why glass had worked as well as the organic materials Reich used. With this idea we embarked on a new series of experiments that resulted in the Manaplate, a format even more convenient than the Manabox.

The original Manaplate consisted of a sandwich of one sheet of copper between two sheets of acrylic or styrene. Some models consisted of up to four layers or sandwiches. This device was found to radiate energy from both sides and was the size of an ordinary index card. We found that the energy effect appeared whenever a conductor and an insulator were put together, and the better they conducted or insulated, the better the effect. Also, unlike the capacitors in radios and such, it did not matter whether the metal was on the outside or inside of the sandwich.

Eventually we found that an extremely thin layer of metal combined with a good insulator would give an excellent energy effect. The next model of Manaplate was a sheet of styrene coated with a very fine film of pure aluminum put on by an industrial misting process. The resulting device was lightweight, thin, and gave off a very strong field of energy. And it could be made in a variety of sizes. Unfortunately, the process was too expensive to continue so we looked around for a better insulator.

This came in the form of plastic resin, and thus the first Manabloc was born. This was a small plastic pillbox about two inches square, filled with resin in which we embedded a small sheet of copper or aluminum. The energy effect was very good and it was a convenient size, although heavier than the previous Manaplate.

Two more important discoveries led to further improvements. To decorate the top of the Manabloc we used a piece of diffraction grating, also known as "laser foil." This is a very thin sheet of aluminum which has been "grated," or inscribed with ten thousand lines to the square inch or more, and then covered with a very thin sheet of plastic, either clear or colored. Far from being a decoration, we discovered that it had an energy effect of its own when it was laid over styrene. Around this time we were also experimenting with the energy effect of two-dimensional patterns, like circle and triangle variations. We first used a concentric symbol on the base of the resin Manabloc and it greatly increased the energy output. Next we found that the symbol would still work even if it was covered up.

We've gone on to produce many variations since then based on the capacitor model which are now called Amazing Managizers regardless of shape or size. While these have strong energy outputs and are as small as a credit card or a thin two-inch disk, don't think you have to buy anything to have your own power source of orgone *kimana*. Here are some cheap and simple ways to make your own devices for healing and increasing your own energy capacity.

1. For an emergency device to use for cuts and bruises, aches and pains, lay a one-foot-square sheet of plastic wrap on a one-foot-square sheet of aluminum foil, and quickly scrunch them together into a ball or a pad. You may even feel a heat effect as you do this. The resulting many-layered device will have a better energy output than most crystals and can be conveniently placed or taped anywhere on the body.
2. Take any plastic container and stuff it with aluminum foil or steel wool. The eggs that stockings come in are great for this, as are the hollow plastic eggs used at Easter. As a variation or addition, coat any plastic container with laser foil.
3. Stuff copper or aluminum pipe with Styrofoam pellets used for packaging. The Styrofoam is such a good insulator that this makes a pretty strong device. Anything anodized, like anodized aluminum, will also generate well because anodizing is applying a thin oxide layer to metal, and oxides are insulators. A lot of commercial energy devices use this.
4. Theoretically, since glass is an insulator and water is a conductor, a glass of water ought to be a good energy device. In fact, it is, especially when such a capacitor is

charged with energy from another source, like the sun, your hands, or another energy device. Plants love it, too.

Now you have the knowledge and the means to increase your power and make the information in the next chapter even more valuable for your urban shamancraft.

THE NINTH ADVENTURE:

FROM INNER PEACE TO OUTER PEACE

E waikahi ka pono i manalo
(It is well to be united in thought that
all may have peace)

Shamans and mystics both use a similar technique for training and focusing the mind, but for different purposes. It is called meditation, which means a continuous, focused attention on something. The basic technique, regardless of culture, philosophy, intention, or style is to use the conscious mind to maintain attention on a limited range of experience until a change occurs inside oneself, outside oneself, or both. Human beings around the planet have invented many different ways or styles of meditating based on mental or physical senses, including visualization, breathing, singing, speaking, humming, movement, hearing, touching, looking, and on and on. But they all have the purpose of focusing attention until something happens.

Of course, there are no hard and fast boundaries, but generally speaking the aim of the mystic is enlightenment, an expansion of the mind and spirit that produces a sense of

oneness with the universe and increases awareness and understanding. For the mystic, intuitive or psychic phenomena
and powers as well as physical relaxation and healing of
mind and body are side effects which are sometimes beneficial and sometimes distracting. Other benefits, such as better relationships, improved financial effectiveness, and a
healing influence in one's environment are also considered
side effects. If they happen, fine; if they don't, that's fine,
too. The shaman's use of meditation or contemplation, on
the other hand, is oriented toward practical benefits for this
world, and if enlightenment happens it's a pleasant side
effect. Oneness with the universe is very pleasant, but can
it help you have a healthier body, be a better friend, pay the
bills, or increase world peace? If it does, go for it. If not,
enjoy it when it happens, but don't bother seeking it.

Shamans and mystics would agree that some phenomena
that arise from the practice of meditation are merely distractions. A well-known story is told of the Zen master,
Dogen. When one of his students reported that during meditation he had seen a vision of Buddha in a brilliant white
light, Dogen replied, "That's nice. If you concentrate on your
breathing it will go away." A shaman reply might be, "Well,
what did you do with it?" There's no particular virtue in
getting visions unless you can make use of them.

In the sections that follow I am going to introduce you to
a special form of shamanic meditation that I was taught
called *nalu*. This word means "to form waves," a metaphor
for broadcasting thought patterns, as well as "to meditate."
Through its roots the word means "peaceful union" or "a
state of unity," with connotations of a cooperative relationship, rather than the oneness of *kulike*. The word *Huna*, the
name of the philosophy being presented in this book, has
the identical root translation as *nalu*, which is not a coincidence. I prefer to use the word *contemplation* instead of
meditation for *nalu*, because the essence of the technique is
a gentle, effortless resting of attention and awareness. In *nalu*
you don't do anything forceful. You just look, listen, and/or
feel. The beneficial effects happen all by themselves because

the continuous attention links your pattern to the pattern you are focusing on. What makes *nalu* so fascinating is the variety of effects that occur depending on your area of focus.

Energy flows where attention goes, says the third principle, and when energy flows into a particular pattern that is being focused on, the pattern itself is energized. An energized pattern has to change, just as energized ice changes to water or energized water changes to vapor or steam. It either expands into a greater version of itself, or it turns into something completely different. If the attention is neutral or positive, the change will be positive. A positive pattern, one that is beneficial and growth enhancing, will become even more positive; a negative pattern, one that is harmful and growth denying, will change into a positive pattern. A negative focus, one of fearful attention, will have just the opposite effect.

Most mystical meditative practices teach you to strive for a neutral focus (some notable exceptions can be found in Christianity and Sufism) as a way of getting your personal desires out of the way. The reason a neutral focus can have a positive benefit, we would say, is because the universe is basically positive. Neutrally energize any part of it and you automatically increase the positivity. It needs to be mentioned, however, that there isn't any truly neutral mystical meditation because the positive intent of meditation itself influences the focus.

With the shamanic technique of *nalu*, you do not attempt to be neutral at all. Nor do you attempt to be emotional. The attitude to have while doing it is one of calm, positive expectation, like you would have just before listening to a favorite piece of music about to be played by a new artist whose talent you respect. You expect it to be different, and you expect it to be good. This kind of attitude greatly enhances the benefits received from practicing *nalu*.

Those benefits come about in several ways. Relaxation generally occurs because the attention is taken off memories and concerns which tend to increase stress and tension, and with relaxation there is often healing, more energy, and greater mental clarity. It hardly matters what you focus on to get those effects. Inspiration and solutions to problems that may be unrelated to what you are focusing on often break through. This is also principally an effect of relaxation plus previous intent or desire. Inspiration and knowledge about the subject of focus will come into awareness because of the linkage of patterns. With continued focus, guided by your expectation, your *ku* will effortlessly learn qualities and characteristics of the subject of focus because of your *ku*'s natural ability as a mimic. And, by simple focus, you will be able to empower, or disempower, anything you choose. Finally, quite apart from your conscious intent, the peaceful union that *nalu* engenders in you will broadcast out and influence all your relationships in the same way. But the purpose to keep in mind is that you are doing this practice to change yourself or change a situation for the better. After a certain amount of practice, *nalu*, like any kind of contemplation or meditation, can become very pleasurable just as a process, and that's great. But when you start doing it just for the pleasure it gives you, and you find yourself upset or uncomfortable when you can't do it, then you have become an addict, no different in essence than an alcoholic or a drug junkie or a jogging fanatic. Mystics and shamans agree that the conscious mind must remain the guide and director of the process so as not to lose sight of the purpose. When the process dictates to you, you have become a slave. Of course, if you are going to be an addict anyway, at least meditation is cheaper than alcohol or drugs, doesn't hurt as much as jogging, and doesn't harm anyone else.

Some people still equate meditation with making the mind a blank, and there are actually teachers who still encourage that kind of nonsense. Yes, it is possible to train yourself to have a blank mind, and it is possible to train yourself to sleep on nails. Why bother? The only way to make your mind a real blank is to teach yourself to exclude all awareness, which defeats the whole purpose of meditation. I think there has been a misunderstanding of the intent of those who first suggested blankness as a proper state. The likelihood is that the intended state was one of quiet receptivity, with no mental chatter or commentary or active thinking. To be aware of something without thinking *about* it would be like blankness for many people. Some forms of meditation encourage or condone momentary periods of blankness, suggesting that these are moments of reaching into higher states. My own experience with myself and others suggests that these blank spots are periods of unconsciousness caused by stress or poor focus. I've never known anyone to derive a practical benefit from them. In *nalu* it is especially important to maintain awareness, although if you don't you just forgive yourself and practice more.

Meditation is usually considered to be a discipline, a practice that you must commit yourself to if you are to derive any benefit from it. In a way that's true, and in a way it's misleading. There are two aspects to meditation: the purpose, and the process. If you commit yourself to a process (like chanting a mantram or gazing at a flower) it is possible to gain the beneficial side effects of meditation (relaxation, etc.) without necessarily making any other changes in your life. Or such changes may come only after a very long period of doing the process, in which case the process may or may not be a critical factor in the change. After all, meditation is only a focus of attention, and a process is only a pattern that may become a habit. If you perform a habit long enough it becomes pleasurable to do, even if it was difficult to learn. You can train yourself to meditate on anything and derive pleasure and benefit from it after you've established a new habit pattern. But since energy follows attention and attention follows interest, you'll find it much easier to meditate on something that interests you and all the benefits will come faster. Here is where the purpose enters in. The discipline of meditation, the commitment to it, is much easier and more natural if you commit to a purpose and use the process as a tool to achieve the purpose. In that light, it only makes sense to choose a process that is most closely aligned with your purpose as an urban shaman.

One more thing. Whereas meditation is usually thought

of as something you do once or twice a day for a specified period of time, *nalu* is not so restricted. You can do it that way if you want to, but you can also do it all day long or at frequent intervals. While writing this chapter I received a call from one of my shaman friends who has been practicing a *nalu* of ideas (to be described below) for the past two months. With daily practice he has reached a point of being able to do it three hundred times a day for ten seconds at a time, and reports more ability to be in the present moment, more energy, being more in tune with himself and the world, and a vastly improved problem-solving ability.

The following examples of *nalu* are suggestions, which can be modified, combined, added to, or deleted as you please.

The *Nalu* of Sight

In the second adventure of this book I gave you an exercise for getting in direct touch with your *kane*. If you recall, it was to think of something beautiful. That was actually a *nalu* exercise using inner sight. When you create something beautiful in your mind, there is already a positive expectation built in. As you continue such a focus, your body relaxes, your energy flows, and your *ku* becomes more beautiful.

In the technique of doing *nalu* with the sense of sight, whether inner or outer, you first establish an intentional framework, and then you observe the subject within that framework, keeping your awareness open to whatever happens without judgment while maintaining your focus for whatever period you've decided on. When you observe the beauty of something, for instance, beauty is the intentional framework. It acts like a filter to help sharpen your focus and define the effects you will experience. When you observe, pay attention to shape, size, color, design, and ambience (the setting or relationship of the subject to its surroundings). Keeping your awareness open means allowing thoughts, ideas, and feelings related to the subject to become conscious and then flow on.

Since you're practicing to be an urban shaman and not a

mystic, feel free to take notes if some really good stuff comes
through. Having no judgment isn't necessarily easy, but it
means allowing negative ideas to come up and flow on if
that happens, or allowing nothing at all to happen, without
getting mad or upset or discouraged. Here is where it helps
to remind yourself of your purpose (if you're not clear about
that, start over). Maintaining focus is what you use your
lono for. As you begin to focus in *nalu* you may discover just
how little you know about focusing. Consciously and inten-
tionally keeping your mind on one thing for an extended
period (for some people ten seconds is an extended period)
is a rare skill, in which *nalu* is designed to train you. It's
easy to keep your attention on something exciting, interesting, habitual, or important. It's just that for most people
focusing the mind is neither exciting, interesting, habitual,
nor important. Well, *nalu* won't be exciting unless you are
using it to focus on something you consider exciting; it will
be interesting if you keep the positive expectation and open
awareness; it won't be habitual until you establish the habit;
it will be important only as long as what you are using it
for is important to you. In the *nalu* of sight, you maintain
your focus by keeping your attention on the subject and by
gently bringing your attention back each time it strays. If
you get verbal chatter while you are looking at something,
that's okay. Just use the words to help you keep your focus.
One way is by using words to describe the appearance or
the qualities of the subject to yourself. That will keep your
verbal part busy and helpful at the same time. Eventually,
as you relax more, the words will fade away and you will
just be with the subject, learning more than you realize at
a *ku* level.

Here are some suggestions. For the best effect, do each
one, with the same subject, for at least a week at a time.

• Do visual *nalu* with something fairly small that you consider beautiful, like a piece of art, some jewelry, a flower,
  or a crystal. Just look at it, but look at it in detail. Maintain
  your awareness of what is beautiful about it and be open

to new discoveries. Move it, if you wish, to look at different parts of it, but don't hold it. Every once in a while, close your eyes and see the same object in your mind, in as much detail as possible. You are doing this to train your mind to focus at will, to increase your awareness of beauty, and to increase the beauty and harmony in you.

- Do visual *nalu* with something you don't consider beautiful, only look for beauty. You might use something very ordinary like a kitchen utensil, a piece of chinaware, a tool, or be really daring and try cigarette butts or litter. It's a powerful *nalu*, so don't discard it easily. One of the most wonderful experiences of spiritual harmony I've ever had came from doing visual *nalu* with two paper cups at a shopping mall in Santa Monica, California.

- In a very familiar environment, do visual *nalu* on one part of that environment, say a corner, a wall, or a piece of furniture. Open your awareness to something about it that you've never noticed before, no matter how seemingly insignificant. If you think there is nothing new there for you to be aware of, you can really use this *nalu*. The assumption of sameness severely limits our growth in many ways. The world dream is re-created every day, and it is never the same. This is a good *nalu* for learning how to connect deeply with something familiar in order to establish intuitive communication. I have used it to find things in a messy office, to "know" what to do when my computer, Jonathan, acts up, to talk with pets, and to establish better rapport with friends and clients.

- Do a visual *nalu* outside, with the intent to discover something new about Nature that you never knew before. Be aware of visual details in plants, trees, soil, water, clouds, birds, animals, etc., but pick a restricted area to focus on, like a single plant or group of plants, or the clouds in one part of the sky, or one animal. The new thing you learn doesn't have to be dramatic, just new. This not only enlarges your appreciation of Nature, it also provides rich associations between Nature and your life, and increases your awareness of patterns, natural and unnatural, in the environment. I used this *nalu* once to find a pair of wire-rim glasses someone had lost in a Tahitian jungle.

• Do a visual *nalu* on the world around you in the framework of its being a dream. That is, look at it as if it really were a dream, a projection of your own consciousness and not a separate thing with solid objects. This is one of the most disturbing *nalu*s for many people because as it begins to change the pattern of your habitual relationship to the world, some very strange effects may occur. Just remember that if you don't like it you can simply stop doing it. Some will find that it opens up unparalleled adventure, however. I have used it to discover other dimensions or dreams in the midst of this one, which has given me a greater range of action in my undertakings.

• Do visual *nalu* with a black circle about six to eight inches in diameter drawn on a white background. Imagine a path or a road in the circle that goes over a hill or around a bend and out of sight. Enter the circle with your awareness and follow the path or road, looking for something (without defining what). You may or may not find yourself in a body, and you may or may not feel like continuing the exercise with your eyes closed. You also may or may not find anything in a given time period, but you usually do. Just go along with whatever happens. This *nalu* helps to open and strengthen your creative imagination, and provides lots of good insights.

• Do visual *nalu* on a symbol, picture, or object related to some goal or project. As you maintain focus on the subject your patterns link and change. The usual effect is that initially you begin to get a flow of ideas, old and new, about the subject. If there is tension to begin with in your relationship with the subject or what it represents, your body may express that tension for a while, but as you continue the focus there will be a release and a new relationship pattern. This is a good *nalu* for clearing up relationships with people, places, money, success, or any goal-oriented endeavor, as well as for stimulating a flow of creative ideas in relation to it. Many people are doing this without realizing it when studying, planning, or working. The third thing this *nalu* does is set up a resonance that begins to attract the nearest equivalent to what you are focusing on. Which is why my friend called to tell me about his meditation while I was working on this chapter. It's the third principle at work again.

• A useful variation of the previous *nalu* is to focus on a symbol, picture, or object related to a problem in your life. This may upset a lot of people who say they don't want to give energy to their problems by focusing on them, but a *nalu* focus is different. When you focus on a problem with a calm attitude of positive expectation and nonjudgment, the problem changes because you change. You may get different insights or realizations about it, or conditions surrounding the problem may change without your conscious knowledge or effort, but something will change. We often say that it is easier to resolve a problem if you make peace with it first, and that is what this *nalu* helps you to do.

• Do visual *nalu* on your peripheral sight. What you do is pick something in your immediate environment to center your attention on, and then shift your attention to your peripheral vision, that which is visible around the edges of your vision, without moving your eyes. Let your attention wander all around the outer edge of vision, just don't move your eyes if you can help it. I suggest not more than five minutes at a time to begin with, and remember to blink. In addition to the meditative benefits, the purpose of this *nalu* is to relax your eyeballs, change some mental habits, and expand your vision.

In Western culture many people grow up trying too hard to see things clearly, trying too hard to see what others have told them is out there, trying too hard to focus with their eyes instead of their attention, or trying too hard not to see what they shouldn't and what they fear. The result is often a rigid seeing pattern that verges on tunnel vision and puts great strain on the eye muscles. Since memory is stored in patterns of muscle movement and position, limited seeing patterns may also be linked to memory suppression or memory obsession (when you can't get a memory out of your mind). Because most people have not been trained to use their mind efficiently, they tend to use their body for things the mind is designed to do (like when you try to push a ball in a hole or a basket with your body even after it's on its way). So often they unconsciously use their eyes to push and pull or hold in place.

In addition to helping to relieve the tension produced by such factors, this *nalu* opens up your vision in two curious ways. First, you may begin to see farther around you than seems physically possible. It is not uncommon for people to see things that are behind them while doing this *nalu*. Second, you may begin to see things that people looking with ordinary sight will say aren't or can't be there, like movement, waves of energy, objects, or figures. If you experience it, it's real. You don't have to figure out what it means or why it's there, or whether something's wrong with you because no one else can see it, any more than you would if you happened to catch a glimpse of a wild animal in the woods that no one else around you saw. Simply enjoy the fact that you saw it.

- Do visual *nalu* on a thoughtform. This jumps us into a different range of awareness. In ordinary terms I'm suggesting that you purposely create a hallucination, but in esoteric terms I'm suggesting that you exteriorize a thought. In shaman terms, you just imagine something in your immediate environment as vividly and realistically as you can and observe it as if it were as real as anything else around you. Your imagined subject could be something that is beautiful, that is useful, that represents a goal, or that represents a problem. You'll get the same effects as with previous *nalu*s, and in addition it will be great training for your imagination. An added benefit is convenience. You can carry a thoughtform with you anywhere.

The *Nalu* of Sound

There is sound all around us all the time, simply because there is air or water all around us all the time. Most of that sound we don't hear, either because it's too low or high for us to pick up with our ears or because we are not focusing on it. Sound, of course, is energy, and energy influences us according to its nature and our state, but sound that we are consciously aware of influences us more than sound that is out of our range of awareness or attention. The exception, of course, would be sound that is of such high energy amplitude that it disrupts our body functions whether we can hear it or not. However, we are more concerned here with sounds like words and music that are more or less in our normal range of perception, though we are going to include inner or imagined sound as a part of auditory focus. Before giving suggestions for auditory *nalu*s I would like to talk about "subliminal" tapes, chanting, and music.

I really admire the business sense of the people who produce and market "subliminal" tapes. The profit margin is so incredibly high, especially on the more expensive types, that I may go into the business myself. But my conscience requires that I tell you a little more about them first. *Subliminal* means "below the level of conscious awareness," or "too slight to be noticed," and for most people it brings to mind symbols and words embedded in films and photographs which were intended to stimulate the subconscious into reacting in some manner, preferably by buying a particular product. They are still used in commercials and in some movies to arouse your senses. Just the other day a movie on TV had a glitch and you could see the subliminal messages when the film slowed down. However, the most well-known use today is in audio tapes designed for self-development. Many companies advertise thousands or even millions of affirmations per minute, giving the impression that as you listen your subconscious mind will be bombarded with positive messages that will change your personality without effort as you listen to the sound of waves or birds or whatever. And it's true that a lot of people have derived great benefit as they've listened to such tapes. What you ought to know, nevertheless, is that the benefit comes from your expectation, not from any particular virtue of the taped affirmations. Your *ku* is subliminally aware right now of all the positive and negative statements being made by people, radios, and TVs all around you in this very moment, not to mention the ones you are generating yourself in mind or speech.

What makes the affirmations on your subliminal tape (which may be occurring at an ultrahigh frequency anyway—the only way to get a million a minute) so special? Only your attention and expectation. And the latter is even more important than what's on the tape. One of my students reported that she had played a subliminal tape to increase her confidence and it was having a wonderful effect until she went to turn it over and discovered she had mistakenly played a tape designed to help her lose weight. A scientist named Lozanov who specialized in speed learning said that he got better results from students who just thought they were listening to a sleep-learning tape than from those who actually listened to it. All of this is not to discourage you from using subliminal tapes, but to help you use them wisely. They'll work best for reinforcing something you strongly want to do anyway. And although the price you pay for them may influence how much they help you, any positive tape played at very low volume will give you the same effect. One statement said with feeling can affect your *ku* more than a million all jumbled together at high frequency.

The chanting of a word or phrase is a very old method for achieving focus, and if the usual benefits of meditative focus are all you want—reduced tension, better health, more energy, a clearer mind—then any word or phrase will do. The Indian philosopher Krishnamurti suggested "Coca-Cola," the poet Tennyson used his own name, and Dr. Herbert Benson had fine results with "one." There are no words or phrases that have their own magic apart from the meaning and expectation that people give them. However, if you imbue a word or phrase with magic, if you *empower* it with your belief and expectation, then it will do magic for you.

Now music, on the other hand, has its own magic. It has subliminal powers because it can stimulate thoughts, feelings, memories, and behavior without our conscious awareness (think of toe-tapping, circus or marching music, and music in minor keys), and it can enhance tremendously our appreciation of words and images (think of how dull some famous movies might be without the music). As a subject for meditative focus it is one of the most powerful I can recommend if you use it properly. Not surprisingly, faster music is good to focus on when you want to stimulate your body, mind, or activities, and slower music is best when you want to calm down your body, mind, or activities. Such music will tend to affect you without your focus, but conscious focus intensifies the effect to a remarkable degree. Less well known is that highly structured music, music with a steady rhythm and repetitive melody (i.e., Ravel's "Bolero" or "Greensleeves"), has a good healing effect on people whose minds and lives are too unstructured, and that highly unstructured music with little or no rhythm or melody (i.e., some kinds of jazz and new-age music) has a good healing effect on people whose minds and lives are too structured. Music that will amplify or counterbalance any state you are in or wish to be in can be consciously chosen. One more note: as an aid to learning a new pattern of knowledge or behavior, the *ku* responds most strongly to anything presented in a four-beat pattern. That's the beat that most traditional cultures use, and that's the beat that locks nursery rhymes and commercial jingles into our memories.

Here are some suggestions.

• Do auditory *nalu* with a word or a phrase that represents a quality, characteristic, talent, or skill that you want to increase or develop in yourself. A four-beat chant will impress your *ku* the most. You can phrase it like an affirmation ("I-am-confi-dent") or just use a single word ("confi-dent, confi-dent") or mix them. A word or phrase that gives your *ku* a clear behavior pattern or response to

follow is better than one which is abstract, vague, or implies a fixed condition. "I am feeling good" is better than
"I am healthy," and "I am an achiever" is better than "I
am successful." This *nalu* gives you all the benefits of focused attention plus those of training your *ku*.

• Do auditory *nalu* with verbalized ideas, mentally or vo-
cally. Pick a quote or a phrase and as you repeat it keep
your mind open to ways in which it operates or could
operate in your life. The Bible is always a rich source for
such ideas, as are books of famous quotations. And while
this can be done in a condensed *nalu* of five to twenty
minutes, it can also be done in an extended *nalu* that lasts
all day. The shaman friend I mentioned above who did his
focus three hundred times a day for ten seconds at a time
was using the seven principles of *Huna*. He started out
reviewing them in English, but gradually he was able to
evoke their meaning in Hawaiian, which is why he was
able to review them all in such a short period. A variation
on that technique which I use is to attribute one of the
principles to each day of the week, starting on Sunday. I
start the morning by doing *nalu* with all the principles,
and then I focus on the "principle of the day" all day long,
using it as a background or framework for everything I do
that day. This not only gives me all the benefits of focused
attention, but it helps me to incorporate a chosen idea
deeply into my life pattern while also giving me new insights about it.

• Do auditory *nalu* with music in a special way. Put on the
music of your choice and begin by focusing on the sound
alone. Then shift your attention to the center of your head
and hear the music there (energy flows where attention
goes). Move your attention to your chest and hear the
music there. Then to your navel, and then to your pelvis.
Include your hands and your feet, if you wish, and finally
your whole body. Keep your attention at each location for
as long as you like, and be aware of the sensations of your
body. As you focus on each area the energy of the music
seems to intensify at that point. This is a good *nalu* for

locating areas of hidden tension and releasing them, and for energizing any part of yourself in any way you choose.

• Do auditory *nalu* with the sounds around you. The wind makes a very good focus for *nalu*, as does the sound of water in its many aspects (rain, surf, falls, streams, etc.). But so do all the ordinary and extraordinary sounds of the country or city. As you do *nalu* let each sound exist as a pure sound, without judging its nature or origin. This simple *nalu* can take you into a very deep, refreshing state.

• Do auditory *nalu* with imagined sounds of singing, of music, or of Nature. Besides everything else, doing this will put you in company with many great composers.

• Do auditory *nalu* with your own humming. Besides creating your own auditory focus, you will find that humming actually amplifies and intensifies your personal energy field. This is easily demonstrated by humming as you slowly bring your palms together. Humming while doing *kahi*, for instance (see the Fourth Adventure), will enhance the effects. You can experiment with different tones as you put your attention on different parts of your body to find out which ones stimulate and which ones relax. And you can discover humming tones which will help you resonate with Nature and with people.

The *Nalu* of Touch

The sense of touch includes kinesthetic or body sensations of pressure, movement, position, texture, pleasure, pain, presence, and—just to keep things simple—taste and smell. Your own creativity can think up lots of *nalus* based on any of these, so I will only give a few suggestions.

• Do kinesthetic *nalu* with movement. In one of my shaman courses I teach the students a *nalu* of movement called *kalana hula*, based on a combination of Hawaiian martial art and dance. Such a *nalu* cannot be taught in a book, but you can get similar benefits more easily. Many cultures have traditions of using movement to achieve deep states of meditation. The key is to keep your conscious attention on the sensation of movement itself. One simple way to start is to do a *nalu* on walking or jogging. It's a completely different experience with a *nalu* focus. If you are doing this in a public place you'll have to keep a little more of your awareness open to your surroundings. Dance is another way to do this *nalu*, with rhythmic dance producing the greatest effect. Choose fast or slow rhythms according to your own preference; it doesn't matter as long as the focus is right. A less vigorous process used in some cultures with great effect is to just sit and rock back and forth, again with focus on the movement. This *nalu* will help increase awareness and appreciation of your body and the present moment in addition to the focus effects.

- Do a kinesthetic *nalu* with pleasure. This helps to develop an incredible awareness of your body and a sense of aliveness you wouldn't believe. The essential process is one of increasing awareness of your body first, and then making the smallest possible shifts and adjustments of thought and muscle that will increase pleasure. If you come across pain, instead of fighting or resisting it you try out various shifts and adjustments that will ease it toward pleasure. And whatever sensations arise in your awareness, you keep shifting them toward more pleasure. This *nalu* can enhance appreciation of all your senses, as well as make you feel good. Recalling that the *ku* moves naturally toward pleasure, you can also do this *nalu* with the potential or imagined pleasures of things you want to do, be, or have and thereby build into your plans an automatic motivator.

- Do kinesthetic *nalu* with breathing. Obviously breathing has been around for a long time, so it is one of the oldest and most widely spread subjects of focus that there is. As in many other cultures, the Hawaiians associated breathing not only with life, but with spirit, blessing, and power. The most simple breathing *nalu* is to just be aware of your breathing with the *nalu* attitude. Slightly more involved and very good for relaxing and energizing the body is to focus your breath. This is similar to auditory *nalu* with music, only you are aware of your breathing as you focus your attention on different parts of your body. A bit more involved than that is "dolphin breathing," a *nalu* of conscious breathing where you make each breath a conscious act, like dolphins have to do.

The *Nalu* of Multisensory Awareness

Some of the previous *nalu*s have included elements of this, but now we are bringing the process into full consciousness.

- Do a multisensory *nalu* on a physical activity. If you do this with walking, for instance, be aware of all the sensations of your body, including your breathing; of all the visual and auditory aspects of what's around you; and of all the thoughts that come into your head as you walk. If you do this with eating (it's a real trip), eat slowly and focus on all your sense impressions of the experience, including sight, sound, movement, taste, and smell. This *nalu* helps to expand and integrate your sensory awareness and your connection with your surroundings.

- Do a multisensory *nalu* with writing. Writing, whether by hand or on a typewriter or computer, by its very nature focuses and integrates inner and outer visual, verbal, and kinesthetic awareness. To do it as a *nalu*, write about something you want to do, be, have, or know. I don't just mean write out a list of goals, which is a different technique. I mean focus more intensely and describe or explain or question what you want to do, be, have, or know. This kind of *nalu* will help to clarify your intentions, develop and attract what you want, and open you up to inspiration and related intuitive connections.

- Do multisensory *nalu* with conscious breathing. This involves what may be described as "breathing life" into your entire experience. Another way to think of it is that you are energizing your experience with your breath. All you really are doing is consciously breathing during any experience, with the attitude that you are energizing it or breathing it into continued or increased existence. This can be done in conjunction with any of the previous *nalu*s or with any other technique or experience in your life. During a visual *nalu*, breathe "through" your eyes to energize or create what you are looking at; in a sound *nalu*, imagine that the sound you hear is the sound of your breath; in a touch *nalu* let your breathing give energy to whatever you are touching or let it be a manifestation of your breath. While engaging in any kind of activity, imagine that your surroundings exist because of your breathing. The effects of this may surprise you.

• Do multisensory *nalu* with being. With inner and outer sight, sound, and touch, meditate on being what you want to be. This is almost like grokking, but not quite, because you are playing the role of being you to the utmost. It helps to center the *nalu* on a concept that you want to express in yourself and in your life, like peace, love, or power. Let's take love as an example. In this *nalu* you would meditate on the experience of unconditionally loving yourself, your environment, other people, and the universe; and of being loved by everything in the world around you. You would meditate on thinking, feeling, acting, and receiving as a lover and a beloved. You would use words, images, movement, and touch to guide and reinforce the experience. This *nalu* is potentially the most powerful of all.

THE TENTH ADVENTURE:

THE HEALING POWER OF SYMBOLS

Kukulu ka 'ike i ka 'opua
(Revelations are found in clouds)

The Hawaiian proverb above has a *kaona*, a hidden meaning. In old Hawaii clouds were often interpreted as omens or symbols of events, but clouds were symbolic of thoughts as well. So the above proverb could also be translated as "experience is constructed by thought." This can be taken to mean that everything in our experience is a symbol of a thought, which is the shaman dream concept. Since a symbol is something that stands for or represents something else, a thought can also be a symbol for experience. And round and round and round we go, stopping wherever we choose.

In this chapter we are going to examine different kinds of verbal, visual, and tangible symbols, and how they can be used for healing and change.

Belief Symbols

In one of my courses I start the class by showing what appears to be a plain, wooden pencil, and then I ask everyone to tell me what they think it is and what it's for. Most people quite naturally say it's a wooden pencil and it's used for writing. A few are sure I'm up to something and so they'll say something like, "It's a yellow object made of wood, graphite, metal, and rubber," and a very few will get cute and say, perhaps, "It's something hard that could be used to prop up a window." Then I bend it.

It's really a piece of plastic shaped and colored to look like a pencil, and therefore it could be called a symbol of a pencil. More importantly, it's a symbol of assumptions, the beliefs we have *about* reality. Defining reality as experience, we can also call them our assumptions about experience. It is natural and necessary to make assumptions. We could not operate without them because they not only define experience, they create it by channeling our attention and awareness. Every once in a while I meet someone who says they want to move beyond all belief and assumption. But there isn't anything beyond. If you assume nothing, you experience nothing. Given that assumptions are natural and necessary (I'm assuming that, of course), it seems reasonable to assume that the more effective your assumptions are, the more effective your experience will be.

To make it easier to recognize and change ineffective assumptions, I prefer to call them *kanawai,* which means "rules and regulations." Your *kanawai* are the rules that you have been given or that you have made up about life, about what things are and what they mean, about what's possible and what's not, about what's good and bad and so on. If you begin to think of all your ideas and perceptions of experience as rules *about* experience—symbols, in other words—then you can enjoy a kind of freedom you may never have suspected you had (if you are dependent on such rules for your security, you may undergo a kind of panic).

With rules of life (assumptions, attitudes, beliefs, and expectations) as the basis for experience, it becomes clear that if we want to change experience, we must change the rules. In fact, all techniques for changing experience are only effective to the degree that they help us change our rules of life. Affirmations, for instance, are positive statements that are repeated in order to bring about a change of some kind, but that change won't occur unless the affirmations become our new rules. Visualization is a good change technique *if* it results in a change of rules. Otherwise it's just making pretty pictures. Even if you receive a healing from someone, you will only stay healed if your rules have changed as well. If not, the condition will just return when enough tension has built up to manifest it again.

Many people think that the *ku* is illogical because it doesn't do what they want or because they don't understand what it does. On the contrary, the *ku* is extremely logical and it follows the rules rigorously. Every habitual or spontaneous mental or physical behavior you experience is an example of your *ku* following the rules accepted or laid down by your *lono*. Because of this, your *ku* is quite open to change if the conditions are right. So here are the conditions:

1. Your *ku* will readily accept and go by new rules that don't conflict with old ones. If you make a new rule that says your new diploma or certificate now gives you permission to make more money and you don't have any other rules against making more money, your *ku* will cooperate fully in your new endeavor.

2. Your *ku* will readily accept new rules when old rules have been shown to be illogical. Once when I was helping a woman stop smoking she mentioned in conversation that she had a habit of rebelling against authority, which meant that she had a rule saying no one had a right to tell her what to do. When she was in a deeply focused state and was describing how she would smoke even when she didn't want to, I suddenly said, "You mean that you are letting cigarettes tell you what to do and when to do it?" There was a long pause, during which I knew her *ku* was reviewing the logic of her rules. Then

she said, "No way!" And that's all there was to it. She
never smoked again.

3. Your *ku* will accept new rules when old rules are no
longer useful. When throwing a tantrum no longer gets
people to do what you want, your *ku* will easily drop that
habit and accept a new rule for getting people to do what
you want. Or when the purpose served by a sickness has
been satisfied, your *ku* will drop the rules that produced
the sickness and take on new rules of health.

4. Your *ku* will accept a new rule which is demonstrably
(and therefore logically) more effective than an old rule
for doing the same thing. When the advantages of not
drinking alcohol clearly outweigh the advantages of continuing to drink alcohol, then a person's *ku* will accept a
new rule of abstinence, as long as the advantages of not
drinking and the disadvantages of drinking are kept in
mind in situations where the person used to drink. In
this particular case, that's because not drinking may involve experiencing some pain and tension which drinking
used to diminish. With *lono*'s continued guidance, however, the *ku* will accept the pain which may come with
new rules if their benefits are great enough. That itself
requires a rule that says they are. Because present pain
is such a powerful influence, future benefits of the new
rule or a future worse pain from not following it need to
be kept in conscious awareness. In a different vein al-
together, your *ku* will accept new rules for speaking (as
in using a new language) under conditions in which the
old rules for speaking do not produce the right response.
At a party once I was speaking to a group of Frenchmen
in French, and then I turned to a group of Americans and
spoke to them. It was a full half minute before I realized
from their blank faces that I had been speaking to them
in French, at which point I quickly switched to English.

Now I'd like to pick out and discuss for a bit three rules
or assumptions that cause a great deal of personal and global
grief.

First is the assumption that you know what another person is thinking. Regardless of how familiar you are with a person's habits and attitudes, you don't know what they are thinking at any given moment. You may make some good guesses, and you may sometimes pick up a portion of what they are broadcasting, but to assume that you infallibly know their thoughts is to claim a psychic ability that doesn't exist. Instead of relating to that person as they are, you will be relating to a poor symbol of that person made up of your own limiting rules about them. In doing so you will limit your experience of that person as a changing, growing being.

While visiting with some friends I noted how the metaphysically inclined wife kept saying that her husband wasn't interested in that kind of stuff and that he thought she was foolish to be involved, while he never said a word. Later he and I were up late talking and he turned out be a deeply metaphysical thinker who supported his wife's interests. Some incident must have happened that caused her to make a limiting rule about him and then she continued to relate to the limiting rule and not to him. She didn't have a rule that allowed him to be different, and so she cut herself off from experiencing his metaphysical side.

While we each have to come up with rules that are effective for us, I'll share one that has worked very well for me. It is that people are what they are and they do what they do. This rule allows me to relate to people as they are in the present, regardless of what they've done in the past. It doesn't block my memory of the past, but it does allow me to relate to changes. It is also designed to make their actions more important to me than their words or anything I might conceive to be their thoughts. Finally, it helps to keep me from ever being disappointed in people. No matter what they say, they'll do what they do, and that's what I expect. If it isn't what I want, then I do something to change myself.

The second assumption is that other people know or should know what you are thinking. Wow. If you don't know what others are thinking, and probably more than half the time you don't even know what *you* are thinking, how can you expect others to know what is going on inside your inconsistent head? Yet there are so many people so terribly unhappy in anger or fear because they think that others know or should know what they are thinking. That's like expecting others to be infallible psychics. There are teenagers fearful that others know how afraid they are, husbands and wives angry because their spouses don't anticipate their changeable moods, and people convinced that the government is able to monitor their thoughts. On a more ordinary level, it might be useful to examine your own expectations about this. How often have you been angry because someone didn't know what you wanted when you didn't tell them, or been fearful that someone would know what you thought when you didn't say anything? My rule is that no one knows what I'm thinking. My staff would probably agree (there I go, assuming I know what they are thinking—how easy it is to slip). In any case, it removes another cause for disappointment and fear.

The third assumption or rule I want to discuss certainly operates on a personal level, but is most devastating in its global effects. It is the rule of generalization. This rule says that all similar things are the same. It's a convenient rule in some ways, because it allows us to speak about and deal with things in groups. We can talk about the media, rather than naming each and every radio or TV station or newspaper. We can deal with China, rather than each and every individual Chinese person. Convenient, yes, but potentially dangerous when we attribute individual qualities to the group.

A group is only an abstract symbol that represents an arbitrary mental concept. It doesn't describe a real experience. I remember that once an astronaut remarked on how impressed he was while looking at the Earth from space to see that there weren't any national borders. If we say that the media is too negative, we blind ourselves to millions of examples to the contrary; and if we say that China is aggressive, we ignore millions of Chinese who only want peace.

I have even heard spiritual teachers talk about the masses being unenlightened. There is no such thing as "the masses." There are billions of individual, living, breathing human beings, any one of whom might be completely enlightened for all anyone else knows. However, it's still convenient to say, "I want to reach the masses with my teachings" when you mean "I want to reach as many people as possible." The rule of generalization is so pervasive and at the core of so much intolerance, hate, violence, and fear that it almost seems useless to try to change it, but every little bit will help us move toward more understanding, peace, and harmony. Please do your part by recognizing its negative aspect whenever it appears (that's when a generalization is evaluated as bad) and changing it when you can. Take a good look at your generalizations about specific groups of people; about parents, men, or women; about government and business; about spirit and matter; about money and love.

Language Symbols

Every language is symbolic of a particular way of thinking and perceiving. They all have their rules of grammar and their rules of meaning for various sound combinations, both of which make a language distinctive. But those same rules of structure and vocabulary also help to determine the experience of people who speak that particular language.

One simple example is the Hawaiian word *mana*. Although often translated as "power," "spiritual power," or "energy," none of those are adequate because the word just doesn't translate well. English doesn't have the concepts to handle it. On the other hand, the English word "sex" as a general concept has no equivalent in Hawaiian. To a person who only spoke Hawaiian, "The Sexual Revolution" would only conjure up a change in position by two people making love. Most ancient peoples only had a few words for colors and so they only saw a few colors. Ancient Hawaiians, for instance, didn't distinguish between dark green, dark blue, and black. Today a moderately priced computer can put over

250,000 unique and identifiable colors on the screen that many ancient people wouldn't be able to distinguish because their language had no words for them.

English is an exceptionally flexible language in both grammary and vocabulary, which is one reason it is used so widely around the world. It's so flexible that it's virtually a pidgin language, able to absorb considerable grammatical structure and vocabulary from other languages and still be understood. In fairness, though, another reason for its popularity is the inflexibility of most of its users. I overheard a European say that a person who speaks two languages is called bilingual, and a person who speaks one language is called an American. As flexible as English is in the American style, there are ranges of experience out of reach to its users if that is the only language they know. I read an English translation of a book by Charles Dumas and enjoyed it very much. I read the same book in the original French and laughed and cried. It wasn't that the translation was bad, it was that in French it was different. My point here is that linguistic rules do more than just give us different ways of saying the same thing. They give us different experiences. Your life will be greatly enriched in ways that can't be described in English if you learn to use another language.

Fortunately, there are two other languages that many English speakers use without even thinking of them as languages, yet both of them can express and induce experience that is beyond the capability of English. They are music and mathematics. Sometimes in a course I will ask a student familiar with music to describe Beethoven's Fifth Symphony in English for the rest of the class. The silence itself says a lot. Mathematics is also a good language for describing certain things that English is not adequate for, especially in its dialects of algebra, calculus, and others, but even common arithmetic can tell a person who knows how to read a financial report a great amount of information about a company that reams of words can't say. Mathematics doesn't do well in the realm of feelings, though. Other alternative languages besides music which we have that are better for that are painting, sculpture, mime, and dance. If you think of all these as languages, as symbols that you can use to express yourself and use for a healing influence, you will vastly increase your potential as a shaman and a healer.

Imaginary Symbols

In his very famous book *Think and Grow Rich*, author Napoleon Hill wrote down many excellent ideas and techniques for success. Among them was a very shamanic technique of imagining what he called his "Invisible Counselors." For many years, he said, as he went to sleep he would hold a meeting in his mind with famous men whose qualities he wanted to incorporate into his own life. He would imagine them vividly and address each one, asking them to teach him those same qualities he admired. What he discovered after the first few months of doing this was that the characters became more and more real, to the point where they took on individual personalities, had their own personal experiences, and engaged in lively dialogue with each other. They were not just puppets of the imagination, controlled entirely by his will, but living symbols of creative expression. These conversations were so unusual for him that he stopped them for a few months while he reinforced his confidence that these counselors were his creations. Then he went back to the dialogues and continued them for years because they were so valuable. As Hill said, even though these counselors were products of his imagination, "they have led me into glorious paths of adventure, rekindled an appreciation of true greatness, encouraged creative endeavor, and emboldened the expression of honest thought." He also said that during the meetings he was more open to intuition, that his counselors guided him through many emergencies, and that, while still using other resources, he went to them with every difficult problem that faced himself and his clients. In a later book, *The Master Key To Riches*, he calls these counselors his "Eight Princes," and by this time he had put them each in charge of a specific area of his life. The benefits he attributed to them are too numerous to mention here, but this man who studied the techniques of hundreds of the most successful men of his time called his invisible counselors "my greatest asset."

I am now going to give you some simple guidelines for doing the same thing, for using mental symbols to attract, focus, and communicate ideas that can make your life richer and more effective in many ways. These symbols can be famous people, living or not; gods, goddesses, angels, saints, or heroes from your favorite culture; animals or Nature spirits; or forms of your own creation. If you like, you can think of them as focused aspects of *kanewahine*, your spirit or Higher Self. Some people like to have a special mental place for meeting with what I'll call the Inner Council of Advisors. The Garden mentioned in chapter six would be a good one, or you can make up another one of your own. Other people like to have them appear whenever and wherever they want them, either in the mind or as a thoughtform in their immediate environment. Still others find that a physical symbol of a mental symbol helps them to focus better. For this you might use ivory or plastic carvings of the Japanese seven gods of luck, statuettes representing the Power Animals, or any other figurines or objects that suit your taste. Use the physical symbols to stimulate your imagination, so that with your mind you can bring them to life. You can have as many advisors as you like, but eight is about the practical limit that you can sustain in your mind at one time. I'm going to suggest four below, and you can add what you like according to your needs and desires.

1. **The Health Advisor.** This member of the Inner Council gives you information, ideas, advice, and assistance with everything having to do with your state of health, healing skill, energy, and fitness, or that of anyone you care about.
2. **The Wealth Advisor.** This member does the same for everything having to do with money, prosperity, and abundance.
3. **The Happiness Advisor.** This member helps with love,

peace, harmony, personal and group relationships, fun, and enjoyment.
4. The Success Advisor. This member helps with achieving goals and increasing skills.

Like many others, I had been told about this Inner Council, heard about it, and read about it for years, and never bothered to do it. Be smarter than that and start making use of this incredible resource today.

Of a different nature but in the same category are thoughtform symbols that are designed to perform work. A thoughtform, as you may recall, is an exteriorized thought. In the last chapter they were used as a focus for *nalu*. In this chapter I want to mention their use as tools.

A thoughtform tool is like any other tool, except that it is created entirely by thought, without any physical materials. Depending on the degree of focus and energy put into it, it can last for minutes or years. It does its work by directly influencing the *ku* through intuition, rather than by influencing the body. As an example, I used a thoughtform door to keep my rambunctious kids out of my room on a Sunday morning when I didn't want to get up and close the physical door. They responded as if the physical door were closed. Another time I used a thoughtform of a wolf to chase off an angry dog, and it ran off with its tail between its legs. I felt so bad that the next time we met I used a thoughtform of its owner petting it. That worked so well the dog and I became friends and I've used that thoughtform successfully with other dogs many times since then. Once when I had the flu (when I was much younger) I created a thoughtform healing machine that healed me up in a couple of hours. Thoughtform crystals can work as well as physical ones; thoughtform birds can carry intuitive messages to people; thoughtform animals, people, or objects can help others at a distance; thoughtform environments can help to change moods and emotions. If enough people work together with clarity and focus, thoughtforms can be constructed that would influence world events. You can invent and use thoughtforms in myriad patterns for many things, but here are some guidelines to keep in mind:

1. Your best and easiest results will come from using the thoughtform to influence the *ku* of something, rather than its physical aspect. I'm not saying it's impossible to make a thoughtform so solid or energized that it can directly affect physical matter, but since everything physical is a solidified thoughtform anyway, brought into existence by your *ku* and *kane* using patterns that already exist, why do the same thing the hard way? That reminds me of a story told of the Aborigines of Australia. When someone asked them why they didn't use telepathy to communicate at long distances anymore, one of them said, ''Now we just use the telephone because it's easier.''

2. A *ku* moves toward pleasure and away from pain, so a *ku* can be motivated to change behavior by the promise of reward or the threat of punishment. A thoughtform based on the former takes less energy and is more effective than one based on the latter because there is less resistance to it. In addition, there is the influence on your own *ku* to be considered. Once in a shopping mall with my wife I was in a hurry to get home and I knew there was yet another store she had mentioned wanting to visit. As we neared it I slapped a thoughtform fog over the front of the store. The moment I did that she exclaimed, ''Oh, there's the store I wanted to go in!'' All I had succeeded in doing was drawing her attention to it. It would probably have been more effective if I'd created a thoughtform to draw her attention home in a positive way, instead.

Memory Symbols
The *ku* does everything by memory. All of your assumptions, attitudes, beliefs, expectations, habits, skills, behavior, moods, emotions, experience, language, and creative thought are based on memory. Memories themselves are

patterns of energy that symbolize events which are stored in such a way that an inner or outer stimulus (even another memory pattern) can activate them. Memories, of course, are vital to our functioning as human beings, but if the activation of the memory also activates a negative emotional response, the effect can be detrimental to our health, well-being, and effectiveness. While most techniques that work with emotional memories are designed to change your reaction or relationship to the content of the memory by teaching you a new response pattern (an additional memory), or by changing the content of the memory itself (like changing the events in a dream) so that it no longer evokes the negative emotion, it is also possible to change one or more elements of the storage pattern, and thereby change its effects. In this process you change the context, not the content.

Imagine a painting of a nude hanging in the waiting room of a doctor's office. The likelihood is that for most people it would seem inappropriate and might make them uncomfortable, embarrassed, or even angry. To remedy the situation, the doctor could have the nude parts covered over, have the whole painting covered up, have the paint scraped off and a new painting put on, or hire someone to teach all of his patients a different attitude toward nudity. Or, he could put the painting in his bedroom at home where it would look and feel fine. As another example, a big boulder in a vacant lot might be an eyesore, but a landscaper, without even moving the boulder, could change the surroundings so that the boulder would become the center of admiring attention. As a third example, a poster taped to a wall might draw criticism, but in a nice frame it might draw praise. This is what I mean by changing the context instead of the content. Putting something in a different context can change its effect entirely. When you do the same thing with negative memories they can become neutral or even positive.

In terms of memory patterns, the content is the memory of the event itself, that part of the memory which evokes a reaction in the present. The context has to do with such things as color, size, distance, movement, point of view, props (nonessentials that you add or take away), sound level, setting, and many others. Every *ku* stores memories according to well-defined patterns, with one or more contextual elements being crucial to defining the positive, neutral, or negative emotion of the memory. The patterns can be different with each individual, so you'll have to do some experimenting and exploring on your own. For instance, one of my students found to her great surprise that all of her successful and positive memories were stored in black and white, and all her negative memories were in vivid color. As she began changing her most negative memories to black and white, they either became neutral (they didn't bother her anymore), or she discovered positive aspects to them that she had never noticed before. This also led her to begin planning for future successes in black and white instead of color. It's always easier to work with the *ku* than to try to change its basic patterns. Here are some suggestions for using this very effective process to change your responses to emotionally negative memories. Note that some memories may have to be worked on more than once.

1. Add something to the memory. What works quite well for memories of being criticized, for example, is to put antlers on the criticizer, play circus music in the background, and have clowns behind the criticizer making faces. This puts the event in a completely different context and helps your memory store it in the silly file where it can do no more harm.

   A variation would be to take away something that seems nonessential, like a potted plant or a picture or a cup. Sometimes the *ku* will use such an object for a storage key, and when it is gone the emotional response changes.
2. Change the setting. Try putting the memory in different locations, or different time periods, complete with changes of costume. The emotional key is often linked to time and place. A variation is to change your viewpoint. Usually we always recall a memory from the same point of view, like a fixed camera. Experiment with mov-

ing your viewpoint around. Try it from above, from a different side, from a different level, or from behind. Another variation is to turn the whole thing upside down. With some people this produces a dramatic change in how they feel about the memory.

3. Alter the reality context. One way is to suddenly freeze the memory, as if you've turned it to a thin sheet of glass or ice, and then take a hammer and break it up. Finish by sweeping it up and tossing the remains in a trash can. This is frequently very satisfying. Another way is to put the memory on a screen, as if you were running a movie, and then run it at high speed or in slow motion, and/or speed up, slow down, or vary the volume of the sound-track. A good variation is to make the memory into a play, with you as the director telling the actors to do exactly what they did and praising them on their performance. This gives you a subtle sense of control over the situation and tends to remove feelings of helplessness.

4. Change the elements into their opposites. This is a trial-and-error approach to finding the emotional key to a memory, but it works very well. Color is a good place to start. If the memory is in vivid color, make the colors faded or change them to black and white. If they are black and white or faded, put them in vivid color. If the memory appears close up, push it far away; if it's far away, bring it close up. If you are outside the memory looking at it (even at yourself), put yourself inside and experience it more directly; if you are inside, move yourself outside (although you can leave an image of yourself inside so you don't change the content). If the memory is big, make it small; if small, make it big. If the memory is borderless, put in a border; if bordered, take it away. You get the idea.

As a means for helping others, changing context in any of the suggested ways is an excellent device because you can take them through the process without ever having to know the specific content of their memory. In that way privacy is maintained and embarrassment is avoided. You would just ask the person to recall the emotion-laden event and then guide them into making changes. Silly stuff generally doesn't work well on very traumatic memories because many people have strong rules about treating pain seriously. For traumatic memories I suggest starting with opposites or the viewpoint change.

Environmental Symbols

In traditional societies environmental symbols are called omens or signs. They are really symbolic interpretations of natural events and/or meaningful information about the past, present, or future that comes from apparently random events or sources. The ancient Chinese examined cracks in the shoulder blades of sheep for omens, the Greeks studied the entrails of slaughtered animals, the Persians looked at fire, and one of the favorite Hawaiian practices was reading clouds. Typical scientific types get all hot and bothered about these practices because of course it doesn't make any sense from a first-level point of view. How can there be any correlation between events widely separated in time, space, and essential nature? You might as well try to get stock advice from the tracks of a duck, or psychological counseling from the patterns of raindrops on a windowpane. From a second-level point of view, though, any one of those could work. That's because of the first-principle idea that life is a dream, and the second-principle idea that everything is connected. With his idea of synchronicity Carl Jung came close to explaining the effectiveness of the I Ching, but synchronicity is just another word for coincidence. Shamanism says that duck tracks and stock prices are related because everything is related. Even so, some things are easier to read or interpret than others. While it is possible to make a correlation between duck tracks and stock prices in second-level thinking, it might be more effective to choose something with a closer relationship that would be easier to understand, like past patterns of stock prices.

Omens are all around us, because our thoughts are all around us. That is, everything around us is a reflection or symbol of our thoughts. By paying more attention to the patterns in our environment, we may be able to understand the patterns of our thoughts better.

There are innumerable ways to seek and read omens, but for our purposes here I will only describe the two that I teach in my courses. I might mention, too, by the way, that the only difference between this and the casting techniques discussed in chapter five is that there we were purposely creating symbols, and here we are looking for symbols that already exist.

Bibliomancy is the art of randomly opening a book and getting an answer to a question. It is mostly used with the Bible or a dictionary, but an enjoyable and creative variation is to use any kind of book or magazine picked at random. The creativity comes from figuring out how a paragraph on grilling shrimp can relate to your question about your love life, or what a photograph of an airplane in an advertisement has to do with a question about your career. Frequently, though, the answer to your question will be stunningly obvious no matter where you look for it. And sometimes events come together in such a neat way. In one class held in a library I passed out magazines randomly gathered from a rack. One student had left the room, so I just put one on his chair. When he came back he noted that it was a photography magazine and thought I must have known that was his profession (which I didn't). So he decided to ask where he could find a new type of film he had just heard about. He closed his eyes, flipped open the magazine, and jammed his finger down. His eyes opened onto a full-page ad for the film he had asked about. Fortunately, it was close to lunch break, so he had time to recover from his shock. Sometimes the fact that this stuff works really shakes people up.

The second thing I do is have my students ask the universe a question about their life or their career, and then go off to lunch with an open, expectant attitude. I tell them the omen will come; something they experience will seem significant.

It might come in the shape of clouds, in the shape of spaces between things (like tree branches), in an object that they notice, in a song or a bit of conversation, or in an event. Once in Taos, New Mexico, I asked a question about the relative importance of love and power in regard to a project I was working on. On the way to a restaurant my eye was caught by a message painted in big red letters on the side of an adobe building: "Love is the greatest!"

THE ELEVENTH ADVENTURE:

THE HEALING ART OF CEREMONY AND RITUAL

E 'ao lu'au a kualima
(Offer young taro leaves five times—
*a ceremony to remove sickness of
mind or body*)

Just mention the words *ceremony* and *ritual* and the tendency is to think of Egyptian priests in procession, a Catholic mass, or natives dancing to the beat of drums. The words incline us to think of something strange, mysterious, or exotic, but in fact our modern, urban lives are full of ceremony and ritual (since a ceremony is a kind of ritual, I'll use the latter word to stand for both for most of the rest of the chapter). I know that the word *ritual* can be used to mean any set pattern of behavior that may be carried out consciously or unconsciously (i.e., smoking, driving, exercise), but I'm using it in this chapter to refer to consciously organized behavior intended to impress and influence.

One use of ritual is to mark the beginning of something, so we have rituals like baby showers, ship launchings, grand openings, and ribbon cuttings (a modern version of a ceremony for cutting the umbilical cord). There are rituals for the ending of things, like funerals, bachelor parties, and happy hours. We have completion rituals in the form of graduation ceremonies, toasting achievement, and applause. Transition rituals abound, such as birthday parties, anniversary celebrations, baptisms and bar mitzvahs, confirmations, and crossing-the-equator parties. Connection rituals include marriage ceremonies, church services, debutante balls, and blind dates. With such an obvious abundance of rituals already available, why then are more and more people seeking out rituals of different kinds from different cultures?

Ritual can serve many different purposes, but it won't serve them unless it is effective. An effective ritual is one which leaves a lasting impression and strongly influences people to reinforce or change assumptions, attitudes, or expectations. To do that it must be intellectually and emotionally satisfying to both the *lono* and *ku*. Otherwise it is no more than lifeless habit and dogma and is ineffective for its intended purpose. Our interest in ritual as urban shamans is to use it for healing and for enhancement of positive patterns.

What Determines Effective Ritual

There are very specific elements in a ritual which determine whether it is satisfying and effective.

1. It must have a strong beginning and ending. A ritual that starts weakly loses significance, and it becomes very difficult to focus people's attention. That's why so many rituals begin with drums, bells, whistles, or trumpets. You get a strong beginning by doing something to get people's attention. Similarly, a weak ending leaves everyone feeling unfulfilled or incomplete. You achieve a strong ending by getting everyone's attention again and letting them know clearly that the ritual is over. One of the most common reasons for people being unhappy with the rituals they already have is that those times aren't clearly marked off from the rest of life. This is very important for

making the ritual impressive and influential, because the feeling of most people will be that if the ritual just blends into ordinary things then it can't be very important. When I teach ceremony and ritual in my courses, this matter of a strong beginning and ending is one that the students have the most trouble with. Yet people will forgive a lot of incompetence in between if the beginning and ending are good.

2. It must have strong sensory input. A ritual that you only watch will be impressive and influential to the degree that it is also interesting or beautiful. If it has music and aroma, it will have a greater effect, and if it adds the senses of touch and taste, the effect will be even more intense. Many cultures and organizations have discovered this, and so their rituals include beauty, singing with or without music, fresh flowers or incense, and group participation through prayer responses, sing-alongs, movement or dance, and drinking or eating.

3. It must have a familiar or predictable form. If you participate in a ritual and you don't know what to do or what to expect, you'll be confused and anxious and because of your distraction the ritual will leave less of an impression and have less influence. But if there's enough about it that's familiar, you'll be more comfortable and more affected. Priesthoods accomplish this by using set rituals for specific occasions. The Catholic church used to have a considerable sense of cohesiveness among its members because they knew that no matter where in the world they went, the service in a Catholic church would be the same and they could participate fully even without knowing the local language. The reasons for changing this must have seemed good to those who did it, but the same sense of cohesiveness is no longer there. Shamans satisfy the need for familiarity and predictability by including familiar sensory elements and patterns in every ritual, even though every ritual on every occasion might be different.

4. The meaning of every part of the ritual must be under-

stood by the participants. To whatever degree a part of the ritual is not understood, its effectiveness is lost. Priesthoods tend to neglect this element the most because they tend to think they are doing rituals for one or more spiritual beings, rather than for the people. As long as they know and the spirit knows, what does it matter if the people know? This points up a big difference between priests and shamans. A shaman, if he or she is acting as a shaman, always does a ritual for one or more persons, himself or herself included. Spirits might be acknowledged, but the effectiveness of the ritual is determined by how well it impresses and influences the people involved, and a good shaman knows that. So in shamanic rituals you will usually find everything explained before or during the ritual.

5. It must be special. A ritual that doesn't look or feel any different from any other occasion loses its effectiveness. A major reason why so many of our modern rituals seem empty is that so many of our leaders no longer treat those rituals as special. This is particularly evident in our holiday rituals. For most people, Halloween is a costume party, Thanksgiving has practically disappeared except as an excuse to eat turkey and cranberry sauce, Christmas is a shopping frenzy, New Year's Day is a hangover and a football game, and the Fourth of July is a picnic. Of course there are exceptions, but not enough to make these ritual times into occasions of positive reinforcement of cultural values. Rituals of other cultures that have retained their specialness are very attractive to those who feel a lack of it in their own culture.

What Makes a Ritual Special
There are four basic aspects to a ritual's specialness:

1. A special area. An area can be made special in several ways. One way is by consecration. This means doing a ritual blessing that is designed to indicate the specialness

of an area for all time. This could be to protect it, bring good fortune to it, or to reserve its use. Graveyards are often made special in this way, as are buildings designated as churches or temples. In Hawaii it is still common to consecrate (bless) any new building or land project. Another way to make a place special is by setting it apart, either by erecting fencing (as around a park), by location (as the Statue of Liberty), or by reserved use (as a school). Outlining can be done, either with plants or marks on the ground, as well. The easiest way to make a place special for ritual purposes, however, is by encircling an area with people, especially by having them hold hands. Such an enclosed area is automatically felt to be special.

2. Special objects. This includes a wide range of things, but first I'll mention clothing. Special clothing in the form of robes, sashes, uniforms, hats, masks, costumes, or special variations on normal clothing (i.e., traditional dress, formal gowns or tuxedos) has been used for untold ages to help make an occasion special. Jewelry used only on ritual occasions helps increase the sense of specialness. The famous flower leis of Hawaii given for greeting and honoring are a variant of this. Special decor to aid the ritual effect includes flowers, banners, furnishings, and arrangements designated for the ritual. Special tools could be batons, staffs, cups and bowls, crystals, statues, or anything used in the ritual itself. And special food can add a lot to the ritual. Sometimes this is food that is only prepared when the ritual is performed, like Christmas cookies or *hallah* (a special bread eaten only on the Jewish sabbath or holidays), and sometimes it is regular food made special by consecration or designation for ritual use. In old Hawaii, squid was a popular food, but it was made special in a healing ritual by the shaman who would remind the patient that the word for squid, *he'e*, also means "to flee," and by eating it the illness would flee. Hawaiian shamans were among the earliest masters of placebos, and they didn't try to hide it.

3. Special movements. In rituals people make movements

that they rarely or never do at other times. There are almost always special gestures, ways of moving the arms and hands to emphasize, point out, or bless something that's going on. Special postures may be used by one or more of those present, usually the leader unless the whole group is doing the same thing (as in meditation rituals). And special dances can be done. Most people are familiar with the Hawaiian hula, or at least the modern *auwana*, or entertainment hula. Not nearly as many (although this is changing) are aware of the *kahiko*, or ancient style of ritual hula. Even though it is beginning to be presented as entertainment, it is still mostly done as a ritual opening of a show, and it is still used for various rituals to make them very special.

4. Special sounds. Apart from opening and closing sounds to get our attention, there are special sounds for use in the ritual itself. One of these is intonation. Ritual words that are spoken like ordinary conversation don't have nearly the impact as the same words spoken in a special voice reserved for rituals. If you can remember the intonation used by someone asked to give the opening prayer or blessing at a meeting you may have attended, you'll know what I mean. Also there may be a special rhythm which involves voice, as in chanting, or it may involve some kind of percussive instrument (snare drums, Hawaiian gourds) used to emphasize or set off ritual words. Music naturally is included, but it's special music designated, designed, or traditionally used for the ritual. Specialness might be indicated by the style of the music (a church hymn), by its content (the folk song "Greensleeves" becomes "What Child Is This?" at a Christmas celebration), by the instruments used (the Hawaiian gourd is only used in ritual hula), or by the context ("Let There Be Peace On Earth" can be sung anytime, but has greater impact at a ritual gathering). Special sounds also include the special words used only for ritual purposes, like prayers and blessings, and the use of a special language. A special language that isn't understood by most

of those present—whether Sanskrit, Japanese, Hebrew, Latin, Hawaiian, or whatever—will have some impact just because it sounds special, but the impact will be more significant if it is translated at some point, even partially.

Now you've been given all the elements of a good ritual. Let's look at some examples of how they work together.

A while back there was a group visiting Kauai from the mainland that was staying at a camp in the mountains of Kokee. Before arriving they had written to me and asked me to join them for a full-moon ceremony on a Friday night. I thought that would be fun, so my wife and I went up and shared dinner and entertainment with them until we found ourselves seated with everyone in a circle around a campfire. The moon was visible and beautiful, but everyone was just sitting there in a kind of awkward silence and I wondered when it was going to begin. Finally the leader bent toward me and whispered, "Would you like to start the ceremony now?" Well, that was a surprise. I thought I was just a guest. I hadn't prepared anything, and the Hawaiians didn't do full-moon ceremonies (they had ceremonies timed by the moon, but not related to the moon, nor on the night of the full moon). I didn't have any tradition to go by, but as a shaman I did know the elements that constitute good ritual and ceremony. So I had everyone hold hands, said a prayer about the moon, blessed the staves they had been working on for their own training, taught them a brief chant, and finished with another prayer. Everyone was very impressed and happy.

On another occasion at a conference on a college campus in the Midwest, I was asked one evening to come and witness a ritual being given by an American Indian shaman. Something told me to bring along my *kukui*-seed lei and my conch shell trumpet (special objects) and to wear my headband and aloha shirt (special clothing). When I arrived there were about a hundred people in a big circle holding hands (special area). As soon as I was noticed I was asked to enter the circle along with a Hasidic shaman who was there, too. The

Indian started off with a great shout (a strong beginning) and then shook his rattle and named the seven directions both in his language and in English (clear meaning). Next the Hasidic shaman did the same with his tambourine in Hebrew and English, and I followed up with my conch naming the directions in Hawaiian and English. (Actually I had a bad lip that night and my trumpet mostly sputtered, but I continued anyway and no one seemed to notice. In show business you have to learn how to ad lib.) By now the ceremony had fallen into the familiar form of a circle, with a beginning, middle, and probable end, and a rotation of roles. Then the Indian led everyone in a back-and-forth movement accompanied by a chant while he did a little dance in the middle with his rattle. This was followed by the Hasidic shaman doing a dance with his tambourine while everyone sang a song in Hebrew. Then it was my turn. To maintain the effectiveness of the ritual I had to continue the predictable form, but there wasn't anything in Hawaiian tradition to fit the situation. So, like a good shaman, I made something up on the spot. First I got everyone to chant the seven principles in Hawaiian while swaying back and forth, and then I did a dance movement all around the circle that had a hula flavor to it. People loved it, mainly because it felt good and felt appropriate. The ritual finished up strongly and with strong sensory input from mutual hugs all around. Every element had been satisfied.

I even do my shaman training courses as a form of ritual. We always have a formal opening to give a strong beginning and bless the space, which has been previously laid out in a circle whenever possible. There is usually a bit of Hawaiian decor and Hawaiian music, and I have my special headband, shirt, lei, and baton, all of which I explain. The format of the course is laid out so that the pattern will be familiar and predictable, and there is plenty of group participation for sensory input. Also, we always have a strong, formal closing. The ritual framework is a great aid to the learning process.

The basic format for a ritual is:

1. Preparation. Here is where you get all your props and clothing together, arrange furnishings, set up music, plan the steps, and designate the special area. A big ritual could take weeks of planning, or you might find yourself asked to do a ritual at a moment's notice, as in my full-moon ceremony. Once you have the information in this chapter, that shouldn't be much of a problem. In my course I let my students know a day ahead of time that they'll be expected to do a ritual, but I only give them five to fifteen minutes to actually plan and prepare. By then they have learned the basic elements of ritual, so the results are usually pretty good.

2. Opening. A dramatic gesture, words of prayer or greeting, a musical attention getter, or a get-acquainted process of some kind make good, strong openings. One of the best openings I've experienced was at a conference in New Zealand, using a modified Maori model. It was done outside and the hosts were lined up on one side of a lawn, with the visitors on the other. The hosts began by each in turn giving a rather formalized yet improvised greeting to the land and the visitors. Then volunteers from the visitor side returned the greeting. Finally, the visitors lined up and started at one end of the host line with hugs and introductions one by one all the way down the line. As each visitor finished the host line he or she would join the same line so that the next visitor would get another hug and introduction, until everyone had been introduced to everyone else. It was great fun and made a good bond among the participants, but it did take a while.

3. Content. This is simply doing whatever is involved with the purpose of the ritual. Generally, the shorter the content the more formal it is, and the longer the content the more informal it is. A marriage ceremony is pretty formal all the way through, but the Olympic Games are relatively informal between the opening and closing ceremonies.

4. Closing. This is where you get everyone's attention back and make a definite end to the ritual. This vital, yet often

overlooked aspect of ritual can make a big difference in the success of the ritual. A good closing reinforces the group bond, strengthens the memory of the ritual, gives a clear and comfortable transition from formality to informality, and tells people when it's okay to leave. A clear closing can be done with well-defined final statements or prayers; bells, whistles, or gongs; group singing; handshakes or hugs; or that popular old favorite, applause.

In the remaining sections I am going to give examples of specific rituals that may be of use to modern, urban shamans. As always, feel free to modify, add, or delete.

A Healing Ritual

Here is a very effective group-healing ritual, even though it is quite simple. Prior to starting, obtain a pair of short sticks, rattles, or castanets (call them percussives). Depending on the size of your group, start by forming a circle and having one to four people who want to have a healing sit in the center—back to back if more than one person is to be healed. Have them maintain a focus on a positive expectation for the healing they want. Give the percussives to one of the healees in the center to be the primary beat keeper. Do a formal opening, perhaps expressing the desire or intent of the healing, and then have the outer group hold hands. Tell the beat keeper to start a steady four-beat rhythm (about the rate of a relaxed pulse) with the percussives. Any other healees should do the same rhythm with a soft handclap. This keeps the healees involved and attentive. After the rhythm has become steady, get a chant going around the circle to the same rhythm. You can make up your own or use the following one that you've seen before:

> "Be aware, be free, be focused, be here, be loved, be strong, be healed"

Whatever chant you use, be sure to leave room for a breath pause at least one beat long. With the above chant the beat sequence could be like this, with each number representing a chant phrase:

> 1-2-3-4-5-6-7-pause-1-2-3-4-5-6-7-pause-1-2-3-4-
> 5-6-7-pause-1-2-3-4-5-6-7.

A good alternative would be:

> 1-pause-2-pause-3-pause-4-pause-5-pause-6-
> pause-7-pause-1-pause-2, etc.

Remember that the pause is for the chant, not the percussive rhythm, which is continuous.

Keep the chant going until it feels very steady and semi-automatic. This may take from one to five minutes. Then have the person on your left in the circle move forward to the center. Close the circle while that person gently touches the healee(s) on the head or shoulder and softly gives a short blessing, prayer, or affirmation. It will take a lot less time if only one statement is made to serve all the healees. When finished, that person steps back into the circle and the next person to the left goes in. The process continues until everyone in the circle has participated. All this time the chanting and the rhythm continue. After you as the leader have done your turn, let the chanting and the beat go on for about a minute, then bring it to an abrupt end by shouting "Done!" or if you want to use Hawaiian, *"Pau!"* (pronounced "Pow!"). Finish with a group hug that includes the healees and bring everyone back to the present by letting everyone share their experience.

As a practical matter, you may find that because of the high energy and focus required, the beat keeper may tend to trance out a bit and falter with the beat. Then it's up to you to use the chant to strengthen and maintain the beat. Usually that will bring the beat keeper back in line. Sustained focus is the key to the power of this ritual. As the leader I suggest that you keep your eyes open throughout.

A Journey Ritual

One of the most loving things you can do as an urban shaman is a journey to the Underworld on behalf of someone else. Performing a joint ritual with the person for whom you are journeying makes it even more powerful.

For a journey ritual, find a quiet place where you can sit with your friend without being disturbed for at least a half hour. The journey itself may only take ten minutes, but give yourself some spare time in case it takes longer and to discuss it. Start by asking your friend what power he or she lacks or would like to have in order to heal a condition or achieve a goal. Note that your role is not to heal this person, but to find power for them to do their own healing or changing. Continue by establishing a deep rapport with mutual *kahi*. The physical contact doesn't have to be maintained during the journey. When you are ready, close your eyes, go to your own Garden, and focus there with sight, sound, and touch. Then call upon a Power Animal and find a path that leads to your friend's Garden. Once there, look for a hole in the ground as the entrance to *Milu*, jump in, and go forward on your quest, dealing with whatever challenges come up on your way to the Power Object you are seeking. When you find it, bring it back through your friend's Garden, where you leave the form and bring the spirit or essence back through your Garden and into the present moment. Holding the spirit of the Power Object in your hands as if it were physical, place it in your friend's body with a blessing at whatever place seems appropriate and finish with a hug. Now what I haven't said yet, and what makes this ritual exceptionally powerful, is that you are to describe out loud to your friend everything that happens from the time you first enter your Garden until you place the spirit of the object in his or her body. This has the dual effect of greatly increasing your own focus, and of adding the focused attention of your friend to the journey. Thereafter you will have a shared inner experience that neither one of you is likely to forget.

A House Blessing

Blessing the finished construction, new purchase, new rental, or new opening of a house, apartment, condo, office, or store is a nice service to do for someone. It makes everyone feel good and gives the sense of a positive fresh start. While the possibilities are unlimited, here is one modified from Hawaiian practice. Its purpose is to ensure good things for the location and the people who use it.

1. Prepare by wearing something special that sets you apart as the one doing the blessing. The simplest thing would be something you wear around your neck like a lei, a necklace, a pendant, or even a ribbon. Also have a small bowl of fresh water and something you can dip in it and use to sprinkle the water. In Hawaii this would be a *ti* leaf or a fern frond, but any long leaf or even a crystal or wand would do. If nothing else is available, use your fingers. And drape a ribbon across the main doorway. In Hawaii this would usually be two *maile*-leaf leis tied together. Real traditionalists would hang *lauhala* leaves or ribbons from the top of the doorway, representing extra thatch that was left uncut in the old days until the time of blessing.

2. Open the blessing ritual at the doorway with any appropriate words, such as, "Everyone and everything bear witness. So begins the blessing of this house." Then cut or untie the ribbon or lei. As you do so, say something like, "The cord is cut (loosened). Born is the house (apartment, etc.) of so-and-so." Then breathe upon the bowl of water four times and step inside.

3. Inside, sprinkle a small amount of water in each room as you say a blessing. A rule of thumb is to sprinkle large or important rooms in every corner plus the center, and to sprinkle small rooms once or twice from a doorway. You can say anything you want for a blessing. The simplest form would be "I bless (or blessed be) this living room," but it's nicer to be more specific, like "Let this

room be filled with love and peace," or "May this office enjoy success and prosperity." Be sure to include an outside yard or garden if that's appropriate. Usually it's sufficient to sprinkle the corners.

4. A good closing would involve the owner/tenant and/or guests. A nice finish would be for the owner/tenant to light a candle, turn on a lamp, or put a special object in a special place, and for the guests to give their personal good wishes or blessings. Your final closing words, perhaps "This house (apartment, etc.) is blessed, let the celebration begin," would probably fit better right after the lighting of the candle or lamp and before the good wishes of the guests. This would also be an appropriate place for applause.

A Land Blessing

You might want to do a land blessing ritual when land is purchased, when escrow closes, or when a construction project is about to begin. It may be combined with the previous blessing.

1. Prepare with a bowl of fresh water, a leaf or wand for sprinkling, a bell or rhythm sticks or rattles, and something special to wear. Also have four plants (in Hawaii it would be *ti* plants, but on the mainland any favorite plant or one you know that signifies good luck can be used) or four stones (crystals are okay, but any stone will do), and a digging tool. A shell trumpet would add a nice touch. I like to include a Hawaiian nose flute, but any flute is good if you or someone in the group can play it. If there is too much to carry, use an assistant or a carrying bag.

2. Open at the center of the land, if feasible, or at any corner, by sounding a percussive or blowing the trumpet and saying words like, "We are here to bless and give birth to the land (or project) of so-and-so."

3. Walk to a corner if you start in the center, sounding your percussive as you do, or just sound the percussive for a

while if you are already at the corner. Then thank the ground for letting you dig a hole and dig one for the plant or stone. Present the plant or stone to the seven directions (east, south, west, north, above, below, and center), then place it in the hole, telling it silently or softly to do a good job of bringing harmony and good fortune to the land. Fill in the hole and play a little tune on the flute to make the plant or stone feel comfortable in its new home (use a percussive instead of the flute if you wish). Then breathe on the bowl of water four times and sprinkle some on the plant or stone, saying, "I bless (or blessed be) the power of this plant (stone) to bring harmony and good fortune to this land (project)." Then head for the next corner playing your percussive and repeat the performance. You can have the owner/tenant participate in any part of this. If the land is too big or inconvenient for walking to each corner, you can do the holes closer in, saying out loud that these holes symbolize the corners. If it's not feasible to dig holes, simply place stones, leaves, or potted plants at the corners, saying that they symbolize the good fortune being planted at the corners. After the main ritual is over, pick them up and say something like, "Your purpose has been served, now you are free for other things." Remember the seventh principle—there's always another way to do anything.

4. When all four corners have been blessed, go back to the starting point. Now have the owner/tenant dig up a bit of earth and turn it over as you say, "May everyone and everything bear witness to the birth of this land (project) to so-and-so. Its name is (and here you insert the name of the land or project, which might be its address or something more elaborate). Let the celebration begin." And then you start the applause. I always like to end a blessing ritual with a celebration of some kind.

A Car Blessing

In ancient times it was quite common to bless personal belongings like horses, chariots, carriages, boats, and even more personal items. This kind of blessing helps us maintain a good shamanic relationship with the other kinds of life that we interact with. The following blessing is designed for a car, but can be adapted to anything else.

1. Prepare a bowl of fresh water, something to sprinkle it with, and something special to wear. If you don't want to get water on your car or whatever else you are blessing, fill the bowl, empty it, and carry on as if there were water in it. No problem.
2. Start at the front of the car (or other belonging) and say, "Everyone and everything bear witness to this blessing."
3. Sprinkle the front and say, "May this car always provide useful and harmonious service to its owner." Of course, you can change that wording any way you like. Move around and do the same thing on the three other sides.
4. When you are back at the front, say, "The name of this car is (whatever the owner has told you). The blessing has been done." Although I haven't mentioned this yet, it's always appropriate to use a closing gesture of some kind for a real sense of finish. In my tradition we do a hand movement that looks like you are wiping a window with your right hand in a clockwise direction and then closing your fist. Use whatever suits you.

A Cleansing Ritual

It happens sometimes that a location or an object becomes associated with negative feelings or experiences. It may be due to something unpleasant that has happened at the location or with the object, or it may just be that the "vibes" don't feel right or people don't feel right when they are around it, or things just don't seem to go right in that place or presence. Whatever the cause, a cleansing ritual may be appropriate either to change the pattern of the place or thing, or to settle down the kus of the people involved. The following ritual is quite simple, but quite effective too, if done in a state of strong confidence.

1. Prepare a bowl of saltwater or salted water, something to sprinkle it with, and something special to wear. The Hawaiians would use fresh water for blessing and seawater for cleansing. You can use sea salt, table salt, Epsom salts, or bath salts. For this ritual, salt is salt. About a teaspoon is sufficient for any amount of water you would use. Also bring an object with you that represents peace, harmony, or whatever quality you want the ritual to instill.
2. Start with a strong statement like, "Let everyone and everything bear witness. I am here with the power to harmonize this place (object)."
3. Sprinkle the place or the object five times, saying each time something like, "In this moment, here and now, the harmony increases."
4. Finish by placing the object you've brought in a prominent place at the location or next to the object being cleansed, saying, "I empower this (name the object that you've brought) to complete the cleansing by tomorrow at twelve o'clock noon. So be it done. This is my word." Then make a closing gesture and leave.

As a symbolic object you may want to use something that you know the person you are doing the cleansing for would relate to well, like a religious symbol, or you can use something a little more neutral, like a crystal. I would use a *kukui* nut, which symbolizes enlightenment. The main thing is not the prop you use, but how confident you are. It is your confidence that will change the pattern, and if there is also confidence in the symbol, so much the better.

A Peace Ritual

Just before a big peace-related ritual you may have heard of called the Harmonic Convergence, some people asked me if our group on Kauai was going to do something for it. We hadn't planned to because there were certain assumptions involved with it that we didn't care for, but as more people asked and we thought about it more we decided, why not?

Any excuse to gather for peace is a good one. On the big day, we gathered about two hundred strong at one of the most special places in the Pacific, on a ridge above the Wailua River next to a *menehune* temple called *Poliahu* (the *menehune* were an ancient race that inhabited Kauai before the Hawaiians arrived), and we did the following ritual.

1. We prepared by obtaining enough leis for everyone, cutting a *ti* leaf wand for me, and providing a shell trumpet for my assistant.
2. At the opening we gathered everyone into a circle. Then I said a short prayer of blessing and greeting, and made a statement on love and peace and the purpose of our gathering.
3. To begin the ritual I first had everyone join in pairs holding hands, and had them let their partner symbolize their own parents, siblings, spouse, and/or close friends or enemies. Thinking of their partner as one or more of those, they were to silently give or ask for forgiveness and make peace with them. I gave about five minutes for that and for each of the exercises to follow. After individual peace was made, I had them join in fours, and let that grouping represent their family, friends, colleagues, coworkers, employees, employers, students, teachers, and the like. In the same way I had them make peace with all of them. Then they were joined in groups of eight to represent the people of their neighborhood, town, city, and state, and they made peace with them. Next they were joined in groups of sixteen, to represent their own nation and other nations, and to make peace with all of them. Finally everyone was gathered back into one large circle to represent the entire Earth, including Nature, and peace was made with that.
4. We finished with a song of peace, a final blessing, and a potluck luau.

I did say I liked to celebrate after a ritual. That's a good Hawaiian tradition.

THE TWELFTH ADVENTURE:

THE POOLING OF MINDS

E lauhoe mai na wa'a; i ke ka, i ka hoe;
i ka hoe, i ke ka; pae aku i ka aina.
(Everybody paddle the canoes
together; bail and paddle; paddle and
bail; and the shore is reached)

The real power of human beings, their ability to influence and change the world, comes from their capacity to work together for a common goal. History books, out of a desire for simplicity or in ignorance of the facts, tend to focus on individuals like kings and queens, presidents or dictators, popular politicians and leaders, famous explorers and scientists. Which is understandable because they are easier to focus on. But canoes are moved forward by paddlers not by chiefs, and ships of state reach their destination because of the crew as much as the captain. Leaders are useful, and in some cases perhaps the most significant part of a team, but they aren't critical as such. I've seen symphony orchestras play without a conductor, watched sports teams play without a captain, and once I was a member of the cast of a play with a director so incompetent that the cast ignored him and directed themselves, to rave reviews. I've been told that a bus doesn't go anywhere without a driver, but the driver doesn't go anywhere without tires, fuel, an engine, a chassis, etc., and without passengers there's no point in going at all. When I was in Africa doing community development work, it was necessary protocol to speak to the chief of a village first when we were going to do a project. With that ritual out of the way, the villagers gave themselves permission to listen to us. They were really the ones who had to be convinced of the value of the project, because they were the ones who would do the work. Furthermore, I was recently reading a history of Alexander the Great, revered as a military and political genius as well as a god in his own time. But even this outstanding man couldn't do more or go farther than his troops wanted. When they refused to continue fighting he had to turn his attention to maintaining the peace in lands already conquered.

The purpose of this tirade is to emphasize the importance of group energy and endeavors in creating change. Leaders can be useful as symbols and points of focus for the aspirations of a group, but for some things we don't have to wait for leaders. We can just go ahead and act with others of like mind. For effectively changing the world into a better place for everyone and everything, that's exactly what we must do as urban shamans, because there just aren't enough leaders leading in that direction.

Naturally, you can join with existing first-level local and global groups and networks that are concerned about the Earth and that actively engage in first-level projects, but just as naturally I want to share some ways in which you can operate in second-level groups using second-level techniques on first-level projects. To act, in other words, as a modern urban shaman, along with whatever else you may do.

Kokua Groups

Kokua is a Hawaiian word meaning "help, assistance, cooperation." A kokua group, as used by our organization, Aloha International, is a group of three to seven people who use their shaman skills for service to each other and to the community. You can have more in the group if you like, but if it goes much over eight it will have a tendency to turn into a class. That's fine if you want a class, but at that point you tend to lose the benefits of real mutual support. If you do start a group and it grows fast, you'll get better effects if you divide it into smaller teams when it reaches nine. Then during meetings you can have time for team activities as well as whole group activities.

What would you do in such a group? Here are some suggestions for a typical meeting:

1. Start by sitting in a circle holding hands and doing *nalu* on the principles to reinforce the understanding of shamanism and to harmonize your energies.
2. Have each person share a good experience they have had since the last meeting. An experience in the practical use or benefit of shamanism would be preferable, but any good experience would do. This sets a positive tone for the meeting and reinforces the group bond. It is very important that *only* positive experiences be shared at this time. The *ku* moves toward pleasure and away from pain. Complaints and criticisms, no matter how well justified nor what they are about, will weaken the bond and subvert the healing purpose of the group. They have no place in a *kokua* meeting. If negative things must be discussed, pick another time and place for it.
3. Shamanize for your local community (this could be your neighborhood, city, county, or state). To "shamanize" means to use any one of the shaman skills for healing or harmonizing. It would be good to pick a specific project to work on together, but you don't all have to use the same method to work on it. Let's say that you decide to shamanize for the homeless in your area. One of you might surround them with a color of *la'a kea* to help them be successful in their search for housing; another might do *nalu* on a thoughtform of them already being housed; another might grok some community leaders and inspire

them to act more quickly on the problem; and another might tune in to the dream of homelessness and change it. You will have to decide which of the pressing needs of your community to work on. Just remember to work on positive solutions, and not against anyone or anything. Give yourselves at least five minutes to shamanize, and then share your experiences. This helps reinforce memory and bonding, and serves as a form of mutual teaching.

4. If there is a national or international problem of sufficient concern to one or more members of the group, shamanize for that at this time in the same way as above.

5. Now shamanize for each other. Let each person name one thing that he or she would like help with. It could be something having to do with health, with finances, with a relationship, or with personal growth, and it could be personal or for someone outside the group. Shamanize for one person at a time, and share after each person or at the end. The more people you have, the longer this will take. Five minutes apiece is okay for a group of three to four, but in a larger group you may want to keep the allotted time to one to two minutes apiece. Be sure to keep the time the same for each member of the group. If one person has a severe problem, you can do more work on it before or after the *kokua* session. Many groups have broken up because one or two people have monopolized the time, even when they clearly needed a lot of help. You must remember that this is a *mutual* support group for shamanizing. Don't let it turn into a therapy group for a few or it won't work.

6. Do a formal close with a meditation, a song, or a prayer (or all three). You already know why from the last chapter.

7. After the close, allow time for socializing. Again, this strengthens the bonding and is just plain enjoyable. Some groups simply talk, and others have a potluck dinner or snacks, or go out together. For greater effectiveness, do the shamanizing before the socializing and don't mix them.

Meeting once a week is typical and effective. Few people have the time to meet more often. Once every two weeks or once a month will also work, but less than that doesn't work well for such an intimate group. Even a small group like this needs a bit of organizing. Someone will have to call people, arrange meeting space, and perhaps guide the meeting. One solution is to elect a facilitator for a certain period, say a month or a quarter. Another is to have a different facilitator for every meeting, rotating among the members in turn.

A Shaman *Hui*

A *hui* is any kind of organization for working, playing, or joining together, like a company, partnership, club, association, society, or network. Aloha International has seven different *hui*, shaman societies or networks whose members work together on projects of global interest even though they live far apart. Certainly you don't have to belong to a shaman *hui* to do that. You could join any organization working on global problems at first level and simply add your second-level skills to their work. But a description of these *hui* and their areas of activity may help you form your own or give you ideas for where you can put your skills to good use.

1. The Wave *Hui*. One of the projects of this *hui* is assisting the spotted and spinner dolphins, which are at risk of drowning in nets used to catch yellowfin tuna. Because the tuna swim under the dolphins, fishermen capture the dolphins to get the tuna. Shamans are working on this using intuitive communication, grokking, and dream-change either to teach the dolphins how to jump or escape the nets, or to teach the dolphins and tuna not to swim together. This *hui* works as well with whales and other marine mammals and with such things as tidal waves and ocean pollution. If a process solution isn't clear in a given situation (like separating the tuna and dolphins), then the shamans focus on end results (e.g., an oil spill

disappearing). Because of the way second-level reality operates, shamans focusing on a positive end result are indirectly energizing ongoing solutions and inspiring new ones among those who are physically involved. Contributing funds to organizations whose work you believe in is good, and contributing focused thought is just as good or better.

2. The Crystal *Hui*. This *hui* works with earthquakes, volcanic eruptions, soil renewal, and the location and use of mineral resources. The kind of work that can be done with earthquakes and volcanoes has been previously discussed. Soil renewal is an exciting field because ways and means already exist to turn dead clay into living loam, and shaman focus can help spread that to more of the world. The location of new resources and more effective and efficient use of existing resources—including everything from coal to crystals—can be of worldwide benefit. Shamans can use intuition, grokking, and dreaming for these endeavors, as well as other shamanic skills that may be the subject of a later book, such as dowsing and radionics.

3. The Flame *Hui*. Not surprisingly, this *hui* works on fires: forest fires, oil fires, building fires—anything which threatens the human community or which has been caused by humans. It also works with auras, and in this the *la'a kea* is a major tool. As a *hui*, though, it works with communities rather than individuals. As an example, if a community is experiencing civil strife or despair, the members of this *hui* would tune in to the aura of the community and work on harmonizing and changing its quality. Another area of shamanic action is the encouragement of solar energy, nuclear fusion, and similar projects.

4. The Rainbow *Hui*. Weather is the domain of this *hui*. In the short term it helps to avoid or reduce the damage to human communities from hurricanes, tornadoes, storms, and drought. In the long term it will be involved in

weather research and weather management. That takes a deep kind of communication with the elements of weather in order to operate from a state of rapport and cooperation, and not from an arrogant attempt at control. Someone seeking control tries to force the weather to do what he wants, while someone cooperating seeks to know and use the kinds of changes or maintenance that specific weather conditions enjoy. It is not inconceivable that members of this *hui* or shamans working in this area could discover or help to inspire ways of storing and using the vast energies of winds and storms.

5. The Leaf *Hui*. Working on a broad scale, this *hui* concerns itself with plant (including tree) preservation, protection, and propagation. Reforestation, the introduction of new plant species, and crop yields are other concerns. Also the healing of plants and the healing by plants, and the ways in which humans and plants can work more fruitfully together, each serving each other's needs. The study and practice of plant communication is a natural extension of the work of this *hui*.

6. The Unicorn *Hui*. This one involves shamanic work with land and air animals, which includes birds, insects, and bacteria. Helping certain species to survive and flourish is a major concern, as is cooperation between humans and animals and animal communication. The oldest legends of most traditional societies tell of a time when humans and animals communicated easily with each other, and in many cases it was the animals who taught the humans about cooperation with each other and with the environment, as well as about the deeper mysteries of life. As humans became more arrogant, the ability to communicate was lost. It has revived to a limited degree in scientific studies which observe animals in their natural habitat, but it has degenerated to a bottomless pit in the absolutely unnecessary, pseudoscientific experiments on animals that some people carry out. Animal communication is of utmost importance to the well-being of the

planet, as well as to human survival and spiritual growth. Shamanic methods and actions can be of tremendous help in this.

7. The Heart *Hui*. Human relationships with human beings are the responsibility of this *hui*. Using shaman techniques and knowledge to increase peace, harmony, and friendship between groups is what its members do. Also involved is research and the practice of shamanic healing of human minds and bodies. Yes, we must learn to love and cooperate with Nature, but most of all we must learn to love and cooperate with ourselves. We have the knowledge and technology to create a Golden Age, and at the same time we have the knowledge and technology to extinguish ourselves. No matter what we do the Earth will survive. Probably she will revive very quickly even if we devastate the surface, the way ferns shoot up shortly after molten lava and toxic gases wreak their havoc during a volcanic eruption. But even if not, the Earth can take millions of years if she has to. We can be part of her destiny or we can fade or flash out. The destiny will go on. With all she gives, I think it is clear that the Earth loves us, but I don't think she loves us more than her other children, like the dolphins, the ants, and the trees. Still, I think that her love is so great that she will continue to love us no matter what we do. It is not the Earth who will ever turn against us. The danger comes only from us. As does the solution.

Conclusion

Many years ago as I sat in meditation a poem leaped into my mind. It seems so appropriate that I'm using it to finish this practical book for urban shamans.

Ode to a Toad

Grunt and gurgle, little toad
Down there in your mud abode.

Do you ever think of us?
Do we make you fret and fuss
With our wars and waste and greed,
Our rush toward death with reckless speed?
Do you wonder at our fate,
Who preach of love and practice hate;
Who distrust and fear those not like we,
Though they live next door or across the sea?
Do you laugh and laugh at how we talk
Of peace, while one hand holds a rock
Ready to bash our neighbor's head,
Because he's yellow, black, or red?
And at those who cry, "We must disarm!
Our enemies will ne'er do us harm.
When they see we've no weapons or means of defense,
They'll be happy to stay on their side of the fence."
Or at those who say, "Attack and fight!
We'll show them all that might is right.
Who cares about nuclear radiation?
It's important we prove we're the strongest nation!"

Ah, men say this and men say that,
And some change sides and some stand pat.
And some merely glory in tromping on toes,
But few see beyond the thick end of their nose.
They rant and rave with fiery speech,
And preach, and preach, and preach, and preach.
So what is achieved by a thousand words?
And where are the footprints of flying birds?
For words can't grow crops or clothe the poor,
Or find a disease's elusive cure.
They can't feed children or heal the sick,
Or build a dam or wield a pick.
Oh, they have their place, that I concede.
But a word can never replace a deed.

Yes, it's action that counts, not what we say.
We must act and do and lead the way
By DEEDS! if we hope to live at all
In a world without hate, or revenge, or a Wall.
Do we truly believe in the Rights of Man,
Be he black or white, yellow or tan?
Do we honestly think we can live without war,
In trust and peace forevermore?
That there needn't be hunger or sickness or fear;
That death for so many need not be so near?
If we do then let's ACT! and make this old Earth
A place where real joy will attend every birth.

And what if we don't? If we just sit and wait
Till the bombs start to fall and we know it's too late?
These are questions I ask myself, too, little toad,
As I sit at my desk or drive down the road.
If we drop our terrible, monster bomb,
Will you sit there serene, patient, and calm?
Or will you just chuckle, thinking of when
The Earth will no more be troubled by men?
If instead we recognize Earth as our Mother,
And all of her creatures as sister and brother,
The land and the sea and the sky as a friend,
Ourselves as gardeners whose role is to tend,
Then maybe, with love, in an ACTION mode,
We might make it work after all, little toad.